Stories from The Great War Vol. II

Some Came Home

Mick Manise

Grosvenor House
Publishing Limited

This book is published by
Grosvenor House Publishing Ltd
Link House
140 The Broadway, Tolworth, Surrey, KT6 7HT.
www.grosvenorhousepublishing.co.uk

A CIP record for this book
is available from the British Library

ISBN 978-1-78623-659-3

By the same author

Captain Desmond Ellis Hubble
(From Cradle to Grave)

John Banner
(His Life & Times)

Harry Bunn's War

Stories from the Great War
Vol. 1
The Pooley Miners

Dedication

In keeping with the theme, 'Some Came Home', I dedicate this Volume to a representative of both aspects and whose stories are contained within this book;

Private 1852 Walter John Little - 1/5 Battalion York and Lancaster Regiment
(Walter came home)

Barbara Esmée St John - Voluntary Aid Detachment (VADs)

Headstone of Barbara's last resting place in Wimereux Communal Cemetery
Pas de Calais France
(Picture courtesy of Shaun Little)

Acknowledgements

Again, I pay homage to four people in particular whose willing help and outstanding knowledge has made this project possible, Peter Evans, Tim Thurlow, Kevin and Shaun Little, on this occasion they have entrusted me with the stories of people dear to them and for that I acknowledge the great compliment they pay me.

Research has again been undertaken by Jan Lowe. Help with photographic reproduction, my old friend and colleague Graham Bennett. I.T. and all things concerning my computer, including search and information recovery, my lovely wife Christine. Proof reading Simon Westwood.

There are many wonderful people whose encouragement, support and belief is very much welcome, Chris, my sons, Aunt Mary, many friends and total strangers who read my posts in the Face Book group, Stories from the Great War, which I have created as a place to put all the little snippets I glean whilst researching a subject. Kiren Parmar of Radio Tamworth for her live interview time, purchase of my books and exposure in her literary world. GHP Publishing for the ease with which they progress a project from script to book. There are many more and I apologise for not naming everyone.

Every effort has been made to obtain permission to use pictures, where successful due credit is given

Sources

Any information recovered from the internet has been verified from a separate source
The Long Long Trail.
Great War Forum.
Imperial War Museum.
Bovington Tank Museum.
National Archives.
Ancestry.com.uk
Find my past.com
International Red Cross Archives
Face book; World War 1 Photographs, Great War Reads (Kevin and Shaun Little), WW1 Colourised Photographs. Stories from the Great War (Peter Evans).
Books;
The First World War (IWM)
Tracing your prisoner of war ancestors Sarah Paterson (IWM)
Beneath Flanders Fields, P Barton, P Doyle, J Vanderwalle
The First Day of the Somme, Martin Middlebrook
With a Machine Gun to Cambrai, George Coppard
The 11th Royal Warwicks in France 1915-16, Colonel CS Colinson DSO
World War 1 Gas Warfare, Tactics and Equipment, S Jones
The Battle of Lys 1918, Chris Baker
On the Trail of the Great War, Birmingham 1914-1918, Alan Tucker
Fields of Death P Slowe and R Woods
The First World War, Malcolm Brown (IWM)
24 Hour Trench, Andrew Robertshaw

Contents

Foreword

As a long serving member of the Royal British Legion and a witness to the sacrifices made in the name of freedom by men and women of the Armed Forces, I cannot emphasize just how important the whole issue of remembrance is. Whilst we continue to work hard throughout the year and in particularly during the Poppy Appeal to support members of the three services and their families, we take time each meeting and any opportunity to remember those who have fallen whilst protecting our way of life and freedom.

The scale of loss to be honoured is so great that remembrance is mainly conducted in a blanket manner and the issue of individual recognition largely left to family, friends and communities around local memorials. Those who remember the first great conflict of the 20th Century are now all gone and we rely on historians, authors and archivists to preserve the memory, as we will in the future for the conflicts which follow

This book selects people from the Western Front and tells their stories in such a way as to give an insight into the lives of them and their families. They were hard times for working people both in employment and domestically. Infant mortality was high and the physical statistics of the men on joining the forces gives a picture of physical development for the time, due to poor diet men were statistically shorter than we are today the average height in 1914 being about 5'5".

The royalties from this book, as with Mick's other four books, will be donated to the Royal British Legion to aid in its extremely important work. By buying this book you not only contribute financially, but share the knowledge gathered in the book's preparation, thereby contributing to remembrance in two ways.

Terry Dix
Alderman of Staffordshire County Council
Chairman of Two Gates and Wilnecote Branch Royal British Legion
Former Mayor of Tamworth
Holder of the Golden Needle for German War Graves Commision

Introduction

Volume 2 of Stories from the Great War was not originally conceived as a book in its own right. Whilst writing Volume 1, The Pooley Miners, I thought it a sensible idea to write about survivors in an effort to elevate my emotions from the sadness of the Pooley stories. It was intended that all the stories would be in one book until it became apparent that the men of Pooley deserved their own volume. This, of course, left many completed stories that had the promise of publication to friends, friends of friends and many total strangers whose relative's service had caught my attention.

Stories from the Great War, Vol 2, Some Came Home, became a project in itself and the subtitle needs no further explanation. This also explains the randomness of subject selection. I am joined by some other writers in this book who have kindly donated stories and under each title credit is given for that or to the relative who cooperated in completing each subject. Many of the stories written for family and the guest stories, have been written with a full account of that individual's experience. Inevitably there will be duplication of detail in such events as the background to battles and offensives. In an effort to reduce this for the readers benefit, a certain amount of editing has taken place but some repetition is inevitable to make sense of that man's story. Every effort has been made by myself, advisors and proof readers to allow the stories to flow.

I do hope you enjoy the book and thank you for supporting my work and of course the Royal British Legion by buying it, as with all my published works the royalties in entirety are donated to that most worthy of courses.

Mick Manise

2019.

Cover Picture

I am very grateful for the cover design for this series of stories to my long-time friend Graham Bennett of West Coast Media Solutions who has donated his services free of charge in order to support the Royal British Legion.

The medals shown have been updated from Volume 1 of this series to reflect the entries in this book, changed is the 1914-15 Star to a 1914 Star with Clasp and the addition of a Military Medal. The medals are one of the common characteristics of the stories as all subjects, regardless of their fate, earned at least two if not all four of them.

The Stars

The first medal to be authorised was the 1914 Star following relentless pressure from King George V who ardently believed that the men of 1914 deserved a distinctive award. The army resisted this move until late in 1917, believing that a simple clasp on a campaign medal would suffice as had previously been awarded, for instance, in the Boer War. 378,000 of these stars were awarded for active service between 4thAugust and 22nd November 1914. Most went to the original members of the British Expeditionary Force (BEF), sometimes known as 'The Old Contemptibles' following a derogatory remark made by the Kaiser, who said that the BEF was a contemptible little army. The cut-off date for this medal was 22nd November 1914, which was determined to be the last day which satisfied the above criteria but also marked the stabilisation of the Western Front and the commencement of the static nature of that theatre of war.

There was some resentment from other branches, such as the Royal Navy who were at war at sea. The only members of the Senior Service who qualified, were some land-based units manning artillery and port defences. The 1914 Star (as shown in the cover picture) was then replaced by the 1914-15 Star, the medals are identical except that on the 1914 version, there is a scroll wound around the crossed Roman swords at the centre bearing the words, *'Aug-1914-1915'*, whilst on the later version the scroll is shorter bearing the dates, *'1914-15'*. This medal was devised following some bad feeling from those who had served in 1914 but had not been entitled to the first award, such as the theatres of war not covered by the qualifying criteria and, as previously mentioned, the Royal Navy. The 1914-15 Star was awarded to those who had served in any theatre of war, regardless of military branch, between 23rd November 1914 and 31st December 1915. Some 2,366,000 1914-15 Stars were awarded and like the 1914 version they were always accompanied by the British War and Victory Medals, this was even to those killed during 1914-15 or whose wounds had curtailed their service.

The fact that the 1914-15 Star was almost identical to the 1914 Star then caused some resentment from the recipients of the latter who claimed they deserved a distinguishable award. To resolve this a dated clasp, (*5th Aug - 22nd Nov 1914*), was produced to be worn on the 1914 Star's ribbon which was awarded to those who had been at the front within range of the enemy's mobile artillery before midnight on 22nd November 1914. This was accompanied by a silver Rose to be worn on the ribbon bar of the medal.

The British War Medal

This circular silver medal was the basic award of World War I. It bears the Monarch's effigy and titles and would have been the award to carry individual clasps as previously awarded but not authorised for this conflict.

This medal was the only one of the four to be awarded on its own, for instance for those on duties around the Empire such as India. A bronze version of this medal was awarded to non-combatant servants or porters enlisted from Africa or India. The recipient's details were impressed around the edge including name, initials, abbreviated rank and unit. Approximately 6,500,000 BWM's were awarded making it the most common British campaign medal.

The Victory Medal

At the Versailles Conference of 1919 the Allies agreed on a standardised medal to be awarded to all those who had entered a theatre of war. The Victory medal was originally struck in dull bronze but later finished with a gold coating. The front has a simple Winged Victory figure and the reverse side the words, *"The Great War For Civilisation 1914-19"* in a wreath. Never awarded on its own, some 5,750,000 medals were distributed.

The medals were subsequently delivered in a small addressed cardboard box with the medal ribbon unattached and, in the case of a deceased soldier, to their nominated next of kin. The Rose and Clasp awarded with the 1914 Star was issued when applied for and that date recorded in the medal rolls for that regiment. The other awards common to all the soldiers killed, was the Memorial Plaque and Scroll. The idea for this was developed in 1916 and reflects the nation's overwhelming sense of loss which had been a feature of this terrible conflict. The Scroll was designed and worded by a committee set up to discuss the issue but the Plaque was a result of an open design competition offering a prize of £250 to the winner. The wording of the Scroll reflects the sacrifice made and the Plaque depicts Britannia in mourning offering a wreath with the British Lion and two dolphins to represent sea power. Around the front face are the words, *"He Died for Freedom and Honour"* and the name of the fallen person was printed in a frame. A small number with the wording commencing with *'She'* were produced for eligible women casualties which included victims of U-boats at sea. The dates for eligibility were 4th August 1914 to 30th April 1920 to encompass those who died of wounds or disease after the war had concluded. 1,360,000 plaques were issued to the nominated next of kin to the subjects from Britain and the Empire.

Picture Tim Thurlow

The example above was kindly made available for use by Mr Tim Thurlow who has a collection of World War I artefacts which has taken over 30 years to accumulate; Tim is a Battlefield Guide and has been a valuable source for my research. Henry Blackstone, Corporal L10497, was serving with 7th Battalion the Queen's (Royal West Surrey Regiment) when he was killed on 10th August 1917 and is remembered at Tyne Cot Cemetery.

The Military Medal

The Military Medal was established on 25th March 1916 and was awarded to other ranks for acts of bravery and devotion to duty under fire on land. It ranked below the Distinguished Conduct Medal and was initially poorly received by veterans who saw it as a means for the military leadership to award less DCM's. The award was made retrospective to 1914 and many medals were then awarded for previous acts of bravery which had been deemed not worthy of the DCM. The award was published in the London Gazette but not the citation, this makes researching what a particular medal was awarded for very difficult, very often legend in family is the only clue. A Royal Warrant issued in June 1916 extended the award to women recognising the gallantry of women serving in various capacities at the front and it was discontinued in 1993 when the Military Cross was made available for all ranks as it had previously only been available to commissioned ranks. In the event of a soldier being awarded a disability pension, as a result of his military service, the pension was enhanced by a gratuity of sixpence per day, but only once, there was no extra for recipients of more than one medal.

Chapter 1

How they got there

The introductory chapter in Vol. 1 of this series is entitled, 'Why they were there', it follows nicely to describe how they got there. As previously the chapter is meant to be informative and relevant to the men in the stories, therefore it is again confined to the army and Western Front.

In July 1914 the British army was distributed around the Empire engaged in Garrison duties wherever there was a need for an armed force to protect British interest from aggressive external or internal elements. As the threat of war became an inevitability, Regiments based in Britain were mobilised and from wherever they could be spared, Battalions were brought home for re-equipping,(many units were equipped with inappropriate uniform such as tropical kit) and mobilised to form the British Expeditionary Force (BEF) which was despatched to France.

At this time the German army was supplemented by a system of reservists and had the capacity to mobilise 4.5 million men, the French army had a similar system and manpower reserve. Britain's army was organised following the 1908 Haldane reforms and consisted of a permanent professional army, supplemented by Territorial reservists raised, equipped and trained on a local basis and affiliated to favoured Regiments. For instance, the Tamworth Territorials consisted of local men who met and trained on a regular basis at the Drill Hall Tamworth and who were affiliated to the Staffordshire Regiment. They were allowed to wear the Regiments identifying features and enjoyed the associated history and esprit de corps. The total establishment of the British army was 975,000 men, the original BEF six Divisions, 100,000 men.

Following the mobilisation of the BEF to France, reservists were called to duty on a permanent basis (embodied). As fully trained soldiers they were the obvious choice to follow the professional army, either as reinforcements or replacements. A national recruitment drive was commenced with the expectation of 200,000 acceptable respondents. By acceptable, certain criteria needed to be fulfilled, a minimum height of 5'3", age of 18 (19 to serve abroad) to 38 years and a reasonable standard of health determined by means of medical examination. The call to arms created a national fervour responded to by so many men that long queues formed outside recruitment offices, this was dealt with by opening further facilities at public buildings such as town halls.

On successful application the recruit was given the King's shilling, part of a very old tradition, and either sent home to await orders or given travel papers to a regimental depot to commence basic training. Each infantry Regiment was comprised of two Battalions but with the outbreak of war this was increased as needs dictated to accommodate the demand. A training Battalion was formed, quite often 3rd Battalion and these units remained in Britain throughout the war often forming part of home defence.

Battalions were aligned to a regiment for administrative purposes but in reality formed part of an Infantry Brigade. At the beginning of the war four Battalions comprised a Brigade but this was later reduced to three due to manpower loss. Each Battalion was commanded by a Lieutenant Colonel with a Major as second in command. There was a Headquarters Company plus four Companies, usually A, B, C and D but sometimes 1, 2, 3, 4, or W, X, Y and Z. Each Company, commanded by a Captain was divided into Four Platoons commanded by a Lieutenant. The Battalions total establishment was 30 officers and nearly 1,000 other ranks. The headquarters staff also included the Regimental Sergeant-Major plus a number of specialist roles filled by Sergeants: Quartermaster, Drummer, Cook, Pioneer, Shoemaker, Transport, Signaller, Armourer and Orderly Room Clerk. A Corporal and four Privates of the Royal Army Medical Corps were attached for sanitary and clean water duties; a Corporal and 15 Privates were employed as Signallers; ten Privates were employed as pioneers; 11 Privates acted as drivers for the horse-drawn transport; 16 acted as stretcher-bearers (these often being the musicians of the battalion band); six Privates acted as officers' batmen and two as orderlies for the Medical Officer. For transport the battalion had 13 riding and 43 draught and packhorses to draw its six ammunition carts, two water carts, three General Service Wagons (for tools and machine guns), four mobile kitchens and the Medical Officer's Maltese (a lightweight two wheeled Cart drawn by one horse). The battalion signallers had nine bicycles. When on route march the transport and men stretched out over 800 yards.

Each soldier carried: Clothing; boots, braces, service cap with badge, identity disc and cord, woollen drawers, service dress jacket with metal shoulder titles and field dressing, clasp knife, pay book, puttees, shirt, socks, trousers, cardigan waistcoat. Total weight 14 pounds 11 ounces.

Weapons: Lee Enfield bolt action .303 calibre rifle with oil bottle, pull through, sling, bayonet and scabbard, 150 rounds ammunition. Total 19 pounds 8 ½ ounces.

Tools: Entrenching implement and carrier. Total 2 pounds 9 ½ ounces.

Accoutrements: Water bottle with carrier, web equipment 1908 pattern. Total 8 pounds 4 ¼ ounces.

Contained in the pack: Cap comforter, holdall with laces, toothbrush, razor and case, shaving brush, comb, greatcoat with metal shoulder titles, housewife [mending kit], mess tin and cover, socks, soap, towel. Total 10 pounds 1 ¾ ounces.

Rations and water: bread, cheese, emergencyiron ration, water. Total 5 pounds 13 ½ ounces.

Total weight on the soldier; 61 pounds 0½ ounces.

To meet the huge response to the call to arms large areas of open land and country estates were made available to the army to create camps and training areas, Salisbury Plain and Cannock Chase were two such areas. The barracks vacated by the departing BEF were soon filled and tented camps were erected to accommodate the men whilst wooden barracks were built to create better and more permanent accommodation. The chaotic situation is described in a more than one story but equipping the men was a big problem initially until the war industry got up to speed with the production of weapons, clothing and the equipment needed.

When a Battalion was deemed sufficiently equipped and trained for war, mobilisation orders were sent which precipitated a few days of frenetic activity, recalling men from leave, checking stores, transport and quite often the training schedule of the men was confined to musketry on the ranges. On the appointed day the Battalion would form up in Company order, officers on horses, transport to the rear and march to the local railway station. If they were lucky enough to be billeted near to their local town a parade for the locals would be held and with great pomp the men would march past local dignitaries to the railway station where they entrained for the next leg in their great adventure.

It may seem rather odd to describe, what we now think of as a horrific period of world history, as an adventure, but try and place yourself into the shoes of a young man from a working background, miner, farm labourer, nail maker, factory worker, newspaper print setter, earning a pittance for long hours, having left school at 12 years of age, whose future was firmly mapped to their current situation. The media and propaganda of the day reports atrocities, committed by men portrayed as beasts, everything those men hold dear is threatened and their King and country asks them to step forward to right a horrendous wrong done to a tiny peaceful country. It is firmly embedded in the British psych to stand up to a bully and protect the underdog, this together with the rally to serve touched the hearts of a generation of men and women who flooded to the colours for an opportunity to travel to a foreign land and with the promise of, ‘it will be all over by

Christmas', there was a fervent desire to be involved whilst the opportunity was available.

Three trains were made available for a Battalion, but often the transportation would take place over two or three days, the destination being a sea port such as Southampton or Portsmouth. At railway stations and the sea ports the men were met by volunteers, mainly women from various organisations, who provided them with sandwiches and hot drinks. The Battalion travelling as part of its designated Brigade would board transport ships (TS) in the chaotic atmosphere of docks loaded with equipment waiting to be placed on board, officers, NCO's and Military Police barking orders under the guidance and authority of naval personnel, but all this added to the excitement of the moment. On board ship there was no luxury accommodation waiting for the men but the journey to Le Havre or Boulogne was not a long one, often overnight for security purposes. The disembarkation was a reversal of the experience in England and the men formed up in marching order and marched to one of many rest camps in near to the ports. On this march, many of the men met a foreign person and culture for the first time. Local people greeted the marching columns with much enthusiasm and often benefited from this influx of men with money to spend by setting up small bars called Estaminets or serving food to supplement the army fodder, a very popular dish became egg and chips, surprisingly.

From the rest camp, the Battalions marched to camps near to the front line, here the training in trench warfare, which they had undergone in such locations as the low tides of Western super Mare, became reality. By small unit or Company the men accompanied seasoned Battalions into the front line and the remainder formed working parties to repair, improve or add to the existing system. When everyone had experienced the dangers of artillery, machinegun and sniper fire the fresh Battalions took their place in the line in their own right.

Chapter 2

George, Robert & Ellis Biggin

(For Sally Jowitt)

In title order, courtesy Sally Jowitt

George, Robert and Ellis were brothers, three of Thomas and Salina Biggin's eight children. Thomas married Selina Lowe on 7th July 1878 at Christ Church, Dore, Sheffield, Salina was a local girl born and raised in that village and the couple settled down to raise a family. Thomas was a Scythe Smith by profession and their first home was at 64 Town Head in Dore, by 1881 the first two boys had been born and Thomas's sister Lucy was living with them. In 1891 the family had moved to 138 Town Head, Dore and the family had swollen to four children, a girl Mary Alice and another boy, Thomas was still working as a Scythe Smith but also worked as a Cutter.

In 1901 the family had moved to 17 Devonshire Terrace also described as the rear of the Devonshire arms, which at the time was run by

William Thorpe who also lived there with his family. The census form shows that next to the Biggin home was an unoccupied blacksmith shop, this is most likely where Thomas made his scythes. Thomas is described as a worker meaning he was employed; the village Blacksmith was John Stones who is described as an employer and living at 12 Devonshire Avenue.

In 1911 Thomas and Salina Biggin had been married for 32 years, they had been blessed with eight children who had all survived to that date. They were now living back at Townhead Road but no number is shown on the record. Of the eight children, five are still living with them including George, Robert and Ellis and there were also two grandchildren, nine family members in four rooms which included the kitchen if there was one, very cosy! Both father and Robert are now working as domestic Gardeners. Robert was only 14 but the school leaving age for the time was 12, George was employed on a farm as a Horseman and Ellis was employed in the silver trade as a Buffer.

Both George and Robert joined the army. George's military file was amongst those burnt in WW2 when Somerset House was bombed, but Robert's file survived. Robert's record shows he volunteered under the Derby Scheme and attested at Sheffield on 4th December 1915, he took the deferment option and returned home until he was mobilised on 20th January 1916. Two clues exist as to when George volunteered; his enlistment place and the War Gratuity paid following his death. This was £6 denoting a service of just over one year and he enlisted at Sheffield. It is not beyond the realms of possibility that these two brothers travelled to Sheffield together and attested on the same day both choosing deferment until called up.

If that is the case, Robert was mobilised before George and reported to the York and Lancaster Camp on Cannock Chase, Rugeley in Staffordshire, having been posted to the 11th (Reserve) Battalion of that Regiment. Private 24062 Biggin began his military life on 20th January 1916 with a medical examination, he was 19 years and one month old, just under 5' 3" tall, weighing 115 lbs. He nominated his father as next of kin, who with the rest of the family were now living in Barkers Row, Dore.

11th (Reserve) Battalion York and Lancaster Regiment had been formed in September 1914 and by the time Robert joined it was a training unit. Robert completed his basic training and along with a draft of other regimental members boarded a ship bound for France on 27th May 1916. His short spell at sea finished the same day when the ship docked at Boulogne. A few weeks was spent in an Infantry Base Depot undergoing further training before being posted to 8th (Service) Battalion which Robert joined in the field on 23rd June 1916 with 95 other men.

8th Battalion had landed at Boulogne on 27th August 1915 as part of 70th Brigade of 23rd Division. On the 23rd the Battalion were in bivouacs in Long Valley, Millencourt, making final preparations for the attack scheduled for 29th June. Heavy thunderstorms occurred that day making life very difficult for the organisers who were busy issuing materials and equipment for the battle. The following day, the largest artillery bombardment of the war commenced, the offensive known as the Battle of the Somme had begun.

The Somme offensive had taken a great deal of planning and was designed to relieve pressure on the French army who had been subjected to a major German offensive based around the City of Verdun just south of the Somme area. The objectives of the British offensive were to divert German resources from the Verdun area, thereby relieving the French, and to go further by breaking the German lines at different locations, sending Cavalry through the gaps with the intention of destroying the enemy front, rear and flank. The planning and organisation had involved the raising of a New Army to create sufficient forces to meet the enormity of the plan, and the production of vast quantities of artillery shells, ammunition and supplies to support the huge number of men in the field.

The infantry phase of the attack was planned for 29th June 1916, to be preceded by an artillery bombardment on the German lines lasting five days. The objectives of the bombardment were to cut the German defensive wire, destroy the front lines and bunkers and kill as many enemy soldiers as possible and to destroy targets disabling the enemy's ability to bring up reinforcements, such as railways. To that end all forms of gun calibre and shell was used, high explosive, shrapnel, smoke and gas. After the fifth day of bombardment it was decided to extend this phase of the operation by two more days pushing the Infantry attack back to a date which will remain in infamy forever, 1st July 1916, Z day. The original five-day bombardment was designated U, V, W and X, the additional two days, 29th and 30th June, were designated Y+1 and Y+2. During the seven-day bombardment over 1.5 million shells were fired (IWM stats).

During this phase, 8th Battalion were making daily preparations for the attack, they were one of the many leading battalions to commence the infantry attack and were placed on the left of 70th Brigade's front; their start point being the British front line in Authville Wood. Not all of the Battalion's strength was deployed on this first day, an element were always left behind in reserve, but Robert was chosen to be with his new comrades on that fateful first day. The preparations for the assault included creating ammunition, food and water dumps at designated locations for each Company to draw on, these dumps were identified by location and a coloured flag, red for S.A.A. (small arms ammunition), black for T.M. (trench mortar), yellow for grenade and yellow and black for the Divisional bomb depot. Each man was issued with the following equipment to be carried into the attack;

- Rifle and personal equipment excluding pack and greatcoat, but including waterproof sheet and haversack. This bag was to be worn of the back and affixed to it was a white disc, the purpose of this was for observers to determine how far the troops had advanced.

- Water bottles were to be filled with a weak tea and not to be consumed prior to the attack without an officer's consent. The two biggest logistical problems faced at this time was the provision of ammunition and water to the front, both were dealt with by the use of dumps.

- Two bandoliers of .303 calibre ammunition for the Lee Enfield to be carried in the haversack in addition to equipment rounds, total carried 220 rounds.

- Bombers to carry equipment and ammunition only
- Machine gunners, 50 rounds each.
- Two days rations
- Three sandbags, one of which was to be used to carry the food ration.
- Two grenades
- Smoke helmets
- Field dressing.
- In addition, every fourth man carried a pick or shovel, along with the sandbags, to consolidate any captured positions. A trench has a fire step in its front face creating a platform for men to fire from, in order to defend a captured trench it is necessary to very quickly build a fire step to repel any counter attack.
- 30 sets of wire cutters per Company.
- Ten wire cutters per special clearing party.
- 30 wire breakers per Company.
- Ten wire breakers per left flank parties.
- 16 bill hooks per Company.
- 25 pairs of hedging gloves per Company to be issued with the wire cutters.
- 12 bridges per Company.
- Each bombing squad, one per Platoon and special parties – not less than 90 grenades.

Provision was also planned for the eventuality of prisoner handling, one guard per 15 prisoners and the guard to then return to his Company following handover. Medical facilities were organised, a first aid post being the foremost facility with an advanced dressing station of the 25th Field Ambulance, situated in Authville Wood.

During the night of 30th June, the Battalion moved up to its start positions. The artillery continued to target the German front line in an effort to prevent them from repairing their defensive wire. On 1st July 1916, 19 mines dug out and placed by tunnelling Companies of the Royal Engineers, were due to be detonated at 7.28 a.m. immediately prior to the commencement of the infantry attack. All but one were detonated on time with devastating effect to the German positions above and in the near vicinity of the explosion. One mine under Hawthorn Ridge was set off at 7.20 a.m. on the orders of the Corps Commander who decided the infantry needed a longer gap for their safety. At 6.30 a.m. The British and French artillery commenced firing on the German line, this instigated retaliatory fire some directed at 8th Battalion's start positions, but casualties at this stage were light. At 7.30 a.m. officers blew their whistles and the men climbed out of the relative safety off the front line and as per their training and instruction walked towards the enemy front line.

Whilst smoke had been laid in most sections to provide cover for the advancing men, none had been laid down in 8th Battalion's front due to an unfavourable wind. The reason for the tactic of slow progressive walk forward was for the very good reason of maintaining connection on the flanks of the various assaulting units, to lose contact could result in a flank being exposed and exploited by enemy counter assault. The other reason was the lack of faith placed in the men of the New Armies by the high command and planners. Pressure to get the offensive underway to relieve the French had meant that the start date was before the time that these fresh units from Britain and the Commonwealth were fully trained; Robert is a prime example of that having arrived with a draft of 96 men a few days before the battle commenced. Regardless of intent, the option to run was not there as the weight that the men were required to carry far exceeded the normal approved maximum weight.

The first wave of 8th Battalion men left the trench in good order, the expectation was that there would be no opposition in taking the German front line as everyone occupying it would be dead. There was almost immediate heavy and sustained machine gun fire from the flanks of the German positions creating an impenetrable curtain of death, most of this first wave were killed or wounded. The first mistake had been realised. The assumption that the artillery barrage would make the infantry assault easy was wrong on a number of counts; the defensive wire had not been cut or had been pulled back together. The German bunker system was underestimated, they were dug very deep and soundly constructed in concrete, for seven days the Germans occupying those bunkers had been subjected to the largest artillery action in history and had survived albeit shaken and hungry. The officers in charge of these positions had made the men practise exiting the bunkers and setting up their machine guns within two minutes, this gave adequate time for them to set a murderous fire down on the walking Tommies. The other issue was that the attack was expected, the concentration and massing of men and equipment for this offensive could hardly go unnoticed by aerial reconnaissance, in addition a deserter from the British line, a man of German heritage had told the defenders what was happening but not exactly when. The tactic of manning the defences in two minutes was effective regardless of when the attack happened.

The Battalion were advancing over open ground and made easy targets for the German guns. In addition, the central area of no-man's land was targeted by German artillery using high explosive and shrapnel shells creating a killing ground. In total four waves of men met a similar fate but regardless of that the survivors managed to breach the German line where they fought hand to hand during the day. Regardless of the danger the men who had reached the first line fought on and captured the German support line, this position was subject of bitter hand to hand fighting and changed hands a number of times during the day, counter attacks by both sides secured the position only to lose it again. A very few men fought on the third line but these brave souls were cut down by machinegun fire. It shows the quality of these men of the 8th when all the officers became casualties, NCO's and even Privates were organising and directing the battle. For those that fell in no man's land and were only wounded, the danger was not over, during the course of the day any movement in these area's brought to bear the attention of sniper's who showed no mercy and finished them off. The frustration and anger of those German's who had spent seven days sheltering in their bunkers whilst the British and French artillery rained death down on them now emanated as revenge, no mercy was to be shown.

Of the 23 officers and 680 men of 8th Battalion who went over the parapet on this day, only 68 men returned unscathed, all the officers were either killed, missing or wounded as were 612 other ranks. That evening the Battalion was withdrawn from the line and the following day when all the survivors had returned, a parade and roll call was held, the enormity of the loss which included the commanding officer and Robert, must surely have been an emotion never to leave these men for the rest of their lives. At 9 p.m. that night (2nd) the remainder of 8th Battalion marched to Dernancourt for entertainment.

Robert was posted as missing but his body was never identified. He could be laid to rest in a grave marked, Known unto God, or he could have been a victim of the high explosive shells leaving nothing behind. He had left his belongings to his father, but nothing personal was recovered and his estate was only £2.8s.5d., which was supplemented by a War Gratuity of £3. He was awarded the British War and Victory medal and along with a usual scroll and Death Plaque these were sent to his family.

George Biggin

George enlisted at Sheffield in the spring of 1916 and was posted to the King's Own Yorkshire Light Infantry (KOYLI), the only records show that he was posted to 1/5 Battalion. This unit landed in Boulogne on 12th April 1915 approximately one year before George enlisted, it is most likely that he was initially posted to one of the reserve Battalions for his basic training and then shipped to France as part of a draft of replacement soldiers to join the 1/5. The record also shows that George had two numbers, 4436 and 241908, the first number was no doubt issued when he first enlisted but a change in the system of numbering in 1917 created the second number which he used to join his unit. The training unit for the KOYLI at this time was 3rd (Reserve) Battalion which was based at Withernsea, Yorkshire. If we allow for three to four months training in England we can roughly estimate that George arrived in the field to join 1/5 Battalion during the month of August 1916. At this time this Battalion was part of 148th Brigade, 49th (West Riding) Division.

1/5th Battalion had taken part in the Battle of the Somme from the first day, George must have arrived after the death of his brother, Robert, but was most definitely treading the same ground. We have no records to show where George was until he was killed on 19th July 1917 and at this time 1/5 Battalion were based in the Somme area and had been spending the usual time rotating between front line, support and reserve. On 13th July 1917, the Battalion entrained at Bethune bound for Dunkerque where they took up temporary residence in a POW camp to undergo attack training on the beaches. This gave those men a golden opportunity to take some leisure time on the beach and the diary notes that a number of men had been stung by jelly fish.

On 17th July, the Battalion relieved 1st Dorsetshire Regiment in the Lombartzyde sector of the line. The following day the support lines were subjected to an intensive artillery bombardment causing heavy casualties in A and C Companies. On the day of George's death, 19th July, there were two actions in which he could have fallen. During the daylight hours, 'A' Company mounted a raid on enemy positions. The Captain leading the action was killed and another officer wounded. Also during the day, an attack was made by enemy troops on B Company's positions but they were driven off. An officer was wounded but again there was no mention of the casualties sustained by other ranks. One other clue is a letter sent to the family following George's death, by the A Company Quarter-Master, this letter states that George was killed instantly by artillery fire and that they could take consolation in the fact that he did not suffer. Whilst the latter part was a standard comment designed to give consolation this was not always the case of course, it does open another possibility though that the artillery fire, targeting both A and C Companies positions mentioned in the diary entry for 18th July, could have spanned the midnight period.

The diary does list the total casualties that the Battalion sustained for the month of July 1917; two officers killed, one missing, ten wounded and 1 died of wounds. Other ranks, 35 killed, 11 died of wounds, two missing believed gassed, 143 wounded, 124 gassed. A total of 329 men in one month, of which George was one, the record showing that hewas killed in action. George's body was recovered and buried at Ramscappelle Road Military Cemetery, West Vlaanderen, Belgium. His family went through the agony of receiving a telegram notifying them of the loss of a second son having barely had time to recover from the loss of Robert. George left £1.3s.9d. too his father which was supplemented by a War Gratuity of £6. He was awarded the British War and Victory medals which along with the usual scroll and death plaque were sent to the family.

The family had an inscription placed on George's headstone which reads;

'When I left Home I little thought that my race was so near run'

They also had a material scroll made which recorded George as a Lance Corporal and bears the below poem;

Like crowded forest trees we stand,
And some are marked to fall,
The axe does smite at God's command,
And soon will smite us all.

Ellis Biggin

Ellis was born in 1894 between George and Robert and was baptised at Christchurch in Dore on 15th July of that year, as already mentioned he was working as a Buffer in the silver trade in 1911. On 23rd April 1916 he married Elsie Greaves at the same church in Dore and they lived on Townhead.

On 20th May 1918 Ellis enlisted in the army and was posted to 1st Battalion Leicestershire regiment. It is most likely he completed his basic training with 3rd (Reserve) Battalion which at that time was a training unit but based at Patrington near Hull and engaged in home defence duty with the Humber Garrison. At some stage Ellis joined 1st Battalion in the field in France; this would have been around September 1918. The only other definitive official record that now exists, is the date of his discharge. Ellis was released as no longer fit for military service due to wounds on 6th February 1919; he was awarded a silver badge number B117044 to wear on his lapel to show he was a wounded veteran. Sometime between September 1918 and Armistice Day, 11th November 1918, Ellis received a gunshot wound to a leg and was hospitalised as a result, without his military file it is not possible to determine when and how he was wounded.

From family records we can see that he was awarded a marksman's badge which he wore on his left sleeve. This was a skill at arms badge, much coveted by infantry soldiers and awarded to the most skilled shooters who attained a high standard, modern day qualification is 85% or higher. To achieve such a high standard in such a short period of service would denote a naturally gifted target shooter.

Ellis was awarded the British War and Victory Medals; he returned to civilian life and lived until 9th February 1965.

Chapter 3

Walter and Ernest Little

(For Raymond, Kevin and Shaun Little)

Walter Little

Ernest William Little

(Pictures courtesy S. Little)

Ernest William Little, (known as William or Bill), was born in 1893 and his brother, Walter, two years later, both in Woodhouse, a suburb of South Sheffield. Prior to the Industrial Revolution this area had beenrural, and families relied on agriculture and its associated industries, such as tanning, for their income. With the growth of industrial Britain, Sheffield, due to the coal deposits found there, became industrialised creating a migrating population from other areas seeking work. The City was built on coal and steel and the name Sheffield became synonymous with quality products such as swords and other bladed instruments. The boys' parents were two such migrants; his father being from Christian Malford in Wiltshire and his mother originating from Stilton in Huntingdonshire.

Their father, Alfred Little, worked in the coal mines as an underground labourer, a gruelling and dangerous life in an industry where families were tied to their employers by virtue of provided homes and at the same time little attention paid to the safety and needs of the workers. The family home at 50, Wolstenholme Road, Woodhouse was run by the boys'mum, Elizabeth Little, her time cut out providing for her husband and at that time six children, aged from one to 12 years of age. All were either in Woodhouse School or at home waiting to be of school age.

In 1911 the family were still living at the same address but Alfred, now aged 50, was employed as a Nursery Gardener, a far cry from shovelling coal deep underground, but a safe and healthier occupation. After 23 years of marriage, Elizabeth was still looking after the family now seven children; an eighth child had died post birth. Walter, the youngest of the five eldest children in employment, was working as an underground Pony Driver at Treeton Colliery. His four elder brothers each had a different employment; a colliery labourer, a Carter (Bill) and a railway Platelayer, giving the family a diversity of occupational experience and providing a reasonable standard of living.

The military record for Bill did not survive the fires of the Blitz in World War 2 when Somerset House was bombed, but from records that do exist, Bill joined up early in 1915 and was posted as Private 17353 to 8th Battalion, York and Lancaster Regiment. This Battalion was formed at Pontefract in August 1914 and mobilised to France on 27th August 1915, landing at Boulogne on that day. Bill landed in France on 23rd September 1915 and joined the Battalion in the field following a short period in an Infantry Base Unit. The difference in dates may well mean that Bill had trained with a reserve unit in England and been posted to 8th Battalion on arrival in France.

On 18th June 1913 Walter, whilst still working as a Pony Driver but now for the Orgreave Colliery, attended Treeton army recruitment office and attested to join the Territorial Army. Walter was 17½ years of age, 5' 4" tall a stature that was an asset to securing a better rate of pay as an underground worker. The medical examiner declared him fit for army service and on Saturday nights he became Private 1852 Little of 5th Battalion York and Lancaster Regiment, signing for the maximum four year period of duty. The Territorial Service had been devised following the Boer War when it was determined that a trained force was needed at home which could be quickly mobilised in times of national emergency. The nature of the British Empire at that time meant that much of the Regular army was spread around the world policing British interests. On mobilisation Battalions needed to return to England to re-equip them for a particular theatre of war and the Territorial Army's primary role was defence of Britain in order that home based units could be mobilised immediately.

Duty as a territorial soldier not only meant regular meetings for drill and training, the men were also required to attend training camps, from eight to 15 days per year.

Walter and family, believed to be taken at a Territorial training camp
(Picture courtesy S. Little)

At the outbreak of war, Walter was with 5th Battalion at a training camp in Whitby Yorkshire. They were recalled to Rotherham. At this time individuals were given the option to serve abroad or restrict their service to home duties, to elect to serve abroad Walter signed what was called the Imperial Service Obligation Form which he was eligible to do aged 19, in September 1914. The Battalion was embodied into permanent service and became 1/5 Battalion York and Lancaster Regiment, the number 1 being placed before the 5 denoted that over 80% of the Battalion had elected to serve overseas, those who hadn't or for some reason were ineligible, were moved to units which were designated for instance 2/5 and assigned to home defence. There followed a four-month period of training at Doncaster which was continued at Gainsborough in November 1914. After this training period, the Battalion took up coastal defence duties in Lincolnshire. On 31st March 1915 mobilisation orders were received and they returned to York where they joined other units to form the West Riding Division. On 12th April an advance party which included the Battalion's machinegun section and transport were sent ahead to Folkestone. This party consisted of three officers, 78 other ranks, 71 horses and 22 vehicles. The following day the main body of the Battalion then paraded and marched through York and over the Lendal Bridge before the enthusiastic cheering of local folk and relatives. This march past was filmed and Walter can be clearly seen raising his cap in salute to the camera, a young man amongst many other young men full of enthusiasm for the adventure ahead.

The Battalion, under the command of Lieutenant Colonel Fox consisting of 28 officers and 930 other ranks, then marched to the railway station where they entrained to Southampton for embarkation to Boulogne. Arriving in France the same day, the men were sent to Ostrehove rest camp arriving there at 5 a.m. on 14th April. On 16th April, the Battalion now part of 1/3 West Riding Brigade, commenced training in trench work under the guidance of experienced units. The Battalion's first casualty occurred on 25thApril when Private Mellor was injured, he was stretchered to 25th Field Ambulance but died of his wounds two days later, the reality of life in the trenches was beginning to be realised. The day that Private Mellor died, 26th April 1915, the Brigade - now designated 25th Infantry Brigade - moved to

Fleurbaix where it manned a front line running for two kilometres between La Boutillerie to Le Bridoux. 1/5 Battalion started their first tour in reserve but soon rotated between front line and support trenches. This area had a high water table and a continual battle was fought to keep the men's feet dry, this particular area the breastworks (front face) of the trenches was built up higher than ground level to provide both protection and a firing step above the ground water line.

Walter Little standing wearing a waistcoat

(Pic courtesy S Little)

In the above picture Walter Is pictured in a trench at this time and the level of the trench is above ground level by use of sandbags. There is available in this story a rather unusual pictorial record due mainly to Captain Henry Colver ignoring regulations concerning cameras and carrying his wherever he went. Captain Colver was killed on 19th December the same year, during the first Phosgene Gas attack on British troops and was buried at Bard Cottage.

This was a relatively quiet period and the Battalion settled to the routine of relief in the trenches, front line, support and reserve. The main activity noted, is exchanges of artillery fire which created a steady flow of casualties; wounded, killed and died of wounds. This also meant that the sandbagged breastworks became damaged and in constant need of repair or improvement. For the period 1st to 4th June 1915 the Battalion suffered six men injured; three each on the first two days in the trench. This figure emphasizes the dangers of trench life even in a relatively quiet period and safe location.

At the end of June orders were received to move north to man the British line on the Yser Canal near to the town of Bosinghe. This location was on the northern side of the Ypres Salient, overlooked by German artillery on the high ground and under constant enemy shell fire. The water table was high, the trenches shallow and often wet, life there was a continual battle to keep water pumped out and feet dry to avoid the dangers of Trench foot. In places the British positions were only a few yards from the enemy's trenches, a high price was to be paid over the next two years denying the City of Ypres to the German army. The trenches were described as "the worst trenches of the allied line" by the Divisional Commander and more casualties were suffered in the first 48 hours than in the preceding two months. The Battalions first tour in the front line was from the night of 9th July taking up their positions by 1.30 a.m. on 10th and was only until they were relieved on the evening of 11th July 1915. The German artillery was very active on the first day causing damage to the trench works, burying one of the machineguns with its crew and causing 27 fatalities, 128 men wounded and two men missing.

During October 1915, Walter had a run in with army discipline when he was charged with losing his smoke helmet, for this he was awarded two days Field Punishment number two. Field Punishment was introduced to punish men in the field by Court Martial or Commanding Officer following the abolition of flogging in 1881. Field Punishment Number One was the more serious of the two and involved the miscreant being tied or shackled, hand and foot, to a fixed object such as a fence for two hours per day. Often the man was tied with arms and legs spread-eagled earning the system the nickname, 'Crucifixion'.

Field Punishment Number Two was less severe in that the man was not tied to a fixed object and could remain with his Battalion; on movement the men under punishment, often described as prisoners, took position at the rear of the column with their escort. Humiliation was the design and in Walter's case was apparently effective, as there are no further references to disciplinary issues. Shortly after this Walter was admitted to 2nd West Riding Field Ambulance suffering Boils, considering the conditions described above any form of open wound would be extremely dangerous and sepsis, without the benefit of anti-biotic treatment, was a major killer. It was during this period when the Battalion whilst in reserve positions that the German army launched its first Phosgene gas attack on British troops. The people most affected by this attack were not the front line but those in the rear. Walter and the whole 49th Division were affected due to a late warning; this incident affected Walter for the rest of his life. The day after the attack, 20th December 1915, 1/5 Battalion's roll call totalled only 290 all ranks of which 100 were still unwell, this evidences the effectiveness of gas to debilitate an enemy but also the problems with accurate deployment. Following treatment, Walter was given a few days in the 49th Divisional Rest Station to allow the open wound to heal and he re-joined his Battalion on 22nd December 1915. The following day the 1/5 went back into the line where they remained for the Christmas period being relieved on 27th December. The diary notes that an attempt was made by the Germans facing them to fraternise but this was resisted. The Battalion made their feelings on this issue very clear with bullets; the recent Phosgene Gas attack which caused so many casualties was still fresh in the minds of Walter and his comrades! Following the unofficial truce which occurred on Christmas Day 1914 the High Command had made it very clear that this fraternisation should never happen again.

January 1916 saw the Battalion moved from the front and entering a period of rest recuperation and training. Training had commenced to prepare the men for the forthcoming Offensive of 1916, the Battle of the Somme. The Battalion moved to the Authuille area during February 1916 where it remained until its involvement in this great battle on 1st July. At this same time Bill serving with 8th Battalion was undergoing preparatory training for the same reasons.

During this period of training it is likely that Walter received specialist tuition in the use of the Lewis light machinegun. In the below picture, Walter is the man kneeling next to the Lewis Gun's stock, the coveted 'LG' badge can be seen on his left sleeve but no badge of rank. It is the beginning of 1916 that the heavy Vickers machine guns were taken from the Battalions and the Machinegun Corps formed, Machinegun Companies were allocated to Divisions and the heavy weapon replaced at Battalion level with the Lewis gun as seen in the picture. Walter was promoted Lance Corporal on 25th May 1916, thus assisting with the date of the photograph.

Walter kneeling next to the rifle stock

(Photo courtesy of S. Little)

In the last two weeks of June 1916 and in preparation for the offensive, 1/5 Battalion was bivouacked in Martinsart Wood providing working parties in preparation for the attack, delayed until 1st July. The work was varied, day and night and involved digging ammunition dumps, water stores, dugouts, depots and assembly trenches. On 27th June the Battalion marched out of camp in full fighting kit, the men were in two main parts those designated to be in the attack starting and those to wait their turn in reserve. They went to billets to await the order to make their way to assembly trenches but the following day they were notified that the start day had been delayed for a further two days, Z day was followed by Z+1 and Z+2 which was in fact 1st July. Bad weather had prevented aerial reconnaissance and artillery spotters from directing fire onto targets the destruction of which was deemed essential to the success of the infantry operation.

Meanwhile, Bill's 8th Battalion had moved up to assembly trenches in Authuille Wood in readiness for the original date of the planned attack, 29th July. They had been in position 24 hours, when the order to delay the attack until 1st July was received. They were relieved and retired to bivouacs in Long Valley. For these two days the artillery bombardment of the German line continued, at night, patrols were sent out to report on the state of the enemy trenches and machine gun fire was used to prevent the enemy repairing the defensive wire.

On Y day, (30th June), the 8th Battalion moved back to its assembly positions in readiness for the Infantry assault. The men assigned to take part in the assault waited all night and then at 6.30 a.m. the artillery delivered what is described as 'an infernal bombardment'. The German artillery replied but for the men waiting their confidence was boosted by the volume and intensity of the fire raining down on the German trenches. The expectation was that when they went over the top, they would be walking towards destroyed positions whose occupants were dead, that the defensive wire would be cut and nothing would obstruct their occupancy of the German front line from where they could consolidate and then press on to the second line objective.

At 7.30 a.m.1st July 1916, the officers blew their whistles and the men left their assembly trenches in good order, at the same time the enemy artillery laid a heavy bombardment on the 8th Battalion's front line but the casualties were few. As the men followed their training and walked in line towards their first objective, German machine gunners came up from their deep bunkers and manned their positions, half way across No Man's Land 8th Battalion were swept by fire from the front and both flanks, at the same time the German artillery who had predetermined the centre point as a target area, commenced firing with high explosive and shrapnel shells. The men started dropping in huge numbers but onwards they pressed regardless of casualties and danger. Most of the first wave were killed or injured and lay in the long grass while the second wave attempted to press the attack, they too were subjected to the same treatment by the machine gunners. Approximately 70 men of the attacking waves from the 8th Battalion reached the first enemy line and some even managed to press on to the second and third line objectives. These men were involved in viscous hand to hand fighting and eventually all were killed, wounded or taken prisoner, only one man returned to the British line. The Battalion providing support 9th Battalion York and Lancaster Regiment were sent forward to assist in the capture of the trenches but were subjected to such ferocious machinegun and rifle fire that only the odd few soldiers reached the places where 8th Battalion were in such dire need of support. The reserve Battalion, 11th Sherwood Foresters were sent into the attack but the same fate awaited them.

At 7.30 a.m. that morning, 23 officers and 680 other ranks had climbed over the parapet to attack the German line, of those men all of the officers were casualties, 18 of them killed, of the 680 other ranks only on 68 returned, Bill was not amongst those men. Bill was 22 years of age when he was killed and his body was not identified, he may rest in a grave marked, 'A Soldier of the Great War Known unto God' or still be lying under the fields where he fell, each year the remains of fallen soldiers are recovered, some identified, but all given the military burial which they deserve. Bill's name was subsequently engraved on the great memorial at Thiepval along with the names of 72,334 other men who have no known grave from this offensive we call the Battle of the Somme, he was awarded the 1914-15 Star, British War and Victory medals

At 3.45 a.m. 1st July 1916, the attacking force of 1/5 Battalion was in its designated assembly trenches in Aveluy Wood awaiting the signal to 'go over the top'. At 1.30 p.m. that day the Battalion went over the top and entered the maelstrom which had developed during the course of the day. Walter with his comrades from C and D Company entered Thiepval Wood with the intention of supporting other units who were already there. The wood had been 'heavily knocked about' by German artillery and bodies and equipment was strewn about all over, shelling continued to be responsible for casualties and Walter was hit in the head by a piece of Shrapnel. Walter was lucky, he was removed from the field and taken to 91st Field Ambulance for treatment and then on to 45 Casualty Clearing Station at Daours, for him the nightmare that had evolved on that day was over. On arrival back in England Walter was taken to 2nd Western General Hospital in Manchester, arriving there on 7th July, where the piece of shrapnel was removed from his head. Walter had suffered not only from the pain of this injury but his eyesight had been affected, no doubt the worry of his wound and what he had experienced on that first day had an effect on his nerves, doctors recorded that he was on edge, the news about his brother Bill may have been a factor. Following treatment and until he was out of dangers such as sepsis, Walter was transferred to a convalescence facility at Ballyvonare Command Depot in County Cork Ireland. In December 1916 he was transferred to 4th (Reserve) Battalion and then in April 1917 to 2/5 Battalion, a second line unit at that time assigned to home defence.

As part of a reorganisation of soldier's numbers, Walter's number had been changed to 240236 and on 12th May 1917 he relinquished his substantive Lance Corporal rank and was posted back to France. On 27th April he embarked once again from Folkestone and landed the following day at Boulogne. Initially stationed at 34 Infantry Base Depot at Etaples he was soon back on the move and joined his brother Bill's 8th Battalion York and Lancaster Regiment in the Field at Ypres.

Walter's arrival in the field with 8th Battalion was in time to take a part in the Battle of Messines which commenced on 7th and finished on 14th June 1917 as part of the offensive known as the Third Battle of Ypres or Passchendaele. The objective was to take the German positions on the Messines Ridge which was one of the high grounds overlooking the City of Ypres and used by German artillery to target both the City and the forces occupying the salient. The attack was preceded by the initiation of 21 mines filled with a total on 1 million pounds of high explosive, 19 of these mines were successfully detonated at 3.10 a.m. on the morning of the attack to be followed up by infantry assault. The 9th York and Lancs went in the first wave and were followed by Walter's Battalion at 6.50 a.m. The battle was successful and the Germans removed from the ridge which they had held since

1914, more importantly the overall casualties were much less than the 50% expected. Walter's Battalion lost 300 men in the attack, killed, wounded or missing and fortunately he was not counted in this statistic. One of the few things which he talked about after the war was finding a cigarette case which had belonged to a German soldier, this item is still in the family. Walter was to take part in several other phases of this offensive before being paraded before the Commander in Chief, Field Marshall Sir Douglas Haig with the whole Battalion.

In early November 1917, 8th Battalion transferred to the Italian Front where they remained for the rest of the war, reinforcing the front which had been weakened by huge Italian losses in the Battle of Caparetto. Walter was involved in fighting on this front twice, on the Asiago Plateau and the last action of the war on this front, the Battle of Vittorio Veneto.

Following the Armistice on 11th November 1918 Walter was part of an Inter-Allied peace keeping force based at Fiume now called Rijeka in Croatia. He returned to England via Le Havre in March 1919, was demobilised from Ripon Camp on 10th April 1919 andreturned to the family home at 50, Wolstenholme Road. Walter went back to working underground as a miner and was eventually promoted to Deputy. A tunnel collapse left him unfit to return underground whilst he was making checks for gas.

Walter married Abigail Edge in June 1922; they set up home at 22, Victoria Road, Woodhouse and had one child. Abigail, a young mother at the time, tragically died in June 1929 leaving Walter to juggle his work/life balance as an employed single parent. Two years later Walter met Annie Elizabeth York while she was cleaning her front door steps. The two fell in love and married in September 1931. Annie was a widow having married Mark Ellis also in June 1922. Annie and Mark had one child a year later, but Mark died of Peritonitis in 1924. Walter and Elizabeth settled down at 136, Sheffield Road, with a ready-made family; each bringing a son, Derek Little and Ken Ellis. The marriage produced one more son, Shaun and Kevin's dad, Raymond in 1933. Raymond was prematurely born, Walter's dad Alfred making the observation that 'he had seen bigger rabbits'! Raymond was bedded down next to the hearth for extra warmth and with the loving care of his mother survived.

During World War 2 Walter returned to uniform and joined the Home Guard earning the Defence Medal to go with the 1914-15 Star, British War and Victory Medals which he was awarded for his service during the Great War.

Walter was typical of his generation, deeply affected by the War, the loss of his brother, his wounds and the effects of exposure to poison gas but he did not allow it to prevent him living a full and productive life. He returned to France on a pilgrimage during the 1920's and visited the Ypres Salient in which he had endured the worst of living and fighting conditions. He dreamed of retiring to Filey in Yorkshire where he had enjoyed many holidays, but this dream was unfulfilled when in June 1957 he died prematurely at the age of 61 in the arms of his son Raymond. Annie, broken hearted, died only four months later when she fell from an upstairs bedroom window.

Chapter 4

Barbara Esmée St John

Picture IWM

Barbara was born 11th September 1885, in the vicarage of Ashby de la Zouch Leicestershire. She was the second daughter of theReverend Henry Beauchamp St. John and Emily Anne St. John. Henry was the Vicar of Holy Trinity Church in that town. The family enjoyed the services of two live-in servants, both young women, who cooked and kept house. Barbara was sent to Eastbourne College in Sussex as a boarder where she was resident in 1901 at the age of 15. By 1911 Barbara had finished school and was again living with her parents who had now moved to Loud Water in Buckinghamshire, they still enjoyed the services of two young women employed in a domestic capacity and living with the family. Barbara, at 25, has no profession or employment; not unusual for a daughter of a middle or upper class family of the time who is still single.

Between 1911 and the outbreak of The Great War, Barbara trained as a nurse and found vocation with the Voluntary Aid Detachment (V.A.D. individuals known as Vads), her service number being Sussex 112. The VAD had been formed in 1909, by the War Office with help from the Red Cross and Order of St. John. Its primary function was to support the Territorial Force medical service and gave training in first aid, home nursing and hygiene by approved medical practitioners; they were also taught how to cook which is a skill which Barbara probably did not have due to her upbringing. By the outbreak of hostilities there were 74,000 Vads of which two thirds were women and girls, the Vads readily offered their services to the war effort but there was resistance initially to them being sent abroad.

In February 1915, the War Office proposed that VADs could help at Military hospitals previously exclusively staffed by members of the Royal Army Medical Corps and the first requests for volunteer help at these hospitals in Britain, came immediately and this was then extended to France in May 1915. Barbara volunteered to work at 5th Southern General Hospital at Southsea Portsmouth, which was a facility opened in September 1914 to deal with casualties returning from the Western Front. Following a year's service at this hospital, Barbara was accepted for voluntary service in France and entered that theatre of war on 17th May 1915. The rest of her story is probably best told by the entry in the British Journal of Nursing, Vol. 57 1916:

> *"We regret to record the death in France of Miss Barbara Esmée St. John, a member of the 112th V.A.D. Sussex, a Red Cross Nurse, thedaughter of the Rev. H. B. and Mrs. St. John, of Ninfield, Sussex. After serving for a year in the 5th Southern General Hospital at Southsea,she was sent abroad to the 25th GeneralHospital, France. Since the great pushbegan, she had charge of a surgical ward of thirty-five beds, with occasional stretcher cases in addition, with only a young orderly of*

seventeento help her, working thirteen hours a day. Asister looked in to help when necessary. She was attacked on October 4th by scarlet fever; butwas making a good recovery, when paralysisset in. She was buried in the soldier's cemetery at Wimereux on the following day with full militaryhonours, much mourned by all who knew her. We have, in this Journal, so often criticised young women not thoroughly trained, being given responsibility, for which they are not sufficiently experienced, in the care of our sick and woundedsoldiers, that we only refer to it in connection with this sad death to point out that the more conscientious the woman the greater the strainupon her physically and mentally; and the chargeof thirty-five acute surgical cases with a Sister occasionally looking-in, under the conditions described, would tax the resources of a highly experienced nurse. It is neither fair on a partially trained person to place her in such a position, nor upon stretcher and other serious cases that theyshould not have the skilled nursing which is their right."

I think this report gives a clear picture of the desperate situation that medical support services found themselves in due to the overwhelming casualty figures experienced throughout the war and, in particular, during and following the Battle of the Somme.

The official cause of death was recorded as Landry's Paralysis which was a Flu-like illness, in this case Scarlet Fever, the muscles in the legs and arms, followed by the chest became paralyzed. With muscles in the chest not working she was unable to breath and asphyxiated. Barbara left at total of £30. 10s. 3d, supplemented by a War Gratuity of £13. Unusually the register does not show a beneficiary but this was probably her father. She was buried in Wimereux Communal Cemetery, Wimereux Departement du Pas-de-Calais, Nord-Pas-de-Calais, France. This cemetery contains 2,847 war graves, mainly soldiers who succumbed to their wounds in one of the ten military hospitals in the vicinity set up during the war and Barbara lies there with several other nurses killed during this terrible conflict.

Chapter 5

Alexander Watt Lee

Sometime between 1871 and 1878, a very young CarolineKynastonemigrated on her own, from her home in Belgrave Road, Edgbaston, Birmingham, to Australia, she had been diagnosed with TB and had been advised to seek a healthy fresh air environment in which to live. Arriving by ship at Brisbane they were met by the usual tug boat which guided their vessel into port and ensued it was birthed correctly. The first officer of this tugboat was a Scotsmen named Douglas Lee, Caroline fell in love with him, they married in 1878 and had 6 children. The fifth child and second son, was Alexander Watt Lee, born on Curtis Island, Kepple Bay, Queensland.

After the 6th child was born, Douglas Lee drowned when his boat sunk at sea during a hurricane, with no one in the world other than her children Caroline decided to return to the UK to live.

By 1901, Caroline with herchildren,were resident at 19, The Limes, Osborn Road, Aston, Birmingham, hardly a location conducive with her condition as it was a highly industrialised area of Birmingham and the main power and heating source was coal. Alexander, whohad attended state schools in Australia, now attended local schools and was tutored in mathematics by a Mr J Clarke Neill B.A. This educational foundation led Alexander beyond school and by 1911, aged 20, he was employed by Birmingham Corporation in the Gas Department as a clerk. He was resident in lodgings with his elder sister, Violet, at 27, Rosary Road, Gravelly Hill; their mother had returned to Australia and was living at 4, Bligh Street, Sydney.

Whilst working for the Gas Department Alexander volunteered for service with the Territorial Army and joined the South Midland Brigade, Royal Field Artillery. He served for 5 years and received instruction with field artillery pieces and as a machine gunner.

At the outbreak of The Great War, Alexander, now aged 24, volunteered for active service and on 8th September 1914, he attended Birmingham Town Hall recruitment facility for attestation. His medical examination records him as 5'6" tall, 113 pounds, with brown hair, grey eyes, a fresh complexion, an abscess scar under his chin and a chest expansion of 2", fit for general service. Alexander, as Private 379 Lee, was posted to 14th Service Battalion of the Royal Warwickshire Regiment based at Warwick. The 14th battalion was formed at Birmingham in September 1914 by the Lord Mayor and a local committee. Alexander was afforded class 2 proficiency pay from day one indicating he had specialist qualifications, probably as a machine gunner gained when he completed his territorial service with the Field Artillery. The Battalion moved to Salisbury Plain in Wiltshire, where they were accommodated near the village of Codford and were billeted in wooden huts.

The situation at this time was rather chaotic. The call to arms had hoped for about 200,000 volunteers as this was the number that could be provisioned, housed and trained with the resources as they existed. The actual number of volunteers vastly outnumbered this expectation and consequently, with no offer being refused, it meant large numbers of men were assigned to hastily formed units, with no uniform or equipment. Many of the volunteers had no previous military service, including new officers and basic training started from the very beginning, how to wear a uniform, salute, bear arms and march.

On 5th June 1915, Alexander married Hilda Goodby, a spinster, at Erdington Parish Church in Birmingham. The ceremony was officiated by Reverend Swindell M.A. and one of the witnesses was Lieutenant Black.

Early in Alexander's service, his age and previous experience showed and he was promoted to Lance Corporal (unpaid) on 8th July 1915;

the paid promotion coming on 24th September. It is highly likely that Alexander's experience was put to good use as a machine gunner and each battalion was equipped with two of the Vickers heavy machine gun and he was promoted to Machine Gun Corporal on 6th October 1915.

The Vickers gun was a heavy piece of equipment - 88 pounds including the tripod, water-cooled from a Jacket around the barrel and belt fed with the standard .303 calibre round. When the barrel became hot, the water cooling system created steam thereby obscuring the firer's view so a condensing system was created with the steam transferred to a jerry can. It was crewed by between six to eight men with a Sgt in charge:one man firing, one man feeding the belted ammunition, assisting reloads and clearing jams and the rest carrying ammunition from stores remote from the firing point.

By November 1915, the 14th was fully equipped and ready for war and duly received orders to mobilise, this order triggering the commencement of the Battalion's war diary. On 21st November 1915, Alexander with the 14th Battalion, shipped to France. Whether he went as a platoon sergeant or in charge of a machine gun section, isn't clear as the Vickers machine guns were taken away from battalions when the Machine Gun Corps was formed in January 1916. At battalion level these weapons were replaced with a light machine gun or LMG, the Lewis. This weapon was air-cooled and, instead of a belt feed, the same .303 calibre round was fed to the guns breech via a circular, top-mounted magazine.

The train journey from Codford to Folkestone was undertaken at night. Arriving at 8 a.m. they embarked immediately to Boulogne. The feeling of excitement was prevalent, all the men were volunteers and had joined for various reasons, mostly it was seen as a great adventure and the war in its early stages was still glorified and had not been sullied by the huge casualties yet to be suffered. On arrival in France they were billeted in tented accommodation, the weather was freezing and the men got little sleep, not the introduction to the great adventure they may have expected.

The following night they entrained at Boulogne and detrained at Conde at 1.00 a.m., then commenced a 12-mile march, over frozen road surfaces the men slipped and slid and arrived at their destination of Bouchon at midday on 27th, exhausted they went into billets.

On 4th December, Alexander was promoted to Machine Gun Sergeant and awarded class 1 proficiency pay.

Training was undertaken and, midway through December, the 14th moved to Bronpay to take over duties in reserve. On 11th December, the first casualty was suffered when a Private Hackett was killed by rifle fire. The duties undertaken were trench repair and improvement and best described by the Battalion commander, Lt. Colonel Murray.

> "*The trenches at the time that the Battn were carrying out this instructional training were in a very bad condition being in many places thigh deep in thick mud; in some sub-sectors nearly all the men's dugouts had fallen in. All ranks suffered somewhat under these conditions but the spirits of the men remained excellent*".

Over the next few days, the men received a baptism of fire in trench warfare, 2 more casualties were taken from rifle fire, the second was a Company Sergeant Major walking outside the trench after dawn, a gift to a German sniper. During the course of a working detail the uniforms, in particular the heavy trench coats necessary for this cold winter weather, became clogged with mud and the men were often exhausted as a result.

On the 18th December, the 14th was relieved and retired to Proissy where they rested in hutments. Every effort was made to make Christmas 1915 special, a meal was prepared and each man given a pint of Bass beer, spirits were very high!

By New Year's Eve the men were back in the trenches and experienced their first artillery bombardment, it lasted one hour from 10.30am and the high explosive shells accounted for a further three casualties, one killed.

Towards the end of January 1916 the 14th suffered an outbreak of Measles and German Measles, and isolating the whole Battalion was the only way to contain this disease. Those infected were removed to an isolation unit but the rest of the battalion spent the whole month of February musketry training, by the end of that intensive period the standard of marksmanship was extremely high. The first 2 weeks of March showed that the measles issue was dying down and by the 15th no new cases were developing. In the meantime, the Battalion had marched to accommodation near Arras where they joined the 13th Brigade of the FifthDivision.

The rest of March was spent in the front line, where they found that the trenches were in poor condition. Much of the time was spent repairing trenches and defensive wire and tunnelling for mines. A steady flow of casualties was experienced caused by a variety of rifle fire, trench mortar and artillery shrapnel. The weather was appalling with snow, rain and freezing conditions but towards the end of the month they were reinforced with two drafts of replacements described as of high quality. This may well have had a boost too morale as when relieved, the 14th had a 10-hour march to billets and they managed to sing for 8 of those miles.

It's not clear exactly where the Vickers machine guns were replaced with the Lewis LMG, but the beginning of April was spent training in musketry and by now nearly all ranks could achieve the high standard of 15 rounds per minute rapid fire. Hand grenade training continued and the machine gunners spent time practising with the Lewis Gun, Alexander's speciality training made him an important part of this familiarisation of the new weapon and he was an instrumental in developing the techniques and tactics for its use.

The months leading up to the battle of the Somme, commencing on 1st July 1916, were a routine of duties in the front line, support and reserve. The front-line work involved carrying ammunition and use of the communication trenches ensured a steady flow of casualties from mortar, artillery, rifle fire and aerial torpedo, whilst in reserve training continued almost without rest.

At the end of June, the Battalion was relieved and went into billets at Agnes. From the beginning of July, they proceeded to practise attack methods in preparation for a special operation, so they missed the first day's carnage of the battle. On the 13th July, the battalion received orders to march to Longueval, where they arrived on 19th July; the daily marches ranged from 8 to 20 miles. On arrival, they took up positions in captured German trenches situated between Longueval and Bazentin Le Grand, the movement completed at 10.30pm.

On 21st July, Alexander went on a reconnaissance patrol to gather intelligence for a proposed attack the following day, the purpose was to take a close look at the enemy positions facing them. The patrol came under fire and Alexander suffered a gunshot wound to his left thigh, with the intelligence, the patrol returned to their own trenches where they came under heavy artillery bombardment. The wounded were treated in-situ until it was safer to remove them to a Field Ambulance. Alexander's wound was complicated by the effects of shell shock.

From the Field Ambulance, he was transported to hospital and then onward back to England where he arrived on 25th July. He was transported and admitted to Belmont Auxiliary Military Hospital in Liverpool arriving there on 26th July. Throughout his journey he was attended by nurses and met at stopping points by volunteer women who provided sandwiches and hot drinks. The transportations were mainly conducted at night to avoid tying up day time transport and also to help hide the number of casualties from the eyes of civilians, the truth of the situation would have had a terrible effect on civilian morale.

Alexander's wound was judged too severe to return to front-line duty and accordingly he was posted to 3rd Battalion Royal Warwickshire Regiment on 14th October 1916. (The 3rd (reserve) Battalion was a training unit which remained in England throughout the war. From its base in Warwick, it moved to Portsmouth in August 1914, then to the Isle of White, the headquarters was maintained at Parkhurst and by the end of 1917 had been moved to Portsmouth).

On 2nd November, after 69 days in hospital Alexander was discharged to Fazakerly in Liverpool, (probably a rehabilitation unit) duty A.

On 16th October, whilst still in Belmont Hospital, Alexander submitted the application paperwork for a commission with a preference for Artillery or Infantry. His application was endorsed by his former employer at the Gas Board who had known him for six years and declared that Alexander was of good moral character. The application was also endorsed by his old Maths teacher, Mr J Clarke Neill B.A., now second master and head of maths at Yardley secondary school in Birmingham, who endorsed that his education was suitable for a commissioned rank.

Alexander attended a further medical examination and was deemed fit for military service, it is interesting to note that his chest expansion was now 3 inches and he was 10 stone, the military life had certainly made him fitter.

This story gives us an example of how short the army had become in respect of the traditional officer material. In 1908, a system of officer training was introduced at the public schools and universities, called the OTC (officer training corps), this was in response to grave losses of officers during the South African War (1899-1902). Designed on a voluntary basis to give boys a taste of military life whilst still in school and hopefully a desire for a military career, the system became compulsory with very few exceptions, to replace the same awful losses experienced in the initial stages of The Great War. Alexander probably left school after age 12 as there was a pressing needs to create income in a fatherless family. He had only attended state schools; hardly the sort of education and background under normal circumstances, that the army of the day would consider officer material. His knowledge, both theoretical and practical, of the workings and tactics of the machine gun placed him in a position of consideration for an officer post, until such time as the status quo could be re-established.

On 8th November 1916, Officer Cadet Lee attended the Machine Gun Corps cadre at Bisley-then and now a famous firing range. Following further instruction in the use and management of the

Vickers heavy machine gun he then attended officer training at the same location with the machine gun corps.

Following successful completion of the officer training cadre, Cadet Lee was discharged from the army on 24th March 1917. On 25th March Temporary 2nd Lieutenant Lee reported for duty with the Machine Gun Corps, his promotion was published in the London Gazette dated 13th April 1917.

Alexander's first posting was at Group C, Clipstone Camp, near Mansfield, where the Machine Gun Corps had one of its training units. Later that year on 2nd September, he was posted to 38th Machine Gun Company, based and fighting in what we now call Northern Iraq but then known as Mesopotamia. On 20th October 1917, Alexander embarked from Devonport aboard RMS Durham Castle. The next leg of his journey was on 30th July 1917, embarking from Durban on RMS Kenilworth Castle. He finally arrived in Basrah on 16th August, disembarking from the steam ship City of Sparta. His journey to join his new unit was then overland and he finally arrived in the company of R.W. Marley of the 5th Border Regiment on 13th September 1917, at a place called Palm Grove Khan Nahwan.

This theatre of war was against forces of both German and Ottoman (Turkish) origin and the weather this month was exceptionally hot. The 28th Machine Gun Company was made up of British and Indian troops. The establishment for August 1917, was nine British officers, 165 British other ranks, one Indian officer, 33 Indian other ranks and eight followers. This last group were Indian non-combatants who followed units undertaking such tasks as carrying water to the troops in the field. They had a tremendous record for bravery under fire taking water to injured men on the battlefield.

There was no action at the time Alexander arrived and, although there was a steady flow of men through the sick system to hospital, the reasons varied from diarrhoea, sores, fever and boils. The company had its own horses and mules for the carriage of persons and equipment, Alexander was allocated his own horse which he rode daily, the heat of the season caused issue with the saddlery as there were never sufficient treatments to prevent the leather drying out.

The diary notes that although there was a plentiful supply of fodder for the animals and that the men's rations were of an excellent standard, general health was only fair and the sickness reasons reflected the heat in which the men had to endure whilst manning their posts, otherwise working and training. One huge logistical problem was the need to supply men in the field with sufficient water. The company was supplied with 16 Pakhals, which was a netted water tank carried by mule but estimated that a minimum of 20 was required to efficiently carry out the task.

Many of these issues prevalent on Alexanders arrival were alleviated when the temperature started to drop, by November the numbers of men reporting sick had dropped to a tiny number.

On 3rd December, an attack was mounted on the Turkish forces by the battalions which Alexander's company was supporting. The infantry advances were covered by the guns which had been hauled to advantageous positions overlooking the ground to be covered. Numerous engagements were made that day with the enemy responding with rapid rifle fire, but the demoralising effect of the machine guns caused not only casualties, but many soldiers surrendered to the advancing infantry. The action was largely a success but delays by some units in achieving their objectives left a route of escape into the hills which was exploited by enemy troops in small groups. The attack took the enemy by surprise who suffered casualties and men and equipment captured including a Maxim machine gun that appeared to have jammed. Some mules in poor health were given good treatment and food and quickly recovered their strength becoming an asset to our forces.

The daily routines of holding the line, training and weapon maintenance was occasionally livened up by enemy artillery fire or a Turkish aircraft dropping bombs on their positions. There was a continual danger from snipers but there is no record of casualties. On 19th December 1917, an enemy plane flew overhead. The machine guns were elevated and 4,000 rounds expended in an effort to bring it down. The only notable event for Christmas Day, was another aircraft flying over their positions but on this occasion at a higher altitude and only 2000 rounds were fired.

January 1918 opened the last year of the war with Alexander directing such work as the creation of new open emplacements for the machine guns, anti-aircraft emplacements, drainage systems and mule troughs. On 6th January there was a large flood and communications were disrupted causing a shortage in milk and sugar. This would have been seen as a serious situation to the British soldiers and they are admired throughout the world, even to this day, for their ability to brew up a cuppa in any conditions, even in the height of a battle. This flood had also created a shortage in grain for the mules and in particular bhoosa which is the chaff from feed grain and used as bedding for the animals. By the 18th of the month the floods had subsided sufficiently for supplies to get through, the men had their cuppa and the animals a full stomach.

During March 1918, Alexander was able to experiment with a new type of machine gun ammunition, the tracer bullet. These are a round which is loaded at determinable intervals with normal machine gun bullets, at a ratio of 1 to 4, which on leaving the muzzle of the weapon leave a visible trace during their trajectory, thus giving the gunner an indication of whether he is on target or not and if not how to rectify the situation. The experiments showed that the better the daylight the harder it was to see the trace and it was better seen from a position near to the gun rather than by the gunner himself. The results and observations were no doubt useful for the development of this innovative idea which became a very useful tool against moving targets such as aircraft.

At 4.00 a.m. on 29th April, Alexander was in action again. An attack was undertaken on Turkish positions near a town called Tuz. The machine guns were mounted and used on mules to support the attacking infantry with cavalry battalions forming the attacking force. At the point where the enemy fire from rifles and machine guns became fierce, the mules were left behind and the guns manhandled from firing position to firing position with the help of carrying parties from the infantry. The plan of the attack was to turn the enemies right flank, attain a position at his rear and then destroy him from all points. The action lasted until midday and was a complete success. The machine guns were used with great effect against machine gun and field artillery positions; 1200 prisoners were taken, 12 field pieces and 25 machine guns were captured, very few enemy soldiers managed to escape.

On 2nd May 1918, Alexander commenced one month's leave and on the 15th boarded RMS Arondato India. Shortly after leaving, heavy rains occurred and again caused supply problems, the men and animals were on half rations due to the condition of the roads. Alexander returned from Bombay arriving back for duty at Basrah, on 27th June. He re-joined 38th Company in the field on 6th July 1918.

Towards the end of September 1918, the percentage of sicknesses rose considerably due to an outbreak of influenza. This was the start of the great pandemic of 1918 which is estimated to have killed between 20 and 50 million people worldwide. By 1st October, there was 57 British other ranks sick with flu. Fortunately the medical officers had seen fit to isolate all those infected thus containing the problem. No further cases were experienced.

The 11th November 1918, came and went without any mention in the war diary. Perhaps that reflects the general opinion that it was difficult to believe it was all over and many expected hostilities to resume; after all the 11th was only a cessation of hostilities! There must have been some elation and celebration, the joy of having survived must have been widespread but not, apparently, worthy of written record.

On the 4th January 1919, Alexander commenced his long journey home. Firstly, to Amara with the 13th Division advance party and then, on the 31st, he continued his journey home, the prize at the end, demobilisation.

Alexander was released from military service on 27th March 1919 He was required to relinquish his temporary rank but allowed to retain the rank of Lieutenant as an honorary gesture. In addition to this, he was awarded the 1915 star, British and Victory Medals. On returning home he returned to his job as clerk at the Birmingham Gas Board and in an effort to improve his situation attended night schools to attain qualifications in business studies.

Two children, Ken and Mary, were a product of a long and happy marriage and his hard work and ambition took him to the joint position of General Manager and Secretary of Birmingham Gas Board. On amalgamation with the rest of the West Midlands boards, he was appointed Deputy Chairman. In recognition of his lifetime service, he was awarded an OBE in the Queen's birthday honours list in 1954, his family accompanied him to Buckingham Palace to collect it from The Queen. Alexander and Hilda celebrated by taking a cruise aboard theWarwick Castle from London to London, the line was the Union Castle Mail Steamship Co. Ltd which went completely around the continent of Africa making stops enroute to deliver mail to the colonies there.

Alexander would never speak of his experiences and appeared not to suffer from his leg wound or shell shock, he did however keep himself very busy with work and family life and no doubt this helped to contain the horrors of his experience. He died the day after Princess Ann married, in 1973, aged 82.

Chapter 6

Frederick Pointon

(Sue O'Hara)

Mr Pointon used the shortened name Fred on various official documents and that is more than likely what he preferred to be called, so Fred was born on 30th November 1895, in Fulford, Staffordshire. The family home was at Green Sytch in the village of Fulford which was a farm run by Henry Fieldhouse; the farm no longer exists or has been renamed. The 1901 census shows two dwellings of this name with no individual numbers; the farm and Fred's home. Fred's father, Charles Pointon, was a labourer married for nine years to Mary Ellen and by this time the marriage had produced four sons; Charles, Fred, William and John, aged from four months to seven years of age.

By 1911, Fred now 15 years old, had left home and was living and working at The Park Farm, Fradswell, near Stafford. The farm was owned by Albert and Annie Heler whose two children were small boys. To run the farm, they employed five young men and women whose employments as dairymaid or cowman show the farm to be mainly dairy. Fred's employment is declared as "worker on farm" so very likely to be a general labourer not yet having achieved a defined role.

On 5th January 1915, Fred now aged 20 years, enlisted to join the army for the 'duration of the war' and following successful medical examination was recruited to the Leicestershire Regiment as Private 9/16794. Whilst Fred's original military file no longer exists, yet another victim of the Blitz of London in World War 2, there is a set of documents based on a post war examination of him and an assessment for a military pension. These pension files often contain copied details from the original file and relevant to the pension board, a medal record shows that Fred was at one stage, a member of both 9th and 8th Battalions, however the papers do not specify in which order. The '9' prefix before Fred's number denoted 9th Battalion and is in a place on the pension forms suggesting it was copied from the 1st document of his military file, the record of Attestation. This would lead us to deduce that he was firstly assigned to 9th Battalion and then transferred at a later date to 8th.

Both 8th and 9th (Service) Battalions Leicestershire regiment were formed in September 1914 at Leicester, to cope with the massive response to the call for arms. Both were assigned, along with 6th Battalion which had been formed in August, to 100th Brigade of 37th Division which was mobilised to France on 29thJuly, 1915. This date coincides with Fred's eligibility for the 1914-15 Star the date of which is the date he entered the relevant arena of conflict.

The situation following Fred joining the army was rather chaotic; the expectation of the recruitment campaign was for 200,000 men but in excess of double this turned up at the recruitment facilities in the initial months. Supplementary recruitment facilities had to be opened in public buildings such as Town Halls to cope with the eager volunteers. The military machine was not equipped for such numbers and soon ran out of accommodation, uniform and equipment. Tented camps were quickly erected around the country and huge quantities of wood cut to provide more suitable hut accommodation. To alleviate the shortage of serge uniform, the Post Office stores were raided and many recruits were dressed in the blue uniform of postal workers. Slowly but surely, the situation eased and battalions became properly equipped and trained. This often meant changes of location for particular training needs but these details were not transcribed to Fred's pension file. At the time of mobilisation orders being received, the 9th Battalion was housed in a hutted camp at Perham Down, a village on the edge of Salisbury Plain in Wiltshire, later to become Swinton Barracks. Embarkation was from Folkestone which was reached via route march and train from Luddershall station and disembarked at Boulogne, where they were initially billeted in a rest camp at Houlle. The logistics for the movement of so many men, (Battalion strength fully manned, exceeded 1,000 men), is exampled in the diary at this point. It records that the transport section mobilised separately and consisted of; three officers, 107 other ranks (including four Army Service Corps ASC), 73 horses, 19 four wheeled vehicles and four - two wheeled. This personnel figure included the machinegun section, grooms, signallers, six bicycles and carts used to carry stores, ammunition, food and mobile kitchens, making them self-sufficient as a unit on the move and in the field.

This independence was put to the test over the next few days with route marches for the whole Brigade and the Battalions kitchens cooked and fed the men in a forest. The weather was hot but thundery with heavy spells of rain, not the best conditions for marching with full kit but the men acquitted themselves well and there is no mention of anyone dropping out. As well as marches, which are designed to not only to test the fitness of the men but also the readiness of the Battalion to deploy. Training was constant and included the usual rifle drill of load and unload to attain a proficient standard when it came to rapid fire. The Lee Enfield Rifle was a very reliable bolt action rifle with a 10 round fixed magazine charged with clip held bulleted cartridges. A trained and efficient rifleman was expected to aim and fire between 20 and 30 rounds per minute, this was known as 'the mad minute'. The current world record for aimed bolt action fire was set in 1914 by a musketry instructor, Sergeant Snoxall, who placed 38 rounds in a 12-inch target at 300 yards, in just one minute. Clearly the practise of operating the bolt to open the action, ejecting a spent cartridge, closing the bolt and stripping a round from the magazine into the breach ready for aim and fire, was crucial training to attain the standard required. Assuming he started with a full magazine, Sergeant Snoxall would also have required three re-loads.

Between 9th – 11th August the Battalion commenced training in trench warfare and by company, spent the time in the front line at Wulverghem, Belgium, receiving instruction from 2nd Battalion Buffs, (East Kent Regiment). The Battalion was deemed ready and on the night of 12th August commenced the routine of relieving a front line unit to take their place in the line. The men took turns in the front line, second or support line and in the 3rd line or relief, until August 15th when their relief started at 10pm. This first time in the trenches was a quiet time and although the German artillery targeted the front line each afternoon no casualties were experienced. The German artillery had been more occupied with shelling the village of Wulverghem during these few days and when the men retired from the trenches, they found it almost completely in ruins. Following a good clean up, the Battalion marched to billets in Armentieres from where they provided daily and nightly working parties to reinforce and extend the trench system.

By the end of August, the first signs of the depravation of trench life start to emerge with the diagnosis of a large number of cases of Scabies, this was attributed to the lack of drinking water available to the men. The two biggest headaches in respect of supply to men at the front became, water and ammunition. Everything had to be carried to the front by either mule load or manpower and the conditions which prevailed around trench warfare meant that any local surface water should be viewed with great caution as it became infected with the waste of man, dead men and animals, and full of hazardous waste such as metals, explosives and gas. Wherever possible the Royal Engineers were tasked with creating deep bore wells to alleviate the transportation problems. All men affected were treated and their clothes and kit disinfected and allowed to dry in the sun; 27 cases were considered sufficiently serious to be admitted to a Field Ambulance.

At the beginning of September 1915, 9th Battalion marched to Humbercamps back in France where they entered billets and prepared to take over a section of trenches which were at that time occupied by the French army. By 4 a.m. September 5th, 1915 the French were entirely relieved and the routine of the trenches commenced. The Germans in the opposite trenches started to call out in English such things as; 'Allies no good', 'You English Tommies' and 'Are you the English from Armentieres?' No reply was made to these taunts which were clearly based on good intelligence and designed to demoralise. Again, this was a quiet time but the Battalion suffered its first recorded casualties on September 9th when an enemy shell scored a direct hit on a dugout and two Sergeants and two Privates were killed.

On 13th September 1915 Fred had his first brush with military discipline; the Battalion was out of the line and providing working parties. Fred was fined two days' pay for misconduct. It is not stated what his offence was, but this would probably be a very minor breach of discipline.

Over the next few months, the routine of time in the line and then reserve - providing working parties both day and night - continued. The working parties were mainly engaged in trench repair and improvement and as the weather became wetter the terrible conditions in the trenches worsened. There were insufficient materials to board the communication trenches at this time and working parties carrying supplies along these routes struggled through deep mud. By the end of November, the casualty count for the Battalion was; six officers wounded, 15 other ranks killed and 43 wounded.

During the early hours of Christmas morning 1915, the Battalion moved into the front line relieving 7th Battalion, Leicester Regiment. It was a quiet day so at 12 midnight three 25-man patrols were sent out from three companies who crept to within a very short distance from the enemy front line and bombed them, there was no retaliation. The weather turned bad and conditions were wet and freezing, the enemy artillery increased its attention on the British lines but the Battalion was relieved on 29th December and they spent the New Year festivities in Billets at Bienvillers providing the usual day and night working parties.

The next few months were spent in and out of the line in the Arras area. Whilst out, working parties were organised digging trenches, carrying supplies, assisting the Royal Engineers at the railhead and training. On 16th of April, a German aeroplane dropped three bombs on their positions near Mondicourt, but no damage was done. Whilst the sight of aircraft by this stage of the war would have been common, to be bombed must have been a very frightening experience and an indication of the way warfare was evolving, where airpower would be the key to the battlefield.

On 21st May, the troops were entertained to an aerial combat between Royal Flying Corps and German planes; the latter was shot down, surely a morale booster and payback for the bombing incident. Whilst casualties were very light during this period, men were still being killed and injured from various causes. Whilst in the trenches, the men were subjected to artillery bombardment almost on a daily basis. Machine guns would sweep the line and snipers were a constant danger. Rifle grenades were a common threat but for the first time, the diary mentions the German Minenwerfer, this was a multi-rocket launching device consisting of a block of tubes, highly manoeuvrable it could move from location to location, fire and move on. Like the Trench-Mortar crews, they were probably not very popular as the firing location usually attracted enemy artillery and by then, those responsible had moved on.

On 30th June 1916, the orders were received to move to Souastre as 7th Corps reserve for the impending offensive. The seven-day barrage which preceded the Battle of the Somme, could be heard back in England. The enormity of what was about to happen must have been all too obvious to the men who were now being moved to take their part in this historic event which was hoped would finally break the deadlock of the trench war. The move on 1st July went without hitch and the Battalion were placed at Souastre in support of 46th or 45th Divisions who were attacking at Gommecourt. That night they were then told to move back to Humbercamp on 3rd July which they did and continued training for the time they would have an opportunity to be involved in 'the big push'.

Various subsequent moves found them on the 10th July 1916, near to Fricourt where, at 9pm they moved into the front line in Quadrangle trench and support lines which had been captured in the initial stages of the offensive. All day on the 11th July, the lines held by the Battalion were subject to heavy artillery bombardment and the following day, the second in command Major Trotter and one other officer were killed and a third officer injured. On the night of 12th July, the

Battalion was relieved and retired to Fricourt. During these few days in the line, 50 other ranks had also become casualties. Following rest, working parties commenced carrying ammunition and grenades to Mametz Wood in support of the troops holding those positions there. Orders were received for the Battalion to take up positions in readiness for an attack on Bazentin-le-Petit Wood.

Section of Trench map (author's collection)

At 12.15 a.m. 14th July, the men, subjected to heavy shelling, reached the reserve positions in Mametz Wood and were finally in position for the forthcoming attack at 3.20 a.m., just in time for an intense artillery bombardment of the German positions to commence. At 5.20 a.m., the infantry assault started. Throughout the day, all Companies of 9th with elements of 6th, 7th and 8th Battalions, Leicestershire Regiment, were engaged in bitter fighting to gain control of the wood. All of C Company officers became casualties. At 6 a.m. some of A Company gained control of a section of German front line and began to consolidate the position, throughout all of this they were subjected to heavy artillery fire. The Battalion's CO, Lieutenant Colonel Haig set up a command post in the wood from which to direct the defence of ground gained against counter attack. At 12 noon D Company captured Colonel Kumme, two officers and 30 men who were removed to the rear as prisoners of war. Between 4 p.m. and 7 p.m., a further attack was ordered on the North West edge of the wood which was still in enemy hands. During this attack, four enemy artillery observers were killed which would have reduced the accuracy of the German artillery, but in the process a Captain Emmett and 36 other ranks were killed by machinegun fire. Reinforcements were sent to finish the capture of this section of the wood who also came under heavy machinegun, rifle and sniper fire. The wood was cleared but at huge cost. The men dug in and consolidated their positions against a counter attack which never materialised, but they were subjected to heavy shelling and rifle fire.

At 2 a.m. on 15th July 1916, orders were received to retire to the centre of the Mametz Wood from where they were relieved at 8 a.m. and returned to their original positions to spend the day cleaning up, re-supplying and resting. Rations which had been sadly lacking the previous day arrived along with rum; this went a long way to assist the men to rest! The depleted Companies were re-organised in preparation for more action. At 9 p.m. that night a 2nd Lieutenant and 20 men returned to take positions on the North West side of the wood but were isolated and all killed. At 3 p.m. the following day a patrol was sent to find them but failed. At 5.30 p.m. that day Captain Bent and two Companies were sent to relieve a like number from the 98th Infantry Brigade in Bazentin-le-Petit village and at 9 p.m. orders were received that the Battalion was to be relieved but this took a long time due to the displacement of units. During the night of 16th July, the final stragglers joined the Battalion who retired to a position near Fricourt at 11 a.m.

During the Battalion's engagement between 14th-17th July 1916 18 officers and 394 other ranks became casualties, this figure is not broken down and presumably includes, killed, wounded and missing, but whatever the causes, it was a grievous loss. One of those men wounded was Fred whose record shows that he received a gunshot wound (GSW) to the right elbow, possibly on 16th July, dependant on the accuracy of the person copying his record and, of course, the record itself. On 16th July, Fred was admitted to 64th Field Ambulance, transferred immediately to 34th Casualty Clearing Station, which would indicate the wound was not a minor one to be patched and the soldier returned to the line. On 24th July 1916, Fred was admitted to 11th Stationary Hospital (SH) at Rouen where he was treated and discharged to 12th Infantry Base Depot to await a posting back to a front-line Battalion. 9th Battalion Leicestershire Regiment had been sent back to the Arras area away from the ongoing battles of the Somme Offensive and, as a result, Fred was posted to 8th Battalion which he joined in the field on 12th August 1916.

8th Battalion Leicestershire Regiment had returned to the Arras Sector following the Brigade's brief but bloody involvement in the Somme Offensive. During the operations 14th-17th July 1916, the 8th had suffered the following casualties; killed in action, four officers (including the Battalion Commander, Lt. Col. J. G. Mignon) and 56 other ranks; died of wounds, one officer and ten other ranks; wounded, 12 officers and 310 other ranks; missing, 39 other ranks. This was a total casualty count of 415 and approximately half the Battalion's start strength.

Due to the focus, both offensive and defensive, of the Somme area at this time, the Arras sector was relatively quiet and the Battalion was able to reorganise, re-equip and receive replacements. They returned to the routine of manning the front line and reserve, providing working parties, both day and night.

During September 1916, Fred was admitted to 105th Field Ambulance, suffering from Pyrexia or high temperature. It is not recorded what the cause of this fever was, but it was sufficient to keep him in hospital for a week and he rejoined the Battalion in the field on 23rd September. During October 1916 the Battalion took over front line duties in the trench system of the Hohenzollern Redoubt.

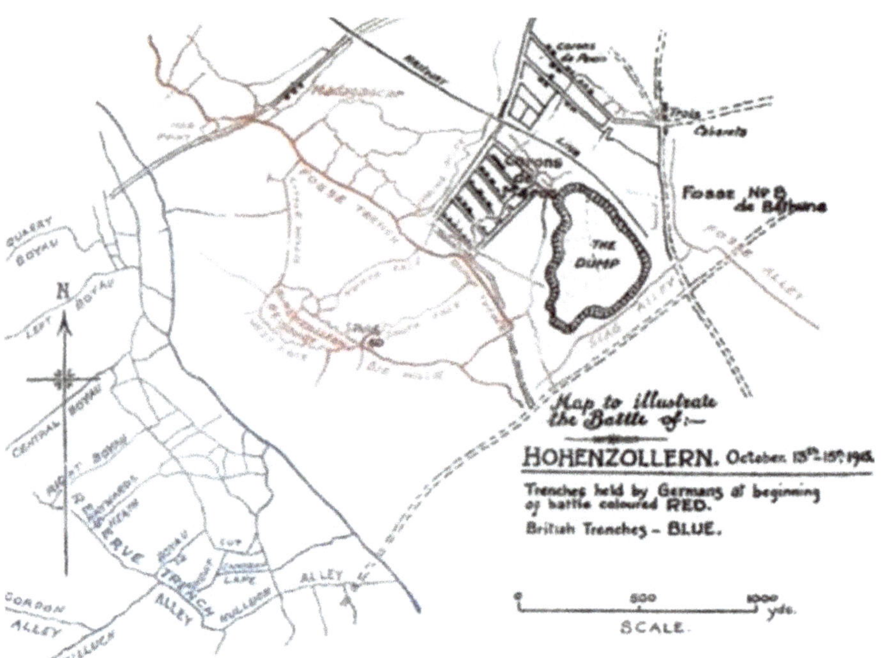

Picture Wikipedia Public Domain.

This location consisted of a bulge in the German front line, which contained a slag heap from local coal mining known as Fosse 8; this had given the Germans an unobstructed view of a large section of the British lines. The whole area had been the subject of fierce fighting since the battle of Loos in 1915 and, during the spring of 1916, the British had gained almost total control. Part of the fight for control had been tunnelling operations by both sides and the blowing of huge mines underneath the trenches. This had created craters which were bitterly fought over as control of such reshaped the attacking front line and pushed back the enemies. Occupation of the craters had been abandoned due to dangers of high trajectory plunge fire artillery, such as the German Minenwerfer or Howitzers. The tactic at this time was to attack and occupy the lip of the craters which were easier to consolidate and defend and gave the occupying troops the protection of an enclosed trench rather than an open space.

Apart from the use of the Divisional baths, Vermelles when out of the line; a cinema had been made available at Sailly-la-Bourse. Each evening approximately 40 NCO's and men were given a pass; they were collected from Philosophe Corner Vermelles, transported to the venue and then returned. This cinema was also used to present divisional concert parties which could be attended by men in reserve when not forming working parties. Life in the front line at this stage was quiet, the main stage still being in the Somme area. There was a daily exchange of artillery fire by both sides on the trenches, snipers were always a menace and any sighting of soldiers in trenches or engaged on working parties drew the attention of mortar or machinegun fire. Night patrols were sent out into No-Man's land to glean intelligence of activity in the enemy front line or concerning their defensive wiring operations, bright moonlight curtailed this activity of course.

On 20th December 1916 the Battalion moved to the Divisional reserve area at Auchel where they occupied Billets; this year they were to be out of the line at Christmas. The week leading up to Christmas was spent with parades, training and church parades for the various denominations. On 22nd December, the Divisional baths were made available to the whole Battalion who enjoyed a good clean, de-louse and fresh underwear, a luxury to these men! On Christmas morning, the Battalion attended Church of England services held in an Evangelical church, marching there in their respective Companies, a Non-Conformist service was also held. Following this, Christmas dinner was served to the men and junior NCO's by the officers and senior NCO's in a school, except B Company, who had their meal in the billets. The record shows that the men thoroughly enjoyed themselves. This type of celebration was usually funded by local donation from home and/or by the profits from the canteens run for the men. On Boxing Day, the afternoon festivities included a football match between the officers and Sergeants played on the Royal Flying Corps ground, the Sergeants won 4-3, surely a popular result! In the evening the men were entertained to a show by the Divisional Concert Party in the gymnasium. New year celebrations were held on New Year's Eve, commencing with the various church parades, the Old Year was played out and the New Year welcomed by the Divisional band in Auchel square. This had surely been a year that the survivors of the terrible conflict would remember for the rest of their lives!

January 1917, was largely spent on an extensive training programme, such activities as bomb throwing, bayonet fighting, PT, gas, saluting and march drills, musketry and rapid firing practice. Some of these activities were included into a sports programme including marching with a shoot at the conclusion, sniping, bomb throwing, and of course the usual tug of war, boxing and cross country runs. By the end of the month with morale at a high, as well as discipline and fitness, the Battalion were ready to return to the reality of War and were transferred back to the front arriving at Bethune in the middle of February.

Towards the end of February, Fred had a second minor brush with military disciple and was deprived three days' pay for an unspecified offence, very likely to be short of a piece of kit, the fine then paying for a replacement. This occurred again in May 1917 when he was fined ten days pay for the loss of a shirt and pants, the cost being ten shillings and thru' pence. The Battalion had a six-day tour in the front line, on 15th February 1917, before going into reserve for six days, thus commencing the return to the routine of trench warfare.

At the beginning of May 1917, the Battalion formed up on the right of the Brigade to become the attacking Battalion at that point, 9th Battalion was placed on the Brigades left. The objective of the attack was the village of Fontaine-les-Cruisilles. To support the infantry attack, two tanks were placed at the disposal of the Brigade but they very quickly broke down and were not used. This was a big disappointment to the men who had high hopes that this wonderful invention was going to be a huge asset, and eventually, of course, it was – but not on this day. At 3.45 a.m. on 3rd May 1917, the attack began behind the cover of a creeping barrage of artillery fire. The Battalion was disposed in two waves of five lines with a final wave of men to mop up behind the main attackers. Visibility was a problem, the attack commenced in the dark and the barrage created smoke and dust, as did the enemies retaliatory fire, no more than a few yards ahead could be seen. The left flank of the Battalion, held by C Company, encountered heavy machinegun fire and their advance was delayed. By 6.30 a.m. it was obvious that the attack was going to fail and 8th Battalion was in danger of being outflanked and cut off, this of course would have been disastrous and resulted in their total destruction. At the point they had reached, the 8th dug in, consolidated the position and held on until relieved at 11.30 a.m. the following casualties were recorded for this morning's work; two officers and 22 other ranks killed, five officers and 101 other ranks wounded, four officers, 168 other ranks missing, total casualties, 11 officers and 291 other ranks. The Battalion marched to Berles-Au-Bois and entered a rest camp, the rest of the month was spent organising a musketry competition, field training and preparing for inspections from the Divisional and Corps commanders.

The Battalion returned to front line duties on 7th June 1917, for a four day tour, the length of time in the line and then reserve had been reduced. During the night of 15th June, the Battalion occupied forward positions in preparation for an attack on the enemy front line. Whilst waiting to move, the German artillery placed a barrage aimed at the ground between the village of Croisilles and the front line, this effectively delayed other units from getting to their start positions and 8th Battalion was split, losing C Company to assist another Battalion. Due to the congestion in the trenches the whole attack was held up proving the effectiveness of the artillery barrage which was aimed at just the right area to create disruption. Another problem encountered was that the wire had not been cut, that and the effectiveness of enemy machineguns resulted in the attack being abandoned only 20 minutes after zero hour which had been 3.10 a.m. During these few minutes two officers and seven other ranks were killed, one officer and 23 other ranks were wounded, one officer and six other ranks were missing and two men were awarded the Military Medal for acts of unspecified bravery. The same day, following a rest, the Battalion was returned to man a section of front line.

On 23rd June 1917, Fred was admitted to 63rd Field Ambulance with Impetigo. By today standards this would appear to be a trivial matter for hospitalisation, but we must remember that there were no antibiotics at this time and an open wound was an extremely dangerous injury to carry due to the terribly unsanitary conditions the men were living with. On this occasion Fred was returned to his unit after one day of treatment but the condition reoccurred during August 1917 and he was admitted to 1/3 Field Ambulance (shown on the file as 1/3 NFA possibly Northumberland). On this occasion Fred was not discharged until 18th August and an indication as to how serious this bacterial condition was viewed.

During the night of 1st October 1917, the Battalion was called into action to support Fred's old unit 9th Battalion Leicestershire Regiment, who had become the target of a ferocious German attack. The enemy successfully gained access to the 9th front line and the SOS was sent out at that point. Heavy fighting during the night eventually resulted in the attackers being beaten off by use of Lewis gun and effective rifle fire, but the Battalion had been subjected to heavy artillery fire and repeated attacks on their exposed right flank. The attack had been mounted on a large scale and the whole of the Brigade became involved, the fighting continued throughout the day and into the night of 2nd October, until the battalion was relieved during the early hours of the 3rd. During this engagement 11 officers and 175 other ranks became casualties, this included the CO Lt. Colonel Utteron, DSO, who was shot through the arm but remained on duty until relieved. The 9th Battalion had also suffered a large number of casualties and on 4th October the two units were amalgamated on a temporary basis.

During the period 15th – 22nd October 1917, 8th Battalion were out of the front line but providing working parties in the forward areas between Clapham Junction and Fitz Clarence Farm near Gheluvelt. The work was digging trenches for the burial of telephone lines, an essential duty to protect the lines of communication which were continually being cut by shell fire. These working parties could obviously be seen and became the target of the German artillery, during this period one officer was wounded and 86 other ranks killed, wounded or missing. Fred received his second wound of the war, when he was hit in the arm by shrapnel on 17th October. Fred was initially admitted to 3rd Australian Field Ambulance and then transfered to 2nd Canadian General Hospital located at Le Treport, Calais.

Fred was out of action until 14th January 1918, when he re-joined his Battalion in the field but was sent home on leave, from 21st January until 6th February. The list of Fred's movements transposed from his original file to this surviving document is comprehensive and there is no doubt that this is the first opportunity he had to return to visit family and friends at home.

On the day Fred is shown returning, the Battalion was holding a front line position, he was likely to have remained with the reserve units until the relief occurred on 9th February when the whole Brigade was relieved. 8th Battalion entrained to Moislains where they went into huts at York Camp.

On 17th March 1918, 8th Battalion moved into the front line east of Epehy in the Somme area. It was well known that the German army was preparing for a major attack in this area. Aerial reconnaissance was by now well advanced and the build-up of troops, artillery and supplies was not something which could be hidden. The front line by this stage in the war, was not a continual line of connecting Battalions but what had become known as a defence in depth. The German army had developed this concept in 1917 and its success made it a tactic to be copied. The front line was now made up of outposts containing snipers, machine guns and raiding parties, making the defensive lines much deeper and a far more difficult target for artillery and mine warfare. Prisoners snatched by the Battalion's patrols were questioned and the information forthcoming was that the attack was planned for a time between 20th to 22nd April. In the early hours of 21st April, one officer and 20 men were sent out to try to identify opposing forces but returned having not seen a single enemy soldier, the mystery of when the attack was to begin ended at 4.40 am that day when the German artillery commenced its barrage of the British lines.

This artillery bombardment was the opening action of the German Spring Offensive which was a final, all out action, to break the deadlock of the Western Front. The German high command realised that for them to win, they had to defeat the Allies on this front before the might of the United States forces could be settled and become effective. The offensive was planned to be in four stages, beginning with Operation Michael in the Somme area commencing on 21st March. The artillery bombardment experienced by Fred and his comrades was the largest barrage of World War 1 and hit targets covering an area 150 square miles, lasting five hours and in excess of 1,100,000 shells were fired.

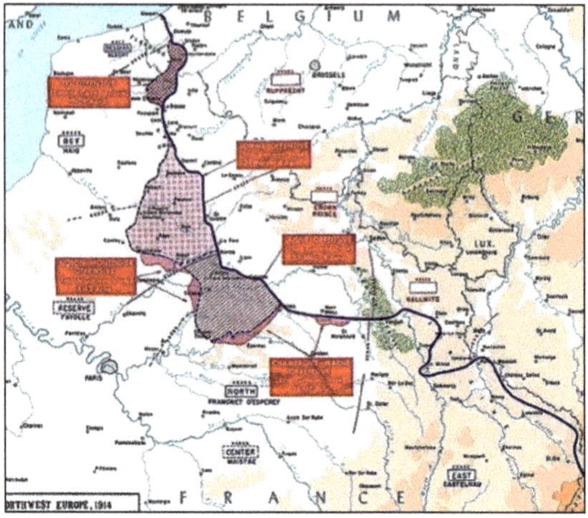

Picture public domain via Wikimedia

Fred's Battalion was positioned in the front line at approximately the centre point of the area covered by this first stage of Operation Michael, if you draw a triangle between Cambrai, St Quentin and Baupaume, Epehy is situated there and the Battalion's positions were just to the east of that village.

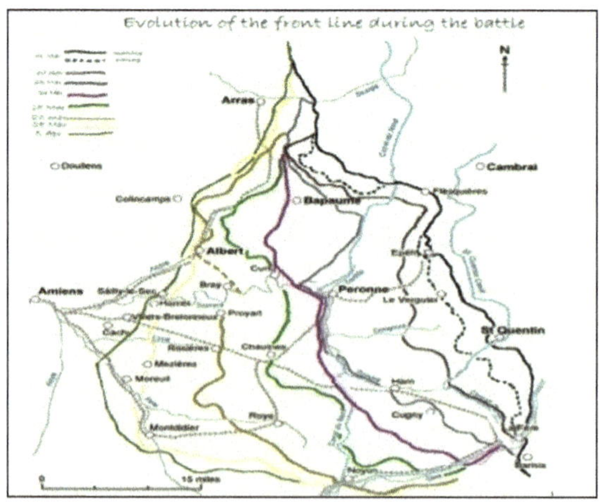

Picture public domain via Wikimedia

The Battalion was subjected to heavy artillery fire using both high explosive and gas shells; the gas used was mustard gas and was in such concentration the men had to wear their respirators for three hours. This gas was a particularly nasty device which caused blistering to exposed skin and if inhaled blistering off the lungs, death was caused by asphyxiation when the lungs became inefficient at recycling oxygen to the system.

At 6 a.m. when daylight started to break through, the mist and dust had created an impenetrable curtain with visibility only possible over a short distance. Just before 9 a.m. the artillery bombardment started to cease and change tactic to protect advancing troops. Communication had been maintained with two of the Battalion's Companies which gave the Battalion command a picture of the events unfolding. The front-line units had been withdrawn to the immediate support line and at 9.50 a.m. enemy infantry were seen to be advancing on their positions. The order to 'Man battle stations' was given. The enemy were engaged by machinegun and rifle fire and started to suffer heavy losses. The practise drill of load and unload came to fruition and rapid fire from units of riflemen competent with the Lee Enfield rifle was almost as effective as machineguns. In fact, captured German reports often stated that they had been engaged by machineguns when they had in fact been engaged by rapid fire from these weapons in the hands of experienced men. The German forces held at the abandoned British front line and dug in, content for the moment consolidate those positions. In these positions the Germans were subjected to very effective Lewis gun and rifle grenade fire, but the visibility was such that forward observation officers could not give accurate reports to bring down artillery fire on the enemy.

During the morning the mist lifted giving a clearer picture of the situation, a withdrawal of units to the Battalion's right had exposed their flank and the enemy had gained access to the trenches at one point but were ejected by fierce retaliatory bombing (Grenade throwing parties). At 1 p.m. that day, a lull occurred in the fighting but was soon over when the enemy commenced heavy trench mortar fire on the Battalion's support positions. During the afternoon, reports came in the enemy infantry had broken through the line to the

Battalion's right and was everywhere; a withdrawal was organised to bring the line together. The mist had cleared and the German infantry was held to account and suffered huge losses. Later in the afternoon, the mist again descended and the enemy were able to continue their advance. The Battalion became involved in a series of retirements to new positions from where the enemy was engaged until another retirement was necessary. This situation then continued for some days and the fighting was continual, day and night. On 25th March 1918, the Battalion's strength was so depleted that it was broken up into different units and attached to other Battalions. By 31st March, what remained of the Battalion was in billets in the village of Allonville and was able to take account of their losses. The total casualties were; 15 officers and 415 other ranks, this included killed in action, wounded, missing and taken prisoner. This included Lt. Colonel Utterson, DSO, who was believed to have been captured on 22nd March with a large proportion of the officers and men missing including Fred.

At this very confusing time Fred was reported missing and a telegram to that effect was sent to his family. Nothing was then heard of Fred's fate until 17th October 1918, when a report, presumably by the international Red Cross, was received that he was a prisoner of war and incarcerated at Güstrow POW camp in Germany. By a failure in communication Fred's family were not informed of this fact and were most surprised after the war when he showed up on the front door step, alive and well.

Güstrow POW camp was situated in a forested area three miles from the town of that name in the area of Mecklenburg-Vorpommern, Germany. The camp was a Mannschaftslager, or other ranks camp; officers were accommodated separately. There were 25,000 prisoners in the camp with another 225,000 men registered at the camp but at alternative accommodation having agreed to work. The pressure on men to work was often harsh often a refusal would be treated with a punishment of standing still all day in isolation with limited rations. Many men were put to work on farms and used the opportunity of the chaos at the end of the war to escape to a neutral country from where they were repatriated back to Britain. Fred would have been held captive behind the German lines with other POW's until they could be transported to a transit camp from where he would have been transferred to Güstrow, arriving there on 24th September 1918.

There is no record of how and when Fred was released from the camp, travelled back to England or what happened when he arrived home. By the end of the war, both 8th and 9th Battalions had ceased to exist. There is an indistinct note on the file of him being posted following being reported missing but before the recorded status of POW. This was no doubt a paper posting for administrative purposes, but the details are indistinguishable. On 23rd February 1919, Fred was examined and assessed for a medical discharge. He had signed the declaration that he did not suffer a disability with regards to his military service but as in the case of wounded men he was examined anyway. The assessment noted the wound scars and deemed that he did not qualify for a pension. On 19th March 1919, almost a year after becoming a prisoner, Fred was demobilised from the army and placed, like all able-bodied men, on the reserve list, category Z. Post Armistice, nobody really believed that the war was completely over until the treaty of Versailles in 1919. The Z list was designed to create an emergency reserve of able-bodied men; discharged but ready to be recalled in a time of emergency. The list was discontinued in 1920.

Fred returned to Staffordshire and in the autumn of 1919, he married Rose Broom. The marriage produced five sons and two daughters. The family subsequently took up residence at Canal Side, Acton Trussell, near to Stafford from where Fred worked as a general labourer.

Fred died in June 1969 aged 73; he had been awarded the 1914-15 Star, the British War and Victory Medals for his service during World War 1.

Chapter 7

Frederick Charles Knowles

(Tim Thurlow)

Frederick was born in Newport, Monmouthshire, on 3rd June 1887. His father, James, a Carpenter and his mother, Harriet, were both from Herefordshire, England and had moved to Wales for work and to start a family. The family home was 31, Bristol Street, Maindee, Newport and where all five of James and Harriet's children were born and brought up there. In 1911, the family unit was still intact at Bristol Road and James, now aged 50, was working as a House Carpenter. The eldest son, also James aged 25, had followed in his dad's footsteps and was employed as a Ship's Carpenter. Frederick, now 24, was a Machine Ruler, Walter, 21 years, was a Crane man in the local docks, Reginald, 18 years, was a Clerk with the Co-Operative stores and the youngest, a girl Hilda aged 11, was attending school.

Frederick had completed a seven-year apprenticeship with Henry Mullock & Son Ltd in Newport to become a Machine Ruler. The owner of this company had been Richard Mullock whose family had run a printing business and produced the Newport Advertiser; this is most likely where Frederick had learnt his trade. Richard was a remarkable character whose achievements included organising the first Welsh Rugby Union international match which ultimately led to the formation of the Welsh Rugby Union from the Welsh Football Union of which Richard was secretary. He was also a referee.

On 2nd September 1914 following the outbreak of The Great War, Frederick attended a recruitment facility in Stroud and attested to join the army. He was also medically examined and found to be fit for military service. The examinations were carried out by the recruitment officers of the Gloucestershire Regiment based at Horfield Barracks in Bristol and Frederick was sent home with his shilling to await orders. Those orders duly arrived and he was instructed to attend Tidworth Barracks in Wiltshire on 12th September, where he became Private 10/18710 Worcestershire Regiment. The 10 prefix denotes he was assigned to 10th (Service Battalion) which had recently been formed at Worcester to help cope with the huge response to the call to arms.

The system for induction of recruits was rather chaotic at this time as the initial expectation for a response to the call to arms was about 200,000 men and this was the figure that the military machine could house, dress and equip. The actual response was far in excess of this and tented camps were hurriedly formed all over the country whilst work commenced to build substantial barracks buildings in wood. Uniform was a big problem and initially resolved by raiding a Post Office store and issuing men with the blue uniform of postal workers. Initially the 10th Battalion was sent to Perham Down on the edge of Salisbury Plain in Wiltshire. Huts were not built until 1915 when the camp became known as Swinton Barracks. The men were accommodated in tents until December 1914, when they were moved to Weston-super-Mare in Somerset. This seaside town was the location of many training camps and during the war, 80% of the trees from the surrounding countryside were cut down to build huts. The beach was used for training men in digging trenches as it is a very slowly sloping beach creating a long low tide and of course the sea filled the works in to make the location ready for the following day. The Battalion returned to Tidworth on 29th March 1915.

A great deal of work was conducted in the initial stages by battalions to properly equip, house and train recruits and by July 1915, 10th Service Battalion was deemed fit for active service and mobilisation orders were issued. Over the two-day period, 17/18th July 1915, the Battalion with all its HQ staff, machinegun detachments, horses, mules, carts and of course the men, entrained to Folkestone. Initially a change of train delayed proceedings due to a collision at Tidworth station, but eventually all embarked and landed at Boulogne on 19th

July where they marched to a rest camp at Ostrohove for the night. The rest of July 1915 was spent marching from camp to camp until they arrived at Laventie, Pas-de-Calais where they commenced training in trench warfare under the instruction of 2nd Battalion, Black Watch and providing working parties. On 28th August 1915, 10th Battalion entered the front line and relieved 1st Battalion, Royal Welsh Fusiliers, the relief was completed by 10 p.m. without incident and the men settled down to the routine of front line, relief and reserve.

(The correct spelling of Welsh in Royal Welsh Fusiliers is actually Welch an old English version of the word. For an unknown reason this was changed to Welsh during The Great War and the various memorials and headstones contain a mixture of the two. If it helps my father-in-law is a very proud Welshman, veteran Welch Fusilier and Welsh speaker who prefers Welsh as that was how he was taught!).

On 7th August 1915 the Battalion was relieved by 10th Royal Warwickshire and during their first experience of trench warfare they had sustained their first casualties; three killed and 17 wounded. At 1.30 a.m. with the relief complete the men marched to Rue des Chavattes where they formed part of Brigade reserve. The days and nights were spent on marches or forming working parties undergoing such duties as carrying stores for the machine gunners and trench improvements. The trench system which prevailed of the Western front throughout the war was still in its infancy and under continual construction and improvement. Spoil removed to deepen the trenches was used to raise the parapet on the trench front face and the three lines, front, support and reserve were interconnected by communication trenches to avoid the obvious dangers and manoeuvre between the three. Little inclusions to the system were developed as experience expanded, small cuts in the communication trenches were added to facilitate passing during relief, and small offshoots were dug to take a machinegun post which gave field of fire in the event of a trench being entered by the enemy. Funk holes were dug in the front face of trenches where the men could take cover during artillery action and take rest. This work continued throughout the war and after heavy rainfall, increased the need to make repairs.

The first mention of a hot bath, occurs of 12th October 1915 when the Battalion spent the day at a brewery in Vieille Chapelle. The brewing vats had been made into bathing tubs manned and supervised by elements of the Royal Army Medical Corps, (RAMC). Fresh underwear would have been issued and an opportunity to rid the body and clothing from lice taken, this experience must surely have raised the men's moral after an extended period of living conditions in muddy trenches and relief camps.

On 5th November 1915, Frederick was admitted to 59th Field Ambulance, RAMC with a condition known as Trench Foot. The following day this diagnosis was changed at No. 9 Casualty Clearing Station, to Frost Bite and due to the serious nature of the condition, he was then transferred to No 6 General Hospital situated at Rouen. Trench Foot is a condition caused when the feet are continually immersed in water and unsanitary conditions, the flesh swells and starts to rot. Untreated, sores and blisters occur creating open wounds and in the conditions associated with Great War trenches, from which the condition gets its name, infection will quickly set in causing Sepsis. This was a common cause of death at this time, as anti-biotics were not yet available and simple things such as boils were sufficient to remove a soldier from the front to a hospital facility. I would suggest that in this case the condition was exacerbated by freezing temperatures and that Frederick was probably very lucky to have survived!

On 10th November 1915, Frederick's war was over and he embarked for 'Blighty' on the Hospital Ship (HS) St. George. No record has survived of where he was treated back at home but it was clearly a lengthy spell in hospital and probably also a rehabilitation centre. A common result of Frederick's condition is the loss of toes and as these are an integral component to the walking process he would have needed to learn to walk again. On 13th March 1916 he was posted to the Regiment's Command Depot at Sutton Coldfield, unable to march he was placed before a medical board who on 23rd June 1916 declared that he was no longer fit for military service and on 12th July he was discharged from the army.

By this stage of the war there was pressure being applied from many sources for apparently able-bodied men to join the armed forces. The military and government used poster campaigns, but also local organisations and individuals. It was common practise for women to carry white feathers which they readily handed to men in civilian clothes whom they judged should be in uniform, this of course was effectively calling the individual a coward. To help identify men like Frederick who had served and been discharged, a Silver War Badge was developed for them to wear on their outer clothing which identified them as veterans. Each badge was officially numbered and issued individually, Frederick's badge was numbered 85401, but the authority for issue is dated in November 1916 and there may have been an uncomfortable period for him until he received his badge, it may also have been that his manner of walking spoke for itself! He was subsequently awarded the 1914-15 Star and the British War and Victory medals.

Silver war badge, author's collection

Following discharge Frederick seems to have remained in the area, he married Ethel Nellie Hopson on 23rd September 1919, in Stonehouse, Stroud, Gloucestershire. This marriage produced one child, a boy James Robert Barrie Knowles, born on 7th January 1923. He had returned to his former trade in the printing industry and by the time of the 1939 census, the family had moved to the Buckinghamshire and were living at Saxhulme, 166 Chartridge Lane, Chesham, where he was employed as a Machine Ruler and Book Binder. Frederick died in Amersham Buckinghamshire on 19th November 1962, aged 74, and his estate of £299.8s.0d. passed to his widow Ethel.

Chapter 8

Henry Thomas Blackstone

(Tim Thurlow)

Henry Thomas Blackstone was born in the second quarter of 1898 and baptised at Christ Church, Sidcup, Kent, on 31st December 1899. Henry's parents were William and Harriet Blackstone of 6, Ashly Terrace, Sidcup. William was a Stoker in the local gas works. Henry was the fourth child, his elder siblings being Albert, aged nine, Daisy, aged seven and Mable, aged five. In 1900 a third boy, George, was added to the family.

By 1911, the family had expanded by a further five children; Ethel, aged nine, Mary, aged seven, Florence aged five, Kenneth aged four and Sidney aged two. In total Harriet had given birth to ten children, all of whom had survived to the date of this census, a remarkable record for the time when a high child mortality rate existed for people of this status. Nine of the ten children were still living at home, and eight were still at school, their ages ranging from two to 15 although the school leaving age for the day was twelve. The only wage earner, other than William, was the eldest son, Albert, who at 19 years of age, was employed as a farm labourer. The missing child, Daisy now aged seventeen, was employed as a General Domestic Servant and living with Walter Grafton and his family in Eltham, London. Walter was the Managing Director of an engineering company which manufactured office appliances. It is interesting to note that living with Walter was his wife and her 77 year old aunt in a ten bedroom house, thereby occupying a maximum of four rooms, whilst William's family of 11 lived in a house with five rooms.

Unfortunately, Henry's military file did not survive the bombing of World War 2, but from the files that did survive, it is apparent that he joined the army before the outbreak of war and because his service number was date issued, certainly before 27th July 1914. His initial training was completed by January 1915 and he was despatched to France on 19th. When he was killed, he was serving with 7th Battalion Queen's Royal West Surrey Regiment but had previously served with 1st Battalion. The 1st Battalion was a regular army unit and had mobilised to France in August 1914, landing at Le Havre on 13th August 1914. At the beginning of February 1915, 1st Battalion's war diary shows their strength to be 27 officers and 453 other ranks. This was the result of the heavy fighting they had experienced during the Battle of Mons and subsequently holding the line during September and October 1914, with renewed efforts by the Germans to break through. A letter in the Battalion's war diary speaks of the dire situation faced by the men at this stage and is reflective of the urgent need to replace the enormous number of men from the BEF killed, wounded or missing. The letter was from Captain J. D. Boyd, DSO, who survived the war and was addressed to 1st Battalion Queens Royal Regiment, Tournay Barracks, Aldershot, dated 2nd March 1923.

Dear Edmonds,

In reply to your letter dated 28th February, the first draft after 31st October, which joined us on 9th November, was a good one, consisting of reservists almost entirely. After that we fell off sadly in quality as well as quantity. The second Battalion was also short of personnel and was filled up prior to the 1st Battalion owing to the latter being in Corps troops.

It was only in January 1915 that a C Company could be formed from a draft which joined the Battalion from Hinges. D Company was formed about February 1915. The men who joined us in January-February were very untrained and any sprinkling of trained NCO's and men amongst them were medically unfit.

I remember 1 draft in particular which joined us at Chocques 1915 and 75 per cent. of whom were returned to the base within a week as medically unfit. I should say that the majority of our drafts after 1st December were only partially trained.

Yours sincerely
(Signed) J.D. Boyd.

Captain Boyd was awarded his DSO personally by the Commander in Chief on 27th December 1914; the Battalion had spent Christmas out of the line in Billets at Hinges near Hazebrouck.

It is very likely that Henry joined 1st Battalion in the field as a replacement with one of the drafts mentioned in the above letter. If he was one of the men returned, due to insufficient training, this could account for the fact that he was, at a later date, posted to 7th Battalion. It is not likely he was returned for being unfit as he had passed the medical examinations to join the army, undergone basic training which would concentrate on fitness and he was only 17 or 18 years of age. There is no mention of any men returned for being underage, which is usually mentioned separately. There are other reasons he could have been reposted, he may have been wounded and following recovery posted to 7th Battalion, returning from home leave or specialist training and 7th Battalion required the replacements at that time, we have no means now of knowing and a long trawl through both war diaries has not supplied the answer. By August 1917, Henry, now aged 21, had served for three years and was posted to 7th Battalion, Queen's Royal West Surrey Regiment as a Corporal, this of course could account for the change of Battalion as he would have been sent to NCO school following promotion to either Lance Corporal or Corporal.

At 7 p.m. on 7th August 1917, 7th Battalion, Queens Royal West Kent Regiment moved to the Chateau Ségard Camp, near Café Beige, Belgium to take part in a planned attack, part of the offensive known as the Third Battle of Ypres or Passchendaele. The objectives of the 7th were to attack and form a line 100 yards inside Inverness Copse, the flanks to be in touch with other Battalions. The four Companies were allotted their individual responsibilities. A and D Companies were the initial attacking units, B Company was assigned to support and mopping up whilst C Company were to concentrate on enemy strong points and mopping up. Any stragglers from other units were to be collected en route and engaged in the attack which was scheduled following relief of the 7th Battalion, Royal West Kents, who were holding the front line. The relief was completed and the men stood waiting for the order to attack in torrential rain, orders delaying the attack were received and at 9.30 pm on 8th August 1917, the enemy commenced a heavy artillery bombardment on the British line which lasted for 30 minutes. At midnight that night an NCO from each attacking Platoon was put out on the start tapes to direct the troops to cuts in the wire. At 00.40 a.m. the lead platoons reached the tapes but a bolt of lightning alerted the enemy to the presence of the attackers, green very lights were sent up to mark their positions and this gave the German artillery spotters the location to call down a barrage. This was followed by a second barrage at 02.28 a.m.

The assault was launched at 04.35, accompanied by an artillery barrage on the German front line and a creeping barrage for the attackers to follow. A problem had occurred that morning with the ration transports and the men had not received a breakfast, however, the rum ration had found its way to the front and each man was fortified with a healthy tot. The attackers found many obstructions in their way such as loose wire or tree trunks, apart from the boggy conditions which makes advance progressively difficult as build ups of mud occur on boots. The German infantry was in Inverness Copse in strength to retaliate with accurate rifle and machinegun fire. The objectives were eventually reached and the positions consolidated, the battalion was relieved during the night of 10/11th August 1917, by 10th Battalion of the Essex Regiment and the survivors retired to Dickebusch New Camp to clean up and recover.

During the course of the day, the total casualties were simply recorded as ten officers and 272 other ranks, this presumably included killed, wounded and missing. Henry's body was recovered and he was buried at Tyne Cot Military CemeteryWest-Vlaanderen, Belgium, grave reference LXVII. F. 15. This cemetery has 3605 identified graves but is the resting place for more than 11,900 servicemen from The Great War. It is the largest Commonwealth cemetery in the world and is famous for its memorial wall to the missing whereon is inscribed the names of 34,997 men with no known grave.

Headstone Picture courtesy Tim Thurlow

Henry left £3.12s.4d. which was reinforced with a war gratuity of £18.10s.0d. to his father, William. He was awarded the 1914-15 Star, the British War and Victory Medals, which were sent to his parents along with the Death Plaque and Memorial Scroll which now form an important part of Tim Thurlow's extensive collection of World War 1 artefacts and memorabilia.

Chapter 9

Arthur William Brown

Arthur was born on 3rd December 1887, the third child of Nelson and Ann Brown of 37, Russett Street, Walton, Liverpool. Nelson, described as a general labourer and Ann, had Arthur baptised on 5th February 1888, in Anfield, Liverpool. By 1891, the family had increased to four children and ten years later they had moved to 65, Rocky Lane, Anfield and a fifth child had been added. Another ten years elapsed and the family had again moved to 45, Rossett Street, Anfield; all four of Arthur's siblings, two brothers and two sisters, had survived to that date. Arthur, now aged 23, is employed as a Compositor for a newspaper; this job involved the arranging of words, letters and pictures on a printing machine, this was skilled work and indicated a good level of education.

On 5th September 1914, Arthur attested at a recruitment facility in Liverpool and was accepted into The King's (Liverpool) Regiment. Assigned the number 2612 he was posted to 1/5th Battalion which had been formed in August 1914 as a Territorial unit in St Anne Street, Liverpool to accommodate the enthusiastic response by the men of Liverpool to the call to arms. Initially, the Battalion's duties involved guarding the London to Brighton South Coast Railway, before being moved to Ramsgate and then Canterbury where the men prepared and trained for war.

On the same day as taking the oath and receiving his shilling, Arthur was subjected to a medical examination, for a man with a relatively sedate occupation he seems remarkably healthy. 6ft ¼" tall, with good vision and a fully expanded chest of 39" with a 4" range, he is described by the examining officer, Captain Monsarrat, to be of good development. The 4" chest expansion would generally indicate good lung capacity and often typical with sports people; perhaps Arthur was a keen football player, he certainly hailed from the right area of Liverpool to show a keen interest in that sport.

The Battalion's War diary is commenced on 1st February 1915, unusually some 20 days before disembarkation and shows that the men were training on a daily basis in Company and Battalion form, mainly in musketry. The objective of this repetitious training was to get each and every man to the high standard required of a rifleman using the Lee Enfield Bolt action rifle. In the right hands, this most efficient of weapons for the time, could be fired at a rate of 15 rounds per minute. The firing discipline was called 'the mad minute' and was in the prone position at 300 yards using the usual man's head and shoulder size target. Firing commenced with a round in the breach and four rounds in the magazine, this was followed by two reloads of five rounds from clips kept in a pouch or bandolier. The effectiveness of this volley fire was very evident when captured enemy reports described the fire they were under as machinegun, when in fact it was the expertise of men like Arthur, highly trained with the Lee Enfield Rifle.

On 6th February the entire transport fleet of the Battalion was replaced with a new issue, this was a good indicator that the men were going to war in the near future. New equipment for the men and ammunition arrived over the next week and on 20th February, the diary notes that the Battalion is fully equipped, not too soon either, as at 4.45 p.m. the same day, mobilisation orders arrived and the following morning the Battalion entrained at Canterbury. Three trains were made available, leaving at intervals from 6.55 a.m. bound for Southampton. The Battalion's strength on this day was 31 officers and 1100 men plus transport horses, mules, wagons and carts. Amongst the organised chaos and excitement, many men had never been on a ship before let alone gone abroad, officers and military police barked orders and eventually the three transport ships at the Brigade's disposal were full. At 5.20 p.m. on 21st February 1915, the 'Duchess of Argyle', 'Queen Empress' and 'Manchester Importer' steamed out of Southampton harbour bound for France. The ships docked at Midnight the same day at Le Havre, but the Battalion did not disembark until 8 a.m. the following morning. At that time the Battalion formed up by Company order and marched out of port to the rest camp at St Adresse, a few miles north of Havre port.

On 23rd February 1915, the Battalion marched to the railway station with orders to entrain but with no known destination, speculation as to where they were headed was bound to have dominated the conversation at all levels, which is the nature of man. On arrival at Béthune, they were housed in a French camp for two days where they found that they had been allocated to 6th Infantry Brigade of 2nd Division of 1st Army. At 2.00 p.m. 25th February, the Battalion was inspected by the Corps Commander, General Horne, and then by route march they proceeded to Vendin-Lèz-Béthune where they went into billets. Over the next few days, each Company in turn went into the front line with 1st Battalion, King's Royal Rifles while the remaining Battalions underwent other training. On 9th March 1915, the Battalion went into the front line under its own command for the first time, relieving elements of the Liverpool and Berkshire Regiments.

That first night, orders were received to take part in a Brigade attack on the German line the following morning. At 7.00 a.m. the artillery opened up with the intention of breaking the German defensive wire and 30 minutes later the target was changed to the enemy front line. This, of course, created retaliatory fire and at 8.10 a.m. the infantry commenced their attack. The Battalion, due to its inexperience was split to join other units in the three separate sections of the attack and therefore had objectives covering the whole of the enemy front line. Under heavy machinegun and rifle covering fire the men advanced but the attack was unsuccessful as the wire had not been broken. The attack faltered and the men returned to the British line. Here the Battalion resumed its front line duty having experienced their first losses of five men killed and 16 wounded, of which one later died of his wounds. The diary notes that the action of all ranks was exemplary and that great bravery was shown in the face of enemy fire and in the recovery of the wounded from the field. Disappointing I am sure, for a first baptism of fire, but the casualties experienced were not by any standards high and worse was to come. The Battalion was relieved on 12th March, and retired to billets to clean up and resume their training programme.

A1 to E3 - German front line objectives (author)

During April 1915, the Battalion resumed the routine of front line support and reserve rotation. Two noteworthy incidents occurred when mines were exploded in front of their positions, firstly on the 6th at 11.20 p.m. when two German mines were detonated but caused no damage as they were 20 – 30 yards short. On the second occasion, 21st April, a single mine was detonated, again short of the line but within a few yards of a sap and 17 men were wounded but none killed. The war diary gives a vivid picture of this event:

> *"This mine made a large crater about 60' long and 40' wide 30' deep and the earth was thrown up 10 to 12 feet high, absolutely blotting out view from a part of our trench. During the night a great deal of bombing was carried out on both sides".*

A regular toll was taken on a daily basis with casualties, killed and wounded.

On 7th May 1915, orders were received for the Battalion to move to positions at Richebourg Saint-Vaast. They arrived there at 3.15 a.m. on 9th May, and stood ready in reserve for the forthcoming battle of Festubert. At 5 a.m. that morning, the Allied artillery commenced a bombardment of the German lines and at 5.40 a.m., the infantry assault commenced. For two days, the men stood patiently waiting, their only updates coming from wounded soldiers returning for medical treatment. The attack was only partially successful, the German line had been broken but the battle raged on. On 11th May, the Battalion was stood down and moved to billets at Le Touret where they waited for further orders.

Over the next few days the Battalion provided working parties on trench improvement and suffered regular casualties from rifle and machinegun fire. On 15th May, the Battalion moved to front line positions to give support to 1st King's (Liverpool) Battalion, who undertook an attack on the German front line which at this point had not been broken. The attack failed and 1st Liverpool suffered very heavy losses. The 5th Battalion held the line and, during the early hours of 16th May, a reconnaissance was made of the German positions. The assessment was that any assault at this point would result in very heavy casualties; the German front line was a distance of 250 yards over open ground but the Brigade commander ordered an attack regardless. At 6.00 a.m. that morning, two platoons were sent forward and almost to a man they were cut down by heavy rifle and machinegun fire. Gallant attempts were made to recover the wounded from the field. During the afternoon German artillery laid an intense bombardment of both high explosive and shrapnel shells on the Battalion's positions and they readied themselves for a counter attack.

Early on 17th May 1915, Allied artillery pounded the German front line and the shooting was described as "magnificent" creating a lot of damage; in some places white flags were seen being waved and German soldiers started to surrender. The Battalion kept up sustained rifle and machinegun fire on the enemy front line and feared treacherous use of the white flags. During the course of the morning, 126 enemy soldiers surrendered and found to be much shaken, but well fed and clothed, a testament to the recent artillery fire. The

German artillery continued to bombard the Battalion's positions and in the afternoon, the 5th advanced and captured the enemy front and part of the second line. Throughout that night the Battalion's positions were the target of enemy artillery and the following day they were relieved and the survivors retied to billets to clean up and recover. The casualty count for these two days was heavy, two officers killed and 11 wounded, 41 other ranks killed with 21 missing believed killed and 265 wounded. Arthur was amongst the 21 missing and was eventually listed as killed in action, his body was never recovered.

Arthur was awarded the 1914-15 Star, British War and Victory medals, these with the scroll and Death Plaque were subsequently sent to his father. Arthur's name was engraved on the memorial along with 13,481 other men, which is situated in the Military cemetery at Le Touret, Pas de Calais.

Chapter 10

Thomas Chilton

(For Kevin Chilton)

Thomas Henry Chilton was born in Brownhills, Staffordshire, on 9 June 1892. His mother Phoebe Chilton, nee Wilcox, gave birth to a total of eight children and all were born in the same given location of Brownhills, Staffordshire. At the time of Thomas's birth, the family were resident at Church Street, Ogley Hay, near to Brownhills and the head of the family, James Chilton, was a coal miner employed as a Hewer. James and Phoebe had married on 5th February 1882.

Sometime after the birth of Phoebe's last child, William, in 1903, the family moved to 3 Piccadilly, Kingsbury, Warwickshire (Now Piccadilly Crescent), where James continued with his employment as a miner at the Kingsbury Colliery. By 1911, of the five children remaining, only William was at school. The other four including Thomas, had followed their father into the coal mines and were all employed as Hewers.

At the outbreak of The Great War, Thomas was still employed as a miner and resident at 3, Piccadilly. Following the establishment of the static nature of the war on the Western Front in November 1914, both sides had identified that tunnelling would be a desirable tactic from both an offensive and defensive perspective. The Royal Engineers (RE) were tasked with creating specialist units to undertake this work and recruitment had taken place of such workers as miners, sewer workers and those men employed digging the tunnels of the London Underground system. These recruits were formed into Tunnelling

Companies, given almost no training and shipped directly to the front in France and Belgium. The first offensive action involving tunnelling was taken by the Germans who on 20th December 1914 detonated ten small mines, each of 50kg of high explosive, dug under the British lines from saps in the German front line. This was followed up by an immediate infantry attack and the resultant casualties were over 800 men from the Indian Corps.

On 2nd October 1915, Thomas attended a recruitment facility in Birmingham and attested to join the Royal Engineers; he was given the number 132459 and assigned to 183 Tunnelling Company. Sapper Chilton was taken on the strength as a Tunneller's Mate at the daily rate of 2s.2d. Per day, the normal pay for a Sapper at this time was 1s.1½d. per day; this differential acknowledged the dangerous work of the underground war. There is no indication on his record that he was subject to the usual medical examination but there is a short description of him, he is recorded as; 24 years and 3 months old, 5' 5 ¼" tall, with a 39" chest fully expanded. Whilst the absence of a specific form is not unusual, perhaps the usual pleasantries were overlooked to speed up the recruitment of men like Thomas - after all, he was being employed in a role he was deemed fit for and not given the recruit training that was usual. On 15th October, with just enough time to be issued with his kit, Thomas was shipped out to France, arriving their two days later on 17th October 1915.

183rd Tunnelling Company was formed on 9th October 1915, at No. 4 Army Base, Rouen in France. This army base specifically catered for the Royal Engineers and was the location all recruits, reinforcements, equipment and logistical support were sent from, for the RE in the field. The establishment for these Companies was five officers and 269 other ranks, which was reinforced by the use of men from infantry units who were attached on a temporary basis and this could sometimes double the strength. The war diary commenced on this first date and records that the Commanding Officer was Lieutenant H.C.B. Hickling and comprised of one Welsh section, specifically recruited Welsh Miners, under the command of 2nd Lieutenant Evan Jones, a Welsh mining Engineer. One Cornish section, likewise made up of miners but from the Cornwall area. A third and fourth sections were comprised at this early stage, of men enlisted from other military units - usually former miners serving in the Infantry. On 11th October 1915, the 183rd marched out of camp its destination Fontaine-les-Cappy south of the Somme. The stay here was short, as this sector was handed over to the French Army and on 6th November 1915, the 183rd marched from its home at Fontaine-les-Cappy, to a new base at Froissy where they came under the wing of 10th Corps, 5th Division. The units new raison d'être was to dig tunnels and saps and prepare mines for the 4th Army in the forthcoming offensive of the Somme.

Thomas landed in France on 17th October 1915, and would have initially been based at No. 4 Army base. It is likely that he received a form of basic training, perhaps tailored to his duties and not as extensive as for an ordinary infantry soldier. The tunnelling war had developed by this stage into a vicious, no mercy given conflict, and both sides were underground and were in a constant search for the enemy with the intention of killing as many men as possible by any means at hand. Listening posts were in common use specifically designed to locate enemy tunnelling operations. When they were found, explosives were laid at an appropriate place and detonated at a time designed to cause maximum damage. On occasion, tunnels came so close that the wall between them collapsed, both sides were then engaged in bitter hand to hand fighting using anything to hand. Weapons used varied but included spades, daggers, clubs laden with nails and a shortened down Lee Enfield rifle as the full version was too long to be useful underground.

On arrival at their destination, the four sections were put to work on various existing mining operations at Mametz, Fricourt and Carnoy and, by the end of October they had improved the situation by creating 900 feet of 'Heading and Sinking' which had greatly increased the safety aspects of the work. Sinking refers to the shafts created but Headers are an airway providing ventilation at intervals along a tunnel. One of the big dangers in any underground mining operation is the likelihood of poisonous gases, these can be naturally occurring, but due to the use of poison gases during the war this added to the danger. Poison gas is designed to be heavier than air and therefore sinks to the lowest places and as the entrance to mines, known as

Saps, were located in the existing trench system the gas gravitated down into them.

It is likely that Thomas joined the 183rd in the field at Carnoy or Fricourt where the unit had moved to when the positions at Fontaine-les-Cappy was handed over to the French army. The war diary records a draft of 35 Tunneller's mates arriving on 22nd December 1915 and another 45 on 29th. The unit had just experienced its first major loss when at 8 p.m. 1st December 1915 the Germans had fired a mine which destroyed two shafts which were being worked. This was in response to the detonation of four Camoflets, (a chamber created by explosive means which does not break the surface causing a crater), each containing 1500 lbs of Ammonal high explosive. Lieutenant H.L.Twite and nine men were killed by this explosion, five men were crushed in collapsed galleries, the officer and two men crushed in the collapsing shaft and two men were gassed to death whilst escaping. The following day another man was killed by gas.

There were insufficient billets for the men near to the work and they had had to build accommodation out of sand bags supported by wooden frameworks. The weather at this time was bad and, in some places, made underground work impossible, due to the poor state of the trenches. The main work of the men at this point was the improvement of trenches and approaches to underground galleries. Listening posts continued in their efforts to identify enemy activity but it appears that they were quiet in this sector.

On 14th January 1916, Thomas was elevated from Tunneller's Mate to Tunneller this would have meant a pay increase to six shillings per day, but only on working days, leave, sickness, punishment and like days were paid at the normal rate for a Sapper.

On 7th February 1916, German miners detonated two underground devices, fortunately their work over the preceding two days had been heard and the Infantry likely to be affected had been warned. Some damage was caused but most of the men had been withdrawn in time, a rescuer, nicknamed the Protoman, was sent down with the use of a 'Siebe Gorman Proto' rebreathing device and two men recovered. A third was in the process of being rescued but there was no response from the officers and men at the shaft head operating the winding gear. It was found that these men had been gassed; two of the men from underground died but all the others made a full recovery. This was the continual cycle of the underground warfare, mining, listening and blowing devices at a time designed to kill the enemy in the largest possible numbers. During the month of February 1916, the Germans fired six separate Camouflets; this included the two mentioned above and four on separate occasions. The British total was four but these were all detonated on the same day, 10th February and consisted of one 9,000lb, two 6,000lb Ammonal Blastine and one combination of 8,000lb Ammonal with 2,000lb of black powder charges. These were massive explosions and designed for defensive purposes, the primary reason was to destroy German works on an upper level close to the British works and to make the positions of their listening posts safer, the Germans were obviously too close for comfort!

On 12th May 1916, Thomas was working in the Mametz area of the Somme when he was overcome by the effects of gas and hospitalised. There is no mention in the diary of casualties on this day but as well as tunnelling the 183rd were also digging Russian Saps from the British lines towards the German lines. These were shallow tunnels intended to allow attacking troops to approach the enemy lines under cover thereby shortening the distance they would be exposed to any defensive fire. Positions for machineguns were also a feature of these saps giving a very advantageous position for the crews to provide covering fire for the infantry. Following the successful capture of the enemy front line, the saps then became communication trenches for the resupply of the new front line and recovery of casualties. The diary for this date makes mention of the unit's work in the tunnels and that the enemy were working so close underground they were heard laughing and shouting, perhaps Thomas's gassing occurred outside of the tunnels and was not noted. Thomas's record does not show to what facility, nor the extent of his injury which would determine the level of care needed and the length of time off duty. This, of course, would vary, dependant on the level of exposure and to the type of gas he was exposed to. Gases were used by both sides and were designed to either incapacitate, such as Tear Gas, or to kill, such as Phosgene.

The care would vary between face washing and fresh air at an aid post, to full hospitalisation back in England. Thomas was treated in France, as his record shows the period of duty there, and returned to duty. One thing is certain, his efforts since joining 183rd were crucial to the forthcoming offensive.

During June 1916, the tunnelling work was hampered by extremely wet weather making it impossible to work in the lower levels; work was concentrated in the upper levels and the Russian Saps. On 23rd June, the work had got so close to the enemy that a hole was bored into a German bunker, loud talking could be heard and the hole was plugged without the occupants noticing. At midnight the following day, 24th June 1916, all work for 183rd ceased. The artillery bombardment preceding the infantry attack of the Somme offensive had started. The 24th was codenamed 'U' Day and the original plan was for this action to last five days, U, V, W, and X days with Z being the day of the Infantry attack. The men of 183rd stood by to observe; the bombardments effects on the tunnels and affect repairs as and when required.

On this first day, the weather was such that aerial observation was not possible and the artillery concentrated on its objective of cutting the enemy wire in front of the objective points to eliminate an obstacle for the infantry. 'V' day saw an improvement in the weather and the Royal Flying Corps were active shooting down enemy observation balloons and observing the effect of artillery fire. The German artillery positions became targets and several large explosions were observed indicating ammunition dumps being hit, the work of the wire cutting shrapnel devices continued. 'W' day saw the return of heavy rain, making aerial observation difficult,but photographic evidence was taken showing the wire had been cut in places and that work continued. Gas was released on the enemy lines and small raiding parties were mounted to take prisoners to determine the effect on them, they were generally disorientated and not expecting anything other than small scale attacks. 'X' and ' days were again made difficult by bad weather and it was agreed to delay 'Z' day until 1st July 1916, thereby giving a further two days for artillery to complete their objectives. 29th and 30th June were designated 'Y1' and 'Y2' days.

During the course of these seven days preceding the infantry attack on 'Z' day, 1,700,000 artillery shells were fired many of which failed to explode and there was limited benefit gained by the bombardment. The German defensive positions had been strengthened and deep concrete bunkers formed where the defenders sat out the storm with their weapons. On 'Z' day the defenders were able to return to their broken trenches and mount an effective defence with the effective pre-planned use of heavy machine guns forcing the advancing Infantry to walk through a wall of lead. The other pre-planned defensive measure, was the targeting of the mid-ground of the battlefield by artillery using both high explosive and shrapnel shells creating a killing ground for the attackers. On this first day limited success was achieved to the loss of 60,000 casualties of which almost 20,000 men were killed. The offensive continued until 18th November 1916, with total losses on both sides of over 1,000,000 casualties and the greatest territorial gain, less than five miles.

As for Thomas and all the tunnelling Companies involvement, their preliminary work resulted in the detonation of 19 mines beneath the German front line. These were amongst the largest non-nuclear explosions of all time. The explosions were heard in London and may be the loudest man-made noise of all time. 183rd Company, still under the command of Horace Hickling now a Captain, were responsible for four mines (the Mametz East Group) and three mines (the Carnoy Group).

The Mametz group consisted of one 2000lb, one 200lb and two 500lb mines, also in this sector the Company had dug dozens of Russian Saps to allow the attacking infantry to break cover nearer to their objectives. These Saps were opened with a small explosion immediately before the attack commenced. Four of these tunnels were also to provide position for devices known as Livens Large Gallery Flame Projectors which were installed immediately before the attack. These devices were a piped projector of flammable liquid which were positioned to spray liquid fire onto the German trenches. These devices were invented Royal Engineer officer Captain William Livens, were 56 feet long, weighing 2.5 tons and required 300 men to transport and assemble it. This device was assembled underground and to fire it a nozzle was pushed up above ground and fuel from several tanks pumped and ignited on exit. It had an eight-man crew and could be fired in bursts lasting from three to eight seconds.

The Carnoy group of three mines consisted of a 5,000lb device beneath a German Salient at Kasino, the miners who observed the effects of this mine believed that it buried three dugouts, four sniper posts and a machinegun emplacement. The other two mines were both 500lb charges and designed to destroy German dugouts and machinegun positions. These mines were through chalk which had gradually become harder and to work this chalk quietly the tunnellers had been drilling holes with an auger and then pouring vinegar down the holes to dissolve the chalk.

It is impossible to say how many enemy soldiers were killed by the mines but the fact remains that it did not give the immediate advantage that was expected and did not prevent the German forces recovering from the artillery bombardment and the concussive effects of the explosions to man their positions and set up an extremely effective defence.

During the month of July 1916, whilst the battle raged above them, the 183rd was employed repairing the tunnel system they had created, connecting it to and repairing the German system which was now available to them. An important immediate task was to locate German mines and cut any leads to them to prevent their use against British troops or even accidental initiation. Much of the rest of the month was spent providing working parties to repair roads and also to dig new wells to provide drinking water to the men at the front. The supply of water and ammunition to the fighting men was always a huge logistical problem and to have a water source near to where it was needed was extremely advantageous. This facility freed up space in the supply columns from the rear and spared some burden for horses, mules and men. The importance of this work cannot be overstated.

During August 1916, the 183rd continued to dig deep wells for water. By now, the battlefield was littered with uncollected corpses and other war debris producing pollutants which made the water near the surface extremely dangerous to use. The unit was also kept busy digging dugouts in the trenches. Attempts were made to place 'Pipe Push' explosives under enemy strong points in advance of infantry attacks but these were unsuccessful. These devices were also known as Bangalore Torpedoes originally developed by a British Royal Engineers officer in India and primarily used for cutting defensive wire. A successful use of the Pipe Push and its operating machine occurred on 3rd September 1916 at 'Lonely Trench' which resulted in a crater 10 feet deep for 60 feet and a further 60 feet at five feet deep, which was then attacked and held by infantry. The rest of 1916 was spent making HQ's for Corps personnel, dugouts and observation posts, one of which was for the use of 4 Field Survey Company and situated up a tree with shelters at its base. Christmas 1916 was spent in camp with all work ceased by permission of Corps from 8 a.m. Christmas Day to 8 a.m. on Boxing Day.

The New Year saw a continuance of the work creating new dug outs for various units and freezing weather which created havoc with already stretched transport means. All of the Company's three lorries broke down with no replacements and the wet muddy conditions meant that often two horses per general service wagon was insufficient, meaning less supplies if any, were hauled. Work continued in these situations using the supplies which had been brought forward and dumped.

Halfway through March 1917, orders were received for 183 Company to move to a new area of the Western Front, their work on the Somme ceased on 12th March and the long march started the following day. The journey from location to location was not completed until 25th March 1917 and transport varied from train, to motorised, to foot-slogging. On this date the Company arrived at its new base in the Swan Chateau and Ridge Wood areas of Busseboom, Belgium. Work commenced almost immediately creating machinegun positions and dugouts, but whilst reconnoitring the area a shell exploded amongst the officers concerned, killing the Machinegun Corps officer and wounding the three 183rd officers including the OIC, Major Hickling. These casualties were evacuated to X Casualty Clearing Station. The work continued, but the water table in this area was high especially at this time of year and in places only a few feet below ground level, the usual drainage methods of streams and the Yser Canal had suffered damage from artillery fire and were not always effective. Excavation work was made very difficult by the continual presence of water and extremely hazardous by the existence of running sand. This running sand or running ground at is it referred to in the diary, is where sandy layers occur in the ground where there is water present; the water can wash the sand away leaving cavities below buildings or dugouts etc which make them unstable causing them to collapse. The work on numerous dugouts continued through to the end of May 1917, the last thing to fit before handing these over to the infantry to use was bunk beds. There are numerous mentions of workings being abandoned due to collapse; this was clearly hazardous as well as hard, filthy, work.

On 1st June 1917, orders were received for work to be commenced in the forthcoming planned operations, these refer to the offensive known as the Third Battle of Ypres or more commonly, Passchendaele. Ypres was a strategically important city which the Germans had failed to take in the initial stages of the war and hadlaid siege to it since 1914. The German forces held high ridges overlooking the city and had reduced it to rubble with continual artillery bombardments. The planned Allied offensive, was to gain control of the ridges to the south and east of the city and the village of Passchendaele (now spelt Passendale) and vital railway links which the German army relied on for resupply purposes.

The offensive was planned to commence on 31st July 1917, and was to be preceded a preliminary attack and the detonation of 21 mines containing a total of over 1,000,000lbs of high explosive. The mining work to facilitate this part of the plan had commenced in July 1915, under Messines Ridge, south of Ypres, the Germans had been aware of this and had engaged in counter defensive mining to disrupt the Allied work. On 6th June 1917, all work on dugouts ceased and the 183rd moved to battle positions at a trench named Queen Victoria Street; their orders were to go over the top one hour after Zero hour and search enemy trenches for dugouts. At 3.10 a.m. on 7th June

1917, the 21 mines were initiated and 19 were blown successfully but two failed to detonate. The infantry attacks following the mines, successfully captured all the day's objectives and the expected casualty rate of 50 percent was much lower. 183rd Company's work continued over the next few days hampered by heavy rains and occasional enemy shelling and gas attacks. Work continued on repairing trench works but this was hampered by a shortage of revetting material. This was wood or sandbags used to shore up the walls which tended to crumble in wet conditions. In this sector, where the water table was high, the depth of the trench was kept shallow but the shoulders built up with sandbags, called breastworks. By 15th June 1917 the trench system was complete and consisted of a main line of resistance (front line), reserve line, support line and connecting communication trenches. The men were now concentrating on improvements such as; breastworks, revetting, drainage, hedge clearing and wiring.

On 17th July 1917 the 183rd were instructed to create cavities in the walls of the Yser Canal (now known as Leperlee Canal). The German and British front lines at this point had been set on the banks of the canal but the British intended an infantry attack to gain both sides. The broken canal would become an obstacle in the supply lines to the front. The purpose of creating these opposing breaks in the canal banks was to facilitate road and railways over this obstacle. That night, a plan having been drawn up, the supplies for this operation were taken forward.

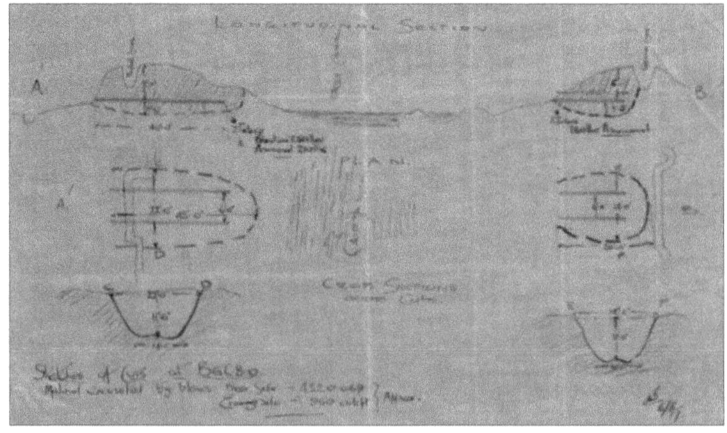

Picture author's

There were two choices to achieve this work. Manpower digging was considered too lengthy and dangerous, as it was to be completed by the eve of an infantry attack and the noise alone would have attracted artillery attention. The other method of course was the use of explosives. As can be seen from the drawing the close proximity of the opposing trench works meant the use of the hole-boring method of placing explosives in the right places. Two eight-inch augers were used to create two 34-foot boreholes underneath nine feet of soil. The British side had a 30' Poplar tree, but each hole was lined with six-inch stove pipes. Attempts to create further holes were thwarted by various problems; tree roots, brickwork from the canal wall or the holes were directed downwards. Eventually two more successful holes were bored but they were wet creating a problem for the placement and initiation of the explosives. Explosives packed into metal tubes were not successful as they fouled on the rivets on the underside of the stove pipes thereby blocking the hole, the answer was to use Blastine tied into bundles and fed into the pipe using a scoop made from an 18-pounder artillery shell.

On 28th July 1917, the German trenches were evacuated and the work to blow and access holes on the east bank was commenced. The Parados (rear wall) of the German trench was not very thick and required less work; another four holes were bored and, on this side, charged with Ammonal. All holes were tamped, (blocked to create a direction for the explosive action) and left for the designed time which was 'Z' hour plus two. All the tubes had been overcharged in an effort to throw all debris clear. The precautions to conduct this explosion safely meant they had to consider that supporting troops would be going forward and injured troops returning.

'Z' hour was set for 3.50 a.m. on 1st August 1917 and, following the infantry attack, the 183rd plan was to blow the charges set in the canal banks simultaneously at 5.30 a.m. Thomas and most of the men were split into groups and sent to assist attacking infantry in a supporting role, which involved the searching and making safe of booby traps and the recovery of useful supplies found in captured enemy trenches.

The detonation of the explosives, despite some of the control wires being destroyed by artillery, gave better than expected results and justified the generous use of explosives (explosives not detonated by their own control lines most likely exploded by means of sympathetic detonation, HE in the close proximity to a high explosion impact will also detonate). The list of stores subsequently recovered by Thomas and his friends is impressive and includes; electrical equipment, petrol engines and tanks, water tanks, shaft boring equipment, drills, microphones and listening equipment, air and water pumps, bells, batteries, a reel of steel winch cable and even a boat!

During August and September 1917, the men's work was largely repairing dugouts discovered in captured trenches and the assembling of a pipe line to transport water from the deep wells previously dug to the forward supply facilities. The diary mentions for the first time, that by section the men were transported to 5th Army rest camp for rest and recovery. The work of the miners was extremely stressful and arduous and it is openly recorded that the men were well supplied with the obligatory rum ration which helped to deal with the constant tensions experienced in the underground war. One section of 183rd was instructed to be kept permanently available for 'tank' work, this was varied but involved making roads fit for the tanks' passage and recovery. This above ground work may well have not contained the same hazards of underground war but men working within view of the enemy were a target for sniper and artillery action and casualties were experienced by these means. On 25th September 1917, 2nd Lieutenant A. Johns was killed by shell fire, there is no mention of other ranks being casualties, but the diary has a poor record for recording this feature of war.

Successive infantry attacks during October and November 1917, were followed by searches of enemy positions for dugouts and materials and towards the end of the month one section was tasked with the destruction by explosives of a damaged tank that was causing a blockage of the road. This task was conducted with such success the section was tasked with several more similar jobs over the following week. Road works continued due to the success of forward movement and were subjected to the usual artillery attention and sniper-fire.

It is impossible to pin Thomas to a particular section during the relevant period for when he was injured. All sections were in the field engaged in either road works, searching of enemy dugouts and recovery of equipment, or the recovery of damaged tanks and creation of more tank tracks. On 15th October 1917, Thomas was hit in the lower right leg by a bullet and evacuated to a forward aid post then to a casualty clearing station and there to a hospital. The injury resulted in the lower third of his right leg being amputated, either at a hospital in France or back in England where he arrived on 22nd October 1917, only six days from the day he was shot. Thomas remained in England for the rest of his service with the Royal Engineers and never returned to France.

Thomas continued to serve with the Royal Engineers throughout the war and it was not until 16th January 1919, that he was discharged, 'No longer fit for war' (as per Kings Regulations), from the Tunnellers Depot at Chatham. He returned home to his parents address at 3 Piccadilly, Kingsbury, and Thomas was judged to have a 60 percent disability and awarded a pension of 27s.6d for 13 weeks and then 16s. 6d. for the rest of his life.

Apart from a short period where he lived at an address in 97, Adair Road, Southsea, Portsmouth during 1923 Thomas spent the rest of his life at Piccadilly, Kingsbury being resident at number 9. Here he set up home with Annie Hollis (Nee Marklew) and her daughter, Beatrice, who was born in 1921. Annie had a troublesome ex-husband and the court records show she had to fight for any financial assistance from him and in fact to get a divorce in order to marry Thomas. Thomas and Annie had five children in total, four boys and one girl, starting with Kenneth Thomas Francis, born on 28th August 1926. Annie finally managed to get her divorce and on 21st March 1944 she and Thomas were finally married at Sutton Coldfield. It is very likely that at some stage Thomas had further surgery on his leg involving further amputation as his grandson Kevin remembers his false leg and the stump was above the knee which would account for more than the lower third of his leg. Kevin remembers Thomas as a gentle chap, not very mobile due to his war wound, his false leg was a very cumbersome device secured to his body by heavy straps around the waist and over his shoulders.

Back at Kingsbury, Thomas returned to the Kingsbury Colliery employed as a Lamp Man; this involved the supervision of the lamp room and the maintenance and repair of the miners lamps used underground. He had a couple of minor run-ins with the law, firstly over an alleged debt he owed for a hire purchase agreement and secondly, when his dog killed a duck on a local farmers pool. Both cases went against him and we don't know whether his dog had the sense to bring the duck home, at least a nice meal could have taken the edge of the resultant fine!

Thomas died in September 1968 aged 76, he had been awarded the 1914-15 Star, the British War and Victory medals for his gallant service during World War 1. During World War 2 his employment as a miner would have been designated essential war work and a continuance of his service to King and Country.

Chapter 11

Charles Whitmore Pink

Charles was born on 13th November 1870, in Lancing Sussex and baptised on 5th February 1871. The fifth child of Fanny and Richard Pink, Charles had four siblings, three boys and a girl, ranged in age from three to 12 years. Richard, Lancing born and bred, was working as a Gardener. In 1881, the family had moved to 8, Clarendon Place, Portslade, Sussex and, apart from an expansion of children their situation was the same. By 1891 the family had moved to Aldrington, Sussex. Richard at 59, is 'living on means' and Fanny is working as a laundress. Charles now aged 20 is the eldest child still living at home and is employed as a painter, his three younger siblings are all employed except for the youngest, Alfred aged 11, who is still at school.

In 1899 Richard Pink passed away and Fanny followed in 1906. During this period the family was broken up and there is no accurate record of where and what Charles is doing. His military record has survived and on joining the army he did declare previous military service with a 4th Battalion (Volunteers) it is not clear what formation this was but likely to be a militia unit and could be the reason he doesn't seem to appear in the 1901 census. In 1911, Charles was living at 5, Frances Court, James Street, Neath and he declared that he was a house painter and married to Elizabeth Pink. The couple have four children; Charles aged eight, Richard aged six, Alfred aged two and Jane, a baby of six months. Elizabeth was born in Dolgelly (Dolgellau) Merionethshire and was bi-lingual. Official records show that the couple did not marry until 1917 and were probably frugal with facts to avoid the stigma associated with their choice of lifestyle and to protect their children from bullying in school.

It would appear that Charles was a fighting man with a taste for a drop of beer. On 17th August 1914, he was convicted at Neath Borough Court for Refusing to Quit (Licensed Premises) and Assault. The record shows Charles to be 44 years of age, 5 feet ten and three eighth inches tall, with grey hair and employed as a painter, he had one previous conviction for Assault at Ruthin Court. He was sentenced to 21 and 14 days Hard Labour to be served consecutively or fines of £1.17s.9d and £1.7s.9d. The record gives a result of the sentence imposed, whether the fine was paid or sentence served, with an option for release date and an alternative with good behaviour. A tick appears on the former date and presumably Charles did his time in full.

On 11th January 1915 Charles attended a recruitment facility in Neath, Wales and attested to join the Royal Engineers. Charles now aged 44 declared his age to be 36 years and 2 months, a sure sign of his determination to serve his country! At this time, Charles was living at 4, Chapel Court, James Street, Neath and was working as a painter. The same day, Charles was subjected to a medical examination which showed him to be 5'10" tall, weighing 154 lbs and to be of good physical development. I suspect he was a fit man, as he managed to keep his actual age from his examiner. Charles was accepted as a Sapper in the Royal Engineers, but on 9th April 1915 transferred to 19th (Pioneer) Battalion Welsh Regiment and then on 30th July the same year, to 21st (Reserve) Battalion. There is no explanation for these transfers but the role of a Private in both the Royal Engineers and a Pioneer Battalion would have involved a lot of manual work and perhaps it became difficult to continue to hide his actual age. The only clue to why he may have been transferred from 19th Battalion to 21st Battalion Welsh Regiment is an entry noting that he was fined eight days pay and confined to barracks for 11 days on 18th June 1915. The offence is not noted but the double punishment is rather severe for a few days overstaying a pass and may have also led to the transfer. On 26th September 1915, Charles was again transferred, this time to the Royal Army Medical Corps, there is no doubt now that his actual age had come to light and he was assigned to a formation with duties more commensurate to his ability. Charles was awarded 5th Grade Corps Pay which was actually the rate for any Private soldier at this time of 1s.2d. per day.

On 8th October 1915, Charles was posted to a Hospital Ship. The earliest note of being posted abroad, is not until June 1916, but he was subsequently awarded the 1914-15 Star which gives the date and duty of his entitlement. He was working as a hospital orderly and the most likely duty was on a hospital ship transferring casualties from France to England. On 30th October 1915, Charles was promoted to Acting Lance Corporal, with pay, but with no vacancy arising he had to revert to Private on 3rd January 1916. It wasn't long before Charles was in need of the services he helped to provide and was hospitalised at the Southern General, Southmead, Bristol between 4th and 27th April 1916 with Jaundice.

On 14th June 1916 Charles embarked on the Hospital Ship (HS) Goor Kha bound for Salonika where he disembarked on 25th June 1916. At the end of July 1916, Charles became ill with Myalgia, or muscle pain, he was hospitalised and transferred by hospital ship to St Paul's Hospital on the island of Malta. On 29th September, he was transferred to England aboard HS Galeka and HS Britannic. From 11th to 24th October 1916 Charles was treated in 2nd Southern Hospital at Bristol for Malaria and then he was transferred to Woodcote Convalescent facility at Epsom until 7th December 1916. It is not certain he contracted this awful illness on this recent posting as he may have contracted it during his previous service and been a sufferer for a much longer period of his life.

It looks like Charles had Christmas 1916 with his family as his next posting was to No. 8 Company RAMC at Nottingham, where he was employed as a Hospital Orderly. Charles married Elizabeth Bright in the first quarter of 1917 and legitimised their union. It is not stated at which hospital Charles was working but he was again a patient suffering from Myalgia from 12th April to 5th May 1917 and treated at Bagthorpe military hospital Nottingham, perhaps he was treated at the facility in which he was employed. The record shows that he was examined by a Major Holmes who judged the condition to be 'trivial' and a recurrence of the disease he had contracted during the course of his duties in Egypt and Salonika. Following discharge for this complaint he returned to work with No. 8 Company.

On 3rd November 1917 Charles was again admitted to Bagthorpe military hospital, this time the situation was serious. He was suffering from pain in his limbs back and body, a slight fever and general weakness, the diagnosis was VDH Cystitis (Valvular Disease of the Heart). The medical report has survived;

3-11-17

Disease (V.D.H. Cystitis) Cause of Death

Malignant disease of spine 90 Myalitis.

When admitted complained of pains in limbs, back and body, slight fever. Urine Alkaline. Gradually although pains in legs have somewhat abated, he has lost power in limbs and the plater and partellar reflexes have become diminished and then abolished. Muscular wasting is general. No incontinence or retention of urine. No albumen or sugar in urine. There is a soft mitral (?????) murmur. The case in the man is one of myelitis accompanied by irritation of the urrer roots possibly due to growth in the spinal cord..Xray no ural or visical calculus. Disease probably in the lumbar, enlargement

T. Davis Pryce.

30-12-17

No definite anarsthesia of lower limbs but some parars-thesiaeg, pin pricks etc. No reaction lower limbs, to farrandie or continuous current. Incontinence and occasional sinking.

27-1-18

Died 27-1-18 *(Sgd) T.D. Pryce*

Charles was buried at Neath Llantwit Cemetery near to his family home which was now 21, Coronation Road, Neath. Elizabeth Pink was awarded a pension for herself and the four children of 33s.9d.0d.

per week commencing from 29th July 1918, until that date a proportion of Charles's pay was given to her to avoid poverty. Charles left £9.4s.9d. which was supplemented by a war gratuity £13.10s.0d. to his wife and he was awarded the 1914-15 Star, British War and Victory medals. Elizabeth was also sent a bronze Death Plaque and commemorative scroll as was the custom.

Chapter 12

Ernest Ash

During the 100 years commemorations of the Great War between 2014 and 2018, the Royal British Legion produced various poppy pins, made from shell fuses recovered from the battlefield and dedicated to individual events. Each pin was accompanied by a card dedicating that pin to an individual who made the ultimate sacrifice, Ernest Ash is the man dedicated by my Passchendaele pin.

Ernest, born in May 1898, was the fifth child born to Edward and Amelia Martha Ash of Notgrove Cottage, Notgrove St Bartholomew, Gloucestershire. Edward worked as a Slater's Labourer and by 1901, the couple had six children; the first four were girls followed by Ernest and a younger brother. The 1911 census shows that the family have moved to Bidford-on-Avon in Warwickshire, Edward is now employed as a farm labourer, Ernest at 13 is still at school and the family has expanded to eight children, three of whom are living elsewhere.

On 10th May 1916, Ernest, just 18, attended Stratford-Upon-Avon army recruitment centre and attested to join up. The following day he was sent home and placed on the army reserve list. The carnage of the Battle of the Somme commencing in July 1916, meant that he did not have to wait long for his call up instructions to arrive. Ernest returned to his parent's home at Salford Road, Bidford-On-Avon and continued in his job as a Grocer's assistant. On 2nd December 1916, Ernest received his mobilisation papers and on 6th December he was posted to 92nd Training Reserve (T.R.) Battalion, based at Chisledon. Private 88497 Ash commenced basic training, and the only noteworthy event at this stage is that he was admitted to hospital on 21st January 1917 for four days suffering from Scabies.

The T.R. Battalions had been conceived as part of a reorganisation commenced on 1st September 1916 to cope with the numbers of men now answering conscription orders. The previous system of basic training had been with the Regiments, who maintained one or two Reserve Battalions devoted to training purposes, this system could not cope with the volume of men now requiring training. This meant that individual soldiers could not necessarily join their local Battalions and following training were posted to where they were needed. For Ernest this meant that following his successful completion of basic training he was posted to the Machine Gun Corps (MGC) on 13th March 1917.

The MGC had been formed at the end of 1915 and commenced active service in 1916. At the beginning of the war, each Infantry Battalion was equipped with two Vickers or Maxim heavy machine guns; this was increased to four early in 1915. After the first engagements in 1914, it was determined that the machine gun sections required specialist training and a Machinegun school was built at Wisques in France and followed by a training camp at Grantham in England. Towards the end of 1915, it was decided to remove this expertise from the Infantry Battalions and form a specialist Corps organised on a Company basis which were then allocated to Brigades. The Battalion machineguns, were replaced with Lewis gun light machine guns (LMG). Both light and heavy guns fired the .303 rifle cartridge, the Lewis from a top mounted drum and the Vickers (which ultimately replaced the Maxim) had a belt fed system. The Vickers was a water cooled weapon, which enabled it to be fired continuously for longer periods without overheating. It did however create a steam cloud which obstructed the firer's view and a condensing tube was added taking the steam to a container. (The two biggest logistical problems on this front was keeping the men in the field supplied with water and ammunition. Ground water, unless obtained from deep wells below the polluted top soil, had to be transported. The recovered water was re-used).

Ernest attended machinegun training and on conclusion, was sent to join the BEF in France on 14th May 1917. On 22nd May he was posted to 11 Company MGC who at that time were allocated to 4th Division and he joined his unit in the field on 25th May.

On the day Ernest arrived, 11 Company MGC was in billets at Buneville, west of Arras. On this day a presentation of medal ribbons was conducted, a Military Cross to Lieutenant Mackay, a Distinguished Conduct Medal to Sergeant Ray and a Military Medal to Corporal Hayton. This brought the total number of medals won by 11th Company to three Military Medals, one Distinguished Conduct Medal and nine Military Medals, since its formation on 23rd December 1915, within days this total was raised by Medaille Militaire (French equivalent to MM) awarded to Private Fairweather. Earnest's next few days were spent fitting into one of the four sections of the Company which was engaged in a rigorous training programme. Each day commenced at 7 a.m. with a run and then a varied programme of range practise with pistol, rifle and machinegun, weapon maintenance, tactics, instruction in ground topography and map reading, construction of emplacements, even instruction in loading and unloading pack animals. The day concluded at 4 p.m. and usually contained football or a forced march to keep up discipline and fitness. At the beginning of June, the Division held a horse show in which 11th Company won third prize, this was followed by a Brigade sports competition in which they fared well. On 10th June, the 11th moved to Billets in Arras in preparation for returning to the front line. The following day during the evening, the Company moved to positions north and south of the Scarpe River (Canal) and relieved 36th Machinegun Company. The commanding officer, Major Westrop DSO, MC, was not happy with these positions and moved the guns to obtain a more advantageous field of fire in Roeux Wood. From these locations the guns conducted a programme of harassing fire on enemy positions, which brought the occasional attention of German artillery, rifle grenade and return machinegun fire. The Company were relieved on 26th June and during this spell at the front had only recorded two wounded men as a result of shell fire. They had taken advantage of a number of incidents where the enemy were forced to the open by artillery and inflicted numerous casualties with deadly fire.

The billets this time were in Fife Camp and the first task was of course cleaning and maintaining the weapons and scrubbing clean uniforms and men. The training programme was resumed with church parades held on Sundays. The Company strength was reduced to ten officers and 184 other ranks when 2nd Lieutenant Jones was removed to a Casualty Clearing Station. During this period the Company had a change of Commanding Officer when Major Westrop was posted 21st Division as Machinegun Officer; command of the company fell to Lieutenant Corballis.

The Company was soon back at the front, this time in front-line trenches with three sections in the front line and one in reserve. During this tour, the Company provided support for operations and raids by 12th Division. No casualties were experienced despite the best efforts of enemy artillery and machineguns. They were relieved and retired to Middlesex camp on 28th July 1917.

On 31st July 1917, the Third Battle of Ypres, otherwise known as Passchendaele, commenced. The City of Ypres was strategically important to both sides and the Germans had failed to secure it in their initial offensive of 1914. The City gave access to road and railway networks and of imperative for keeping an army supplied in the field. The BEF had stood its ground and secured the city under the worst possible conditions as the Germans held high ground and was able to gradually destroy the city by means of artillery fire. By 1917 the importance to the Allied forces, apart from denying the Germans access to road and rail networks, was simply that so many men had given their lives in defence of Ypres it would be unforgiveable to give it up. The Battle for Passchendaele was intended to take the high ground, make good use of that ground against the enemy and relieve the city from continual German attack.

August and September 1917 were spent relieving other Machinegun Corps units in the front line and time at the rear training.

On the evening of 1st October 1917, 11th Machine Gun Company took up positions in the front line with orders to assist in the Infantry attack planned to commence at 6 a.m. 4th October. This phase of the

Battle of Passchendaele is known as the Battle of Broodseinde and the objective was to complete the capture of the Gheluvelt Plateau and occupy the ridge giving name to the battle. The Company allocated two teams to the two assaulting Battalions to their right and left and two teams were allocated to flank defence, each being allocated to a platoon from the 1st Battalion, East Lancashire Regiment. Two teams were in reserve and eight machinegun teams were allocated to 'barrage fire'. Their role was to lay a barrage of machinegun fire on the enemy positions with the intention of forcing them to take cover, or kill them, while the Infantry advanced. There are various forms of Barrage fire and the most likely tactic to be employed in these circumstances would be to fire the guns on a high elevation over the heads of the attacking infantry to avoid causing casualties by friendly fire. This is known as indirect barrage fire, the intended target then determined the rate of fire, the elevation of the gun and the range to the target. The target may have been the enemy front line or behind the front line to prevent reinforcement and supply to the men in the firing line, or a combination of both. The elevated fire enabled rounds to enter trench defensive positions from above and a man lying down to take cover became a bigger target. Ernest was a member of one of these latter teams, probably employed as an ammunition carrier due to his inexperience, the ammunition was not all kept with the gun but at a safe distance away to prevent excessive loss.

As the teams waited for zero hour at 6 a.m. the Germans, coincidentally, launched an offensive of their own and at 5.45 a.m. commenced a heavy artillery bombardment on the British lines. By 6 a.m. the artillery fire was particularly heavy on the locations of the eight barrage teams located at White House and White Trench. Three guns were put out of action with the loss of eight men killed and a further 16 wounded, Ernest was one of the men killed and his body was never recovered, presumably subject of a direct hit. Despite this setback the surviving teams brought their guns into action on time and laid a very effective barrage on the enemy positions.

Ernest left £4.14s.9d. to his sole legatee, his mother Amelia, a war gratuity of £3, based on the length of his service, was added to this sum. He was awarded the British War and Victory Medals and with no known grave his name was added to the Tyne Cot Memorial near to Ypres. This memorial wall stands around the eastern boundary of the Tyne Cot military cemetery and bears the names of 34,991 British and New Zealand troops who have no know grave and lost their lives in the Battle of Passchendaele.

Chapter 13

Henry Seiboth MM

Seiboth Family (Author's collection)

Henry was born in Leige, Belgium on 5th September 1888 and registered by his father as an Austrian subject. He was the third and youngest child of Charles and Agathe Maria Seiboth (Nee Messmer). Charles was born in Germany but registered as an Austrian subject - Agathe was born in Austria. They came to the United Kingdom in 1892 from Belgium and settled in Stourport, where Charles secured employment in the metal working industry as a Tinman (Tinsmith).

In 1901, the family were resident at 8 Foundry Street, Lower Mitton, Stourport. The eldest son, Leonard aged 16 was employed as a Tinman's Apprentice having followed in his father's footsteps. Henry, aged 12, and his sister Maria, aged 14, were both still at school.

On 14th December 1908 Henry joined Birmingham City Police Force. Discipline was very harsh in those days, what would now be deemed as an essential part of community relations, i.e. talking to a member of the public, could be construed as a disciplinary offence then called 'Idling and Gossiping'. On 30th May 1912 Henry was stopped two days leave for neglecting to work a special part of his beat and being found gossiping with a man in Bristol Road, at 7.05am, 15th May 1912.

The 1911 census shows that the Seiboth family are still resident at 8, Lower Foundry Street and intact apart from Henry, who now aged 22, has moved to Birmingham and is living as a border at 2, back off 43, Ladywood Road, Birmingham. This was the home of Thomas Nash, a Gardener and his wife and 46-year-old son who was a Copper Smith.

Not all things in the thin blue line were camaraderie and harmonious teamwork as on 14th December 1913, Henry's police promotion was deferred for two months and to be reported on as to his conduct. This was for fighting with PC B25 Howard Garner in Ladywood Police Station 7.15am, 6th December 1913.

On 8th August 1914, whilst the political situation in Europe had deteriorated into war, Thomas married Lillian Florence Richardson at Kings Norton, then part of Worcestershire. The couple eventually settled at 48, Reservoir Road, Edgbaston, Birmingham, Henry continued in his police career and their first child, a son Leon Henri, was born on 28th April 1915. At this time Henry was a member of 1st Volunteer Battalion Worcester Regiment and prior to his subsequent enlistment in the army he had completed in excess of three years of duty with this territorial force.

At the outbreak of war in 1914, the call to arms was enthusiastically answered by men and women of all ages, keen to serve in any capacity allowed. The original expectation was for 200,000 volunteers, but more than double this number came forward and huge logistical problems were encountered as a result. By mid-1915 the recruitment of men for the armed forces had subsided and with the realisation that the war was not going to be a short-term conflict, an initiative to determine the availability of manpower was devised. The plan was called the Derby Scheme after the Earl of Derby who had been appointed Director General of Recruitment and launched in the autumn of 1915. Each eligible man aged between 18 and 41, not in an essential occupation, was obliged to make a public declaration that he was willing to join the army. This was achieved by a system of Canvassers, usually men who had served or fathers of serving soldiers, who served each man with a letter from Earl Derby informing him of the dire situation the country was facing and asking them face to face if they were willing to serve. Those who were willing then promised to go to a recruitment office within 48 hours where their fitness for war service was judged, they were also paid a signing bonus of 2s. 9d. In this situation, with conscription being planned, many men volunteered rather than wait to be forced.

On 10th December 1915, Henry attended recruiting office number three, Suffolk Street, Birmingham, where he attested to join the Army and was medically examined to determine his fitness. Henry, now 27, was 5' 10" tall with a fully expanded chest size of 37", with good physical development but with a cyst on his left arm and in need of teeth.

Bad teeth were a common feature in working class people of the era and, along with the shorter average height of the time, was the result of poor nutrition. At the beginning of the war the volume of recruits enabled the recruiters to be selective and many men were turned away because of their lack of teeth. The basic diet of people at the time was bread based and it was easier for civilians to be selective with what they ate based on an inability to chew food. The army however, had long before identified the need for a good balanced diet for soldiers but the logistical difficulties in the transportation and presentation of rations meant that there were many things in the food choice requiring teeth to chew, such as biscuit. In October 1914 during the Battle of Aisne, General Haig suffered debilitating toothache and a dentist had to be brought from Paris to relieve his suffering. This resulted in the recruitment of dentists to the Western Front. With the diminishing availability of manpower to replace the grievous losses on the Western

Front, the recruitment system had to be less discriminatory. Men below the minimum height of 5' 3" were allowed to join and special units known as the Bantam Battalions were formed and men with no teeth were fitted with dentures before being sent to the front.

Following the attestation to a magistrate and medical examination, Private 144835 Henry Seiboth was marked medically fit, class A, sent home and placed on the army reserve list to await his call to arms, he continued with his police duties. In March 1917 Henry again had a run in with the police disciplinary system. On 5th March, it was recorded Henry failed to reveal he was of alien enemy birth, his parents being of German nationality. It states Henry subsequently resigned to join HM Forces with the Royal Garrison Artillery, this is not accurate as Henry resigned his post when he was called up to join the army.

During the course of The Great War, hundreds of thousands of civilians were interned in camps by the warring factions. These were civilians either resident in countries foreign to themselves or people such as merchant seamen in ports as they were captured. It is likely that Henry had declared his birthplace as Belgium, a neutral country and its invasion the reason for Britain declaring war, but not the fact that his father was a German born Austrian and, therefore, by reason of parentage not Belgian but an enemy alien. It does give a sense of the anti-German feeling of the time that a loyal servant of the Queen for nine years could be criticised for such a discrepancy. It also raises the issue that if he had fallen into enemy hands and his technical birthright discovered, how would he have been treated? Probably executed as a traitor!

On 6th March 1917, Henry was mobilised and ordered to report to Number 3 Depot of the Royal Garrison Artillery based at the Citadel Plymouth. His rank of Private was altered to Gunner but his number remained the same. Henry packed his bags, handed in his police uniform and reported for military duty. At this time Lillian was four months pregnant, whether she had told Henry or not we do not know but this no doubt added to the tears sure to have been shed on his departure.

The Royal Garrison of Artillery (RGA), was originally formed for garrison duties at locations around Great Britain and the Empire and had been encompassed within the Royal Artillery, along with the Royal Horse and Royal Field Artilleries. The RGA was equipped with heavy and large calibre guns that were positioned some distance behind the front line and wielded immense destructive power that concentrated on strong points, enemy artillery and ammunition dumps. The guns were fired with a high trajectory and were reliant on forward positioned spotters to zero in the rounds, as the war progressed the Royal flying Corps gave great assistance in this role. The Citadel at Plymouth, as well as a defensive fortification was also a training establishment for the RGA. On 28th March 1917, Henry reported for duty and training at 398 Siege Battery based at Weymouth, here he was issued with two pairs of boots, one cap SD (Service Dress), two pairs of drawers, two battle service dress jackets SD, one pair of Puttees, two pairs of Trousers SD, one waistcoat cardigan, one greatcoat drab and one accessories kit.

Henry underwent a comprehensive basic training programme including, drill, saluting, uniform and kit inspections, physical fitness, musketry and field craft. He had a head start over his fellow trainees who had never been in uniform before, he had spent three years with a territorial unit and his police training would have been along similar lines. On 28th July 1917, his basic training completed, Henry travelled to Plymouth where he boarded a troop ship bound for France. The day before, 27th July, Henry's wife Florence gave birth to a baby daughter, Florence Jean Seiboth, it is probable that Henry did not know about the birth of his daughter until a telegram caught up with him in France. The following day he stepped off the ship at Le Havre, this being the closest he had ever been to the place of his birth, which he had left at the age of three. It is most likely that he was sent to Number 1 Base Depot in Rouen which was dedicated to the RGA. This was where all RGA replacements were sent for specialist training and logistical support for the units in the field was despatched from. Henry was posted to 154thSiege Battery which had been despatched to France on 30th August 1916. He arrived with this unit in the field on 5th August 1917, along with two officers and 69 other Gunners and NCOs.

An RGA Battery was typically manned by five officers, in the case of the 154th commanded by a Major, and 177 other ranks. Apart from the guns it was equipped with 17 riding, six draught and 80 heavy draught horses, three two-horse carts and ten four-horse wagons. A Brigade was made up of four Batteries, with its own staff and transport and an ammunition column was responsible for the Battery's supply. This column consisted of; three officers, 104 other ranks, 13 riding horses, two draught, 72 heavy draught horses, one two-horse carts and 16 four-horse wagons.

Unusually for an RGA Battery, there is a war diary for the time he arrived in the field, the diaries for these units were usually maintained at a Brigade level and contain very little detail about the situation on the ground. When Henry joined his unit, it was situated in locations a few miles south of the city of Ypres. The Batteries were moved periodically, in an effort to prevent the enemy artillery gaining an accurate fix on their location and for the rest of 1917 they were located at Moat Farm, Vlamertinge, Dead Dog Farm and Saint Eloi, Voormezele. The Battery was equipped with four 9.2" Howitzers which had been in operation for some time and were showing signs of wear and tear. The science of artillery was quite refined and a record was kept for each gun and how many rounds it had fired, minute calculations were made between shots then adjustments made accordingly. The Howitzers were a high trajectory, plunging fire weapon this made them very effective on targets some distance behind enemy lines and they were used against artillery, strong points, bunkers, dumps, stores, roads and railways. There were two variants of the BL 9.2-inch Howitzer; the Mk1 and the Mk2. The former had a limited range and this was increased in the latter to about 14,000 yards, but the increased propellant reduced the barrel life from 6,000 rounds to 3,500. Each gun weighed in excess of five tons and had to be transported in three pieces, body-cradle, bed and barrel, towed by heavy horses or tractor often referred to as a Caterpillar. As the gun was not mounted on wheels, it was more difficult to transport, but the siege platform was a much heavier mount making this gun the most accurate of the Howitzers. The gun fired high explosive shells which weighed 290lbs, were between 28 and 32" in length and contained between 25 and 40 lbs of high explosive. During The Great War, three million shells were fired by these guns.

9.2" Howitzer picture courtesy Wikipedia Nick-D.

When relocating there was a great amount of preparatory work to do, the platform consisted of a steel section mount bolted to a holdfast sunk flush with the ground. The spoil from this dig was used to fill an earth box at the front of the mount to prevent 'bucking' and this took between 9 and 11 tons of ballast. On top of this trenches and dugouts had to be either dug or repaired and improved

Henry's arrival in the field was six days after the start of the third battle of Ypres, commonly called Passchendaele. The guns were in action on a daily basis and guided by either Royal Flying Corps spotters or forward observation posts situated forward of the British front line accessible by trench or tunnel. These latter positions were very dangerous and brought the attention of all forms of artillery to neutralise them. Recently an exploding shell at the entrance to a post, had injured the officer and killed the telegrapher. On the 12th August, as part of the operations on the Gheluvelt Plateau, the 154th was engaged in counter battery fire to cover the attack on Inverness Wood by 24th Division. Two enemy batteries were put out of action on this day and this work continued on enemy artillery positions daily throughout this part of the battle which concluded on 31st August without satisfactory conclusion for the Allies.

This routine of counter battery shoots continued throughout September and October 1917 without respite. The work was hard and when the shooting was over, the guns had to be cleaned and maintained. On 4th October, a total of 550 rounds were fired commencing at 5.20 a.m. and then on the night of 8th-9th October the guns were in action through the night and continued through the day, a total of 543 rounds were fired. There is no mention of rest days and the men must have been exhausted by this stage but there was no respite, the attacking infantry were dependant on the work of the artillery and every round fired potentially killed the enemy and saved an Allied soldier. This sentiment was a driving force and what made it possible to achieve superhuman objectives, on one day 17 targets were engaged and 500 rounds fired. The total rounds fired for the month of October 1917 was 12,538! This intensity of work continued until 16th November 1917, the official conclusion of the Third Battle of Ypres was on 10th November 1917. On 17th November the Battery experienced its first quiet day and only fired 110 rounds, this lull continued until 24th November with between six and 70 rounds being fired daily. The intensity of battle returned for the rest of the month with hundreds of rounds being fired on a daily basis.

Unfortunately, the month of December 1917 is missing from the Battery's diary and it is during this period, to the end of January, that I think it most probable that Henry won his Military Medal (MM) for bravery. The MM was authorised in March 1916 and was awarded for acts of bravery not deemed worthy of the Distinguished Conduct Medal. The system for issue was based on the need for a quicker turnaround from the time the act of bravery and the award of the medal, this meant that few records were kept of the act, but a citation was issued with the medal and the award placed in the London Gazette. It is now quite difficult to find details of why the medal was awarded unless a mention is made in a diary or on a man's file; this is quite rare as usually the only men mentioned by name in these documents are officers. From available documentary evidence in Henry's file we know he was awarded the medal for gallantry in saving life on the battlefield.

It is possible to get a sense of how Henry won the MM from similar events described in the diary and in fact during January 1918 there is only one event noted which would fit the known facts. Usually it took about three months from the act to the award of the medal and the following event is at the right time and could well be the actual scenario.

The 28th January followed a few days where it had been quiet with no firing which may well have been due to inclement weather and no identified target. A German train became a target and ten rounds were fired at it, as a result an enemy aeroplane took station to spot for the enemy artillery and the Battery started to be bombarded by an enemy 105mm gun. The gun was zeroed with deadly accuracy and a direct hit was taken on number two gun, there followed a barrage fired for effect and then the day continued with harassing fire. In total 300 rounds were fired on the Battery's position resulting in a Captain and three other ranks being wounded and one man killed. Three rounds made direct hits on a sap (entrance to the dugouts) and all lines were cut leaving the Battery without communications. It is this type of action, if not the actual one, where Henry left cover regardless of the danger to himself and rescued casualties recovering them to a safe location where they could enter the casualty chain. There is no doubt that Henry's police training had a bearing, the desire to preserve life is a primary function of a Police Officer and certainly the most important.

In April 1918, Henry was attached to XXII Corps at the anti-aircraft school. This course lasted until early June 1918 when he re-joined 154 Battery. On 23rd April1917, while he was on this course, the notification that he had been awarded the MM was entered in the London Gazette. Henry re-joined his Battery in June and on 21st September 1918 he commenced leave and returned home to see his daughter for the first time. This was an opportunity to catch up with old colleagues and even the Chief Constable, Charles Rafter KPM showed a personal interest by writing in person to the RGA Paymaster in an effort to obtain the medal and award it to Henry in person. This of course would have been a wonderful opportunity for Henry's family to witness but unfortunately the times scales made it impossible to achieve before he had to report back for duty in France.

Henry re-joined his Battery on 6th October 1918, and was there at 11 a.m. 11th November 1918, when the guns fell silent. Of the six million men mobilised from the UK over 700,000 were killed, this was a time to rejoice being a survivor.

On 12th January 1919, Henry left 154 Battery and travelled to England where he reported to No. 2 Dispersal Unit at Chisledon Camp, here he was issued with the necessary identification documents and returned to civilian life on 14th January. Henry's military file contains a document which sometimes has entries and sometimes is just blank. Henry's record of disciplinary action form is marked and certified that no disciplinary action had been necessary during his periods of duty in the army and this fact along with his MM and previous record with Birmingham City Police secured his old job back and he resumed his police career on 10th February 1919.

During the course of his career the record shows he was officially rewarded on two occasions, for the arrest of persons breaking into shop premises and rendering first aid to for a fractured leg. On his uniform Henry proudly displayed the ribbons for his MM and the British War and Victory medals which he was also awarded.

In 1925, Henry's wife Lillian died, they had five children together. On 23rd June 1928 Henry married Louise Gertrude KIBBY of 253, Shenstone Road, Edgbaston, Birmingham. Following a well-deserved retirement, Henry died on 20th November 1954.

Chapter 14

William Ellis Rathbone

William was born on 13th March 1896, at 3, Savoy Street, Oldham, Manchester; he was the first son of William Ellis and Margaret Rathbone. William senior was a Brass Moulder in the Textile Industry and Margaret. The couple had their pride and joy baptised at All Saints Church in nearby Gorton on October 14th that same year. In 1901, Margaret and her two boys, William and Thomas, were living at 181, Anthony Street, Manchester, Margaret was employed at this time as a Handkerchief Machinist working from home. William Senior is not mentioned on this census return and does not appear in records of the time; William Junior attended Armitage Street School, Manchester. By 1911, the family were reunited and living at 74, Henry Street, West Gorton, Manchester. There are now seven boys, but mum has lost three other children who have died post birth, not an unusual rate of child mortality for the time. William senior is still in the same employment and junior has now left school and employed as an Electrical Engineers Fitter, a trade he was to pursue for the rest of his working life.

On 19th July 1915, William attested to join the British army at Manchester recruitment office, he was 19 years and 4 months old and employed as an Improver Electrician. A medical examination the same day found him to be 98 pounds in weight, with a fully expanded chest measurement of 32½" and only 5 feet 2 inches tall. He was accepted to the Manchester Regiment but only for home service, his record was noted; *"Fit for home service only, will develop"*.

The minimum height limit for the British Army at the outbreak of war was 5' 3" and was based on anthropometric studies of the men from

Britain the shortest average being the English at 67.36 inches or just over 5'7". This height issue was for logistical and not just prejudicial reasons; uniform was made and stored for men of certain sizes. Marching pace was set by stride length and speed, and a shorter man would have difficulty stretching to the required stride just as a very tall man would have to shorten his natural stride. The most obvious prejudicial reason was the concept that a tall man looked much smarter in uniform and formation, than a small man.

Initially men less than 5'3" tall were rejected for military service and it may very well be the case that William made efforts to join the army before July 1915, but was turned away. Late in 1914 the height issue was relaxed and Regiments started to form what were entitled 'Bantam Battalions' to facilitate the huge response that men had made, who did not make the height limit. The Lord Mayor of Manchester formed 23rd (Service) Battalion (8th City) Manchester Regiment on 21st November 1914, as a Bantam Battalion. This formation was initially located at Morecombe and later moved to Salisbury Plain, but did not move to France until January 1916. William was posted to 3rd (Reserve) Battalion, a training unit which had been posted to Home Defence on the Humber at Cleethorpes.

Almost one year later on 4th July 1916, William was sent to France to join the British Expeditionary Force (BEF) there. From 30 Infantry Base Depot (IBD) at Etaples he was posted to 17th Battalion, who were fighting on the Somme.

On 1st of July 1916, the Infantry assault stage of the Somme Offensive commenced, the 17th Battalion had gone over the top at 8.30 a.m., attacking German positions East of Montauban. In this first encounter, the Battalion had lost eight officers and 340 other ranks, dead, missing and wounded. They were relieved at 5 a.m. on 3rd July but then on 8th July, they returned to the battle being tasked to attack Trones Wood. During this attack they lost another ten officers and 196 other ranks and only received ten replacement other ranks. They were relieved from the battle at 2 p.m. on 11th July 1916, and the survivors marched to a camp at Bois Celestine, they arrived at 8 p.m. and received a draft of 131 other ranks. The following day a draft of 438 other ranks joined the Battalion and another of 109, followed on 15th July. A reorganisation and refit of the Battalion was undertaken, the shortage of officers was not immediately remedied. Training was undergone as they had now received a total of 823 replacement NCO's and men some of whom would have been straight from basic training and others returning from hospitalisation. There is no mention of men being rejected but there is evidence in some histories of replacements being sent to the front who were too old or in another manner unacceptable and were often sent back to the base depots. In amongst these 823 men was William, not fresh from basic training but certainly not battle experienced was posed to A Company.

Between the 24th and 29th July 1916, the Battalion was situated in assembly trenches between Bernafay and Trone Woods near to Longueval where they made final preparations for an attack on Guillemont. At 10 p.m. on 29th July, they formed up ready for the attack which commenced at 4.45 a.m. 30th July. The journey to the start positions was made difficult by a heavy mist and at 11 p.m. 29th July the German artillery commenced firing gas shells on the British positions which continued until 4 a.m. in the morning. The men were subjected to a combination of two types of gas, Lachrymatory or tear gas followed by a poison gas, the intention being to fill up the gas mask filters with particles rendering them useless and when the mask is taken off the poison gas such as Phosgene kills.

At 4.45 a.m. 30th July 1916, A and C Companies went forward to support the attacking units and at 7.15 a.m., William's A company commenced an attack with elements of C Company and reached the edges of the objective village of Guillemont. Throughout their attack, they came under heavy machinegun and artillery fire from a German strong point situated in a quarry, a gallant attempt to destroy this position was made by a bombing party but this failed. Heavy casualties were experienced as there was little cover for the men to use; and eventually the survivors of the two Companies were withdrawn to the start line. On this very first experience under fire William became a casualty injured by shell fire. The casualty count for the days fighting until relieved at 4.30 a.m. 31st July 1916, was five officers and 274 other ranks, killed, wounded and missing. William was removed from the field to a forward aid post and from there to 5 casualty clearing station. From there he was transported and treated at 1 Australian General Hospital in Rouen for a crushed foot and back injury, discharged on 14th August he reported for duty back at 30 IBD Etaples.

Life at the Base Depots was not always pleasant; the men were subjected to a strict regime of training, both physical and tactical. On 14th August he was posted to 18th (Service) Battalion Manchester Regiment and joined them in the field with 23 other men on 29th August 1916 and allocated to a Platoon of B Company. 18th Battalion had also been involved in the events of July 1916 and experienced heavy casualties in the same fighting as 17th Battalion, at the time of William joining his new unit they were in billets at Le Hamel and Essars.

Both 17th and 18th Battalions were originally formed as part of the eight Manchester Battalions raised under the Pals system. This was a recruitment drive where men were encouraged to join up on the promise that they could serve together with their friends with whom they had worked. 18th Battalion, was the 3rd Manchester Pals (Clerks and Warehousemen's Battalion)' Almost 10,000 men enlisted in these eight Battalions of whom 4,776 were killed.

At the beginning of September, the Battalion returned to the routine of duty in the front line and reserve, casualties were the result of artillery and sniper fire. During October 1916 the Battalion had marched in Company order with the transport sections taking up the rear, to Fricourt Camp to undergo training. Arriving during the hours of darkness someone from D Company, near to the rear of the column, trod on an unexploded bomb and it exploded wounding two officers and nine other ranks. The following day 2nd Lieutenant H.C. Crichton died of his wounds and was buried at Dartmoor Cemetery near Becordel. The burial was attended by all ranks and what should have been a period of work with relatively little danger, was marred by this very sad accident. At the end of the month the Battalion moved to support positions at Bellacourt, initially the men were allocated to working parties, except for D Company manning defensive strong points.

The routine now returned to; front line, support and reserve when the Battalion took over trenches in D2 Sector, East of Brettencourt on 6th November 1916. During December 1916, the Battalion were still rotating between reserve positions, now at Bailleuval and Basseux and the front line trenches at D2 East of Blairville. On 13th of this month two men were wounded one of whom was William by an exploding shell, it is likely that both men were injured in the same incident.

William was taken to 97 Field Ambulance suffering shell fragmentation damage to his right knee and taken directly to 43 Casualty Clearing Station where his right leg was amputated half way up the thigh. He remained at this location for ten days and was transferred on 25th December to 2 Red Cross Base Hospital at Rouen where he remained until 30th December 1916. He was transferred to England where he was treated at 1st Southern General Hospital Birmingham, his amputation was healing well and he was waiting for a place to have an artificial leg fitted. The waiting time for artificial limbs was long and the bed at the hospital was needed for the never-ending flow of casualties from the front and on 28th February 1917 William was discharged from hospital for an indefinite period to await a place at Roehampton.

Queen Mary's Hospital, Roehampton Lane, London, had been opened in early 1915 specifically to cater for all the returning servicemen who had lost limbs. Originally intended to have only 200 beds, the Hospital was forced to expand rapidly because of increasing military casualties. By 1917 some 11,000 officers and men had been treated since it had opened in 1915, and new patients were arriving at the rate of 100 a week. By the end of The Great War in 1918, it had 900 beds and a waiting list of over 4,000 patients. Of 42,000 limbless soldiers, some 26,000 had received prosthetic limbs at the Hospital, which had gained an international reputation as a leading limb-fitting and rehabilitation centre.

It is not recorded when William finally got to Roehampton, but he was admitted to The King George Hospital London between 25th May and 21st June 1917. On 11th July 1917 he was discharged from the army, declared no longer physically fit for war service and also permanently exempt from further medical examination. William was awarded Silver War Badge 211792 to be worn on his lapel to show he was a wounded veteran and subsequently the British War and Victory medals.

Chapter 15

Charles William Davies

Prior to the World War 1, Charles was employed as a Telegraph Messenger and Postman. At the time, these were posts within the civil service. His father Noah Davies was also a Postman and his mother Elizabeth a housewife. Charles was born on 9th November 1895, and baptised on 1st December 1895, at Turnastone, a small village near to the border with Wales, as was his elder sister, Minnie. By 1901, Noah had moved his family to 7, Mostyn Street, Hereford and they were still at that address in 1911 when Charles, at the age of 15, was employed by the Telegraph Service.

Charles attested to join the army on 3rd April 1915 and was initially posted to 3/1st Battalion, Herefordshire Regiment, which was the training unit based as Abergavenny, Wales. All the Battalions of the Hereford Regiment were Territorial units, the Regiment did not have Battalions of the Regular Army. Private 3330 Davies was clearly a man with leadership skills as he was promoted Lance Corporal on 12th May 1915, Corporal on 1st September 1915 and Sergeant on 7th June 1916. These positions were in an acting capacity whilst serving with 3/1st Hereford Regiment.

On 22nd September 1916, Charles was posted to the King's Shropshire Light Infantry and travelled to France where he arrived at a Base Depot on 30th September, his stay with this Regiment was very short and he was posted to A Company, 11th Battalion, Border Regiment on 11th October 1916. Retaining the pay and rank of Acting Sergeant, Charles's number was changed to 27725; he joined his unit in the field near to Beaumont Hamel where the Battalion had been fighting during the Great Offensive of the Battle of the Somme. The final battle of the Somme offensive, known as the Battle of Ancre, occurred between 13th - 18th November 1916. This last British action was designed to exploit German weaknesses and fatigue and gain ground from which the offensive could be renewed in 1917. Whilst fighting continued along the front after 18th November 1916, this is the official last day of the offensive. On this last day, Charles was wounded in the knee by a piece of shrapnel from a German artillery shell which also buried him and rendered him unconscious. When he returned to consciousness, he found that he was in a German dugout and a prisoner of War, initially he was posted missing and his family received a letter reporting that he had been killed in action.

Charles was put with other prisoners and they were marched to a place known as the Citadel at Cambrai, approximately 45 kilometres away, his wound was very minor and did not prevent him walking but he received no medical attention and eventually removed the shrapnel himself with a knife. On the last leg of their journey one of the prisoners fell to the ground dead, the men were not allowed to carry him and he was pulled to the side of the road to await a burial detail. At the Citadel, which was a large barracks used as a collection point for POW's, the prisoners were put in a room above a large stable and told not to sleep until they had been fed but no food or drink was offered to them until the following day. Charles was kept in this room for an indeterminable time as the windows were boarded and they were kept in the dark. On occasion they were paraded outside and given a meal of bread and soup, but he did not think this was every day. The room was extremely crowded and not ventilated. The only sanitation was 4 large tubs which were emptied when they were full. It was difficult to move without stepping on anyone and this ensured that the atmosphere was not pleasant. A few days before Charles was removed from the room, the men - British, French and Algerian - were given some straw to lie on. With no medical attention given, not even to those with wounds, all the men started to suffer the effects of Dysentery. On one occasion whilst outside on parade, a German NCO handed out cards for the men to write on and send to their families, on completion he laughed and tore them all up.

On 8th December 1916, the men were visited by a Parson who found Charles and some other men too weak to go outside and he demanded that they be afforded medical attention. They were taken to hospital in Cambrai. Charles was given clean pyjamas and a good bed at the hospital, the food daily was good but inappropriate for his condition, after eating he suffered severe pains and the German staff were indifferent to his plight. On 21st December, Charles, with two other British prisoners, was transferred by Red Cross hospital train to a hospital at Aachen, Germany where they were cared for by German nuns. The conditions here were clean and the food better and Charles started to improve. Whilst in hospital, Charles and the other prisoners had been allowed to write postcards home. On 31st December 1916, Charles's family received one of his cards and this was the first occasion they had been given any positive information about him. What a New Year's Eve party was held at 7, Mostyn Street, Hereford that year! Charles father wrote to Hereford Territorial Forces Comfort Fund, including the postcard as proof that his son was alive, asking for information as to his whereabouts. Eventually, they were provided with an address to send parcels to Charles.

On the 11th January 1917, Charles and his two fellow British prisoners with him in hospital, were sent to Friedrichsfeld prisoner of war camp near Wessel, Germany, they travelled there on a normal passenger train under an armed guard. The prisoners were housed in large wooden huts mounted on brick foundations, these buildings were split into half and in each section between 250 and 300 men were resident. There were approximately 32 of these buildings which were well ventilated by windows, lit at night by electric light and heated by four stoves in each half. The sanitary arrangements were good and once a week the men were allowed a hot shower, but no soap was provided as it was scarce.

Charles was put to work as a supervisor in the Packet Office where the parcels were received and distributed; his previous employment as a postal worker was helpful. He received sufficient packages from home not to need the food provided by the Germans and he gave this to the Russian prisoners who had nothing. Possession of many things was banned, toothpaste, Vaseline, medicine of any kind and boot polish, these items were removed from the packages when they were censored prior to handing them to the addressee. One item which the Germans were particularly fussy about was Wills and Black Cat Cigarettes which contained pictorial cards which they disapproved of; the example below is self-evident why - good fighting moral was not what they wished to encourage in POW's!

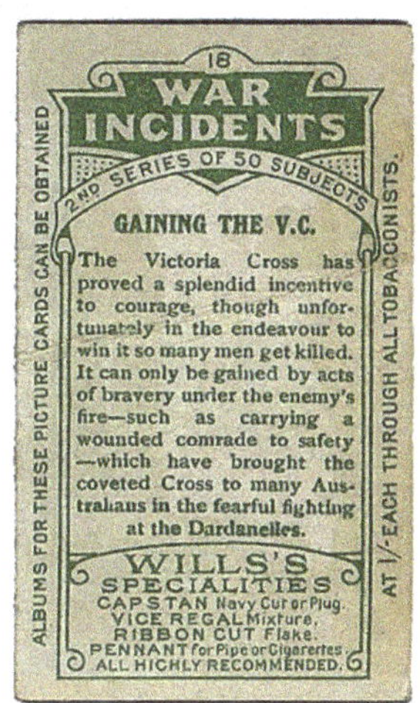

Picture author's collection

On 7th January 1918, Charles managed to escape from the camp and made his way of foot to the nearby Dutch Border where he surrendered himself to the Dutch authorities and was soon repatriated back to England arriving there on 23rd January. Charles was granted an immediate 2-month furlough which he spent with his family in Hereford, he applied for financial assistance as he had no money but this was slow in being processed and in March 1918 was forced to ask for £10 on account of what he was owed.

Charles was posted to A Company of 3rd(Reserve) Battalion Border regiment and his file was clearly marked in red ink that he was an escaped POW in the event of him being posted overseas any posting should take this factor into consideration. In the event, he was not sent abroad again and remained in the army until being disembodied (demobilised) on 19th March 1919, but before that event Charles married Ellen Dorothy Upward on 3rd June 1918, at Holy Trinity Church, Hereford.

Following disembodiment, Charles and Ellen set up home at Malt House, Ewias Harold, near Hereford and he resumed his career as a Postman. The couple had two children; Dorothy Joan, born on 23rd December 1919 and Alfred, born 23rd September 1921 both in Hereford. Charles had been awarded the British and Victory Medals for his service abroad during the war, but during December 1919 a Police officer was despatched to his home at the behest of the War Office to determine whether he was still alive, the reason for this was that he had been awarded the Military Medal for his escape from German captivity, this award was published in the London Gazette on 30th January 1920.

Charles lived out the rest of his life in the Hereford area, working as a Postman Driver and looking after his family, he died in December 1968.

Chapter 16

Edward James Raisbury

Picture courtesy of family.

Edward was born in the Norfolk town of Walsingham on Thursday 25th June 1896. His father, William Edward Raisbury, was a Railway Platelayer, whose job involved the laying and general maintenance of the railways. Edward's mother, Alice Dorothy Raisbury (nee Salmon), was a full-time mother who, by 1911, had given birth to ten children in total, of which two had died; not a bad mortality rate for the day.

In 1901 the family, consisting of Edward's parents, elder sister and brother, lived at Gate House, Little Walsingham, Norfolk and by 1911, they were resident at Luggar Yard, Wells next the Sea, Norfolk. Edward's father was still a Plate Layer for the Great Eastern Railway and his mother was at home caring for the seven children still resident with them. Edward, at 14, is the second eldest of the seven children and his elder brother, William at 16, is described as '*at home*'. As

Edward and his younger siblings are all at school, we can assume that the standard of living for the family is good for the day, the school leaving age was 12 and fewpoorer families could not afford the luxury of missing a potential extra income by allowing children to pursue an education. One other interesting point arises from these two census documents. Both Edward's parents were born in Wells and most of the children were born at the two addresses identified therein. It appears that Alice did not comply with convention and take her confinement with female family but stayed at home to deliver her children.

Following the outbreak of The Great War and the call to arms, on 28th August 1914, Edward, now 19 years of age and employed as a Groom, enlisted at Norwich and was posted to the Royal Norfolk Regiment as Private 12482. On that same day of attestation, he was subjected to a medical examination, Edward stood 5'3" tall, weighed 108 pounds, had a chest expansion of 2" to 34" when fully expanded and for physical development was described by the medical examiner as *'fair'*. The minimum height for the British Army in 1914 was 5'3" and many willing volunteers under this height were turned away from the recruitment offices. There was no lack of volunteers at this stage of the war. On the contrary, the recruitment offices were flooded with men eager to serve King and Country and emergency recruitment facilities were opened in Town Halls and the like to cope with the demand. Edward's minimum height and fair physical condition was more than matched by his determination to serve and he passed the examination. The training he would undergo would make huge improvements to those indicators describing him as only fair!

Edward was posted to the newly formed 7th (Service) Battalion and underwent basic training at Shorncliffe camp near Cheriton in Kent.

This training continued when the Battalion moved, in January 1915, to Romney in Kent and then, in February 1915, to a more permanent location at Malplaquet Barracks at Aldershot. The first two locations were probably being used at the time as staging posts, to collect the newly forming Battalions and to equip them. The recruitment drive at the outbreak of war had an expectation of 100,000 volunteers but almost half a million men answered the call and there was great difficulty finding accommodation and uniform for the men. Initially, 500,000 blue Post Office uniforms were made use of coining the name, 'Kitchener Blues', but as the weeks and months went by, the Battalions of the New Armies, as they were called, became dressed in Army Khaki and equipped with the Lee Enfield .303 bolt action rifle.

There is no hard and fast rule as to when the training of these New Army Battalions was complete. The logistical issues experienced in the early months hampered many aspects of the very basics, such as rifle drill and weapon discipline. Prior to moving to musketry practice as it was then called, no rifles made this somewhat a problematic! What is clear in each case, is that training continued until mobilisation and then at all stages until the front line. On 29th May 1915, the 7th Battalion commenced the business of carrying out their orders to mobilise and at 6.55 a.m. that day, the carts, horses and some of the men set out for Folkestone from Farnborough on the London and South West Railway (LSWR), the first step on the grand adventure. At 4.35 p.m. and 5.20 p.m. the same day two more LSWR trains set out from Aldershot with the rest of the Battalion. The destination was Folkestone to Boulogne on board the SS Invicta. The war diary lists the number and type of carts that the Battalion had at its disposal and gives an insight into the equipment needed to supply and support a Battalion on the move:

> *5 Carts SAA* (small arms ammunition)
> *4 Machinegun* Carts (Battalions equipped at this time with 2 Vickers heavy machineguns)
> *1 Maltese Cart* (light 2 wheeled cart)
> *2 Water Carts*
> *4 Field Kitchens*
> *2 Tool Carts*
> *2 Machineguns*
> *14 Riding horses*
> *52 Pack and Draught horses*

The Battalion strength is recorded as 30 officers and 954 other ranks.

A series of daily marches and periods in billets led the Battalion to Oosthove Farm near Armentieres on the French Belgium border on 14th June 1915, where they were to undergo training in the various aspects of trench warfare. Over the next few days, by Company, the officers and men received lectures at the farm, individual instruction in the trenches and dug out communication trenches. Instruction and practice were given in techniques for assaulting an enemy trench and German patrols in front of their own trenches and how to capture prisoners from these patrols. The weather during this period was extremely fine and hot, the reality of trench warfare was yet to be realised by these men. The Battalion received two further drafts during this period and the establishment was swollen to 30 officers and 1012 other ranks. Whilst walking in Armentieres a soldier became the first casualty when he was hit by shrapnel, this was recorded as an accident!

On 4th July, Edward and his comrades went into the front line for the first time, they occupied trenches near Ploegsteert Wood and relieved 6th Royal West Kent Regiment. The relief was carried out between 10 a.m. and 2 p.m. without incident, this daytime relief became very dangerous as the enemy artillery targeted communication trenches at times when they were full of men and the reliefs were then mainly carried out under the hours of darkness and as quietly as possible. This first front-line tour lasted seven days and was quiet. Occasional shelling resulted in three casualties but only wounded, the most notable events were action taken by Canadian forces to the Battalions left, who blew three mines, successfully followed up and occupied the resulting craters. A succession of seven-day periods followed in and out of the front line. Time out of the frontline was spent in a subsidiary line and the men were engaged day and night forming working parties developing the trench system under the guidance of the Royal Engineers. Shelling was a constant danger but this was added to by periodic sniping, by the end of July the Battalion reported five men killed, one officer and 22 other ranks wounded.

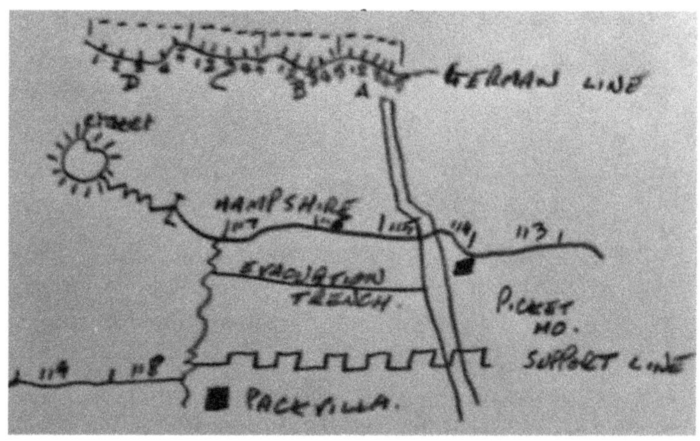

Author's picture

During the month of August, a particularly successful series of maps was produced of the Battalion's front line and the opposing German line. These simple maps were developed from aerial photographs taken by the Royal Flying Corps and in the possession of each Company Commander and his opposite number in the artillery battery he called for support. By use of this simple coded drawing accurate artillery fire could be brought down on enemy positions and silenced several snipers and trench mortars which had been causing casualties to the men in the front line. Time out of the line was spent on yet more working parties creating trenches, communication trench systems and slits, 18" wide by 7' deep, dug into the sides of in the communication trenches for seven to eight men to take cover in the event of shelling.

September 1915 brought rain and the Battalion, experienced one of the worst aspects of trench warfare for the first time, mud. Special attention was paid this month to grass growing long in front of the line, presumably it blocked the view of soldiers watching for enemy activity and was cut at night. Snipers, working from Picket House (see above sketch), managed to destroy enemy periscopes when they appeared over the parapet. At the end of the month the Battalion moved by motor bus to new positions near Loos, the trenches were found to be shallow and constant shelling caused a steady supply of patients for the field ambulances. Casualties for the first four days in October were; 56 killed in action and 65 wounded.

On 13th October 1915, the Battalion took part in an attack on the German line, preceded by an artillery bombardment. A trench mortar unit was given the task of destroying German machinegun emplacements and a smoke screen was to be laid down. At 2 p.m. Edward and his comrades went over the top, the smoke screen had prematurely cleared and the machine guns were still in operation, most of the casualties occurred were within 20 yards of the British line, mown down by German machineguns. The enemy could be clearly seen manning their parapet, one soldier to every 1½ yards, the British soldiers walked into a devastating fire. A 200-yard length of German trench was taken but as no support could reach them, they were forced to retire when their bombs and ammunition ran out. Casualties in this action were; three officers killed a fourth later died of wounds, seven officers wounded, 66 other ranks killed, 196 wounded and 160 missing.

The only noteworthy event occurring in November 1915, was Edward being promoted to Lance Corporal on the 16th. As was usual, this was an unpaid position and usually several men were promoted for each available position and then the best was confirmed in the rank and then paid. Edward soon proved himself worthy of the assessment made of him as he was made substantive Lance Corporal after only one month, on 16th December 1915.

On 23rd December 1915, the 7th Battalion came out of the line at Givenchy, and went into billets at Hingette, near Bethune in France as Divisional reserve. The following day, Christmas Eve, the Battalion had all day use of the baths and took the opportunity to clean themselves and their equipment. On Christmas day, following a Divine Service, sporting competitions were held in running and bombing and Christmas dinner was served at 2 p.m. On 27th December 1915, the party was over for Edward and his companions and during the afternoon and early evening they marched to the front line and took up positions at Festubert, the relief was completed without incident by 9 p.m. During this period in the front line, there was no notable activity just the usual shelling from both sides and some German machine gunners were active but not effective. On 29th December 1915, Edward was shot in the right shoulder, probably by a sniper and evacuated to an aid post then Casualty Clearing Station and then on to the 37th Field Ambulance for treatment, arriving there on 30th December 1915. The Field Ambulances were a mobile hospital unit and an intermediate level in the system of dealing with casualties in World War 1. They were situated away from the front outside of the range of the enemy's artillery.

Edward's war was over for the time being, he now spent some time in the care of the Royal Army Medical Corps. He was posted to the 70th Field Company Royal Engineers from 9th to 19th January 1916 but returned to the 37th field Ambulance on 10th February 1916 with an ankle injury caused on duty. When not in the Field Ambulance he was resident at 12th Divisions rest station. On 28th February 1916, he was again back in 37th Field Hospital with boils, this condition was treated seriously during World War1, anti-biotics were not available yet and an open sore such as this in the conditions which soldiers lived would very quickly become infected and likely to result in blood poisoning.

For administrative purposes, he was posted to the 8th(Service) Battalion Norfolk Regiment in July 1916 and, on 18th September 1916, Edward began his journey home to England. On board the troop ship Jan Breydel, Edward had an accident and injured his left knee, but apart from that he arrived safely back in England on 19th September. Edward was admitted to the Northumberland War Hospital, Gosforth, where he was treated for his various injuries including synovitis of his left knee; a particularly painful condition where the synovial membrane lining lubricating the knee joint becomes inflamed. Treated with rest and no doubt appropriate physiotherapy, Edward was discharged from the hospital on 22nd November 1916.

It's not clear in Edward's record where he was posted to next, but he was stationed 'at home' until 25th August 1917 when he returned to France. During this time, he was again hospitalised with Synovitis of his left knee at a military hospital in Tipperary, Ireland, from 30th January 1917 to 7th July 1917, after 158 days he was declared fit category A. On 26th August 1917 Edward arrived back in France and joined the 1st Battalion Norfolk Regiment, arriving on 12th September 1917.

The 1st Battalion Norfolk Regiment had been stationed in Belfast at the start of the war and had been mobilised and sent to France as part of the British Expeditionary Force in August 1914. When Edward joined them, they had just come out of the line and were in billets in the North Eastern area of France. In total the Battalion received three officers and 206 other ranks during the month of September 1917, and from the day Edward joined they were training or involved in sports days. At the end of September, the Battalion received orders to move and by train and daytime march, relocated to Westoutre in Belgium, the Battalion prepared to go back into the line. On 30th September 1918 Edward was promoted to full Corporal, it hadn't taken him very long at all to return to the life of a professional front line soldier and impress on his superiors that not only did he deserve the rank he carried but that he was ready for the next one as well. On 5th October 1917, they went into the front line at Tor Top, the trenches were in very poor condition and over the next few days they were subjected to shelling on a regular basis, on top of this the weather was cold and wet and the men had no great coats. On 8th October, orders were received to mount an attack on Polderhoek Chateau in conjunction with 16th Royal Warwickshire Regiment. At 4 a.m. and following the usual artillery barrage, the two Battalions lined up and commenced their attack at 5.20 a.m. The attack was unsuccessful and the companies returned to their original lines by nightfall the same day. The men had been caught in machinegun crossfire and bombing from wing trenches, casualties recorded were; four officers killed, four wounded, 28 other ranks killed, 144 wounded and 112 missing.

November 1917 passed with the usual trench routine but quite quiet and then, towards the end of the month, the Battalion received orders to mobilise to Italy.Before the commencement of World War 1, Italy had aligned itself with the Austria-Hungary and German Pact but had declined to take part. A flurry of British and French diplomatic Activity had persuaded the Italians to negotiate the Treaty of London, join the allied cause and declared war of Austria in May 1915. The Italian Forces had engaged the Austrians in the Alpine area on their border and had not been successful, British forces were sent to help them hold the line. Where the line occurred in the mountains every crack and fissure had been opened with explosives to create a trench system, it was not as complex and organised as the trench systems created in Belgium and France. Dugouts did not exist except where caves were available, the rock was a lime stone and many shelling injuries were from fragments of rock as well as steel shrapnel. Out of the mountains the front existed on plains to the French border, these were an unhealthy place to exist due to the existence of the Malaria carrying mosquitoes there. In 1917 the Germans were sending forces to assist their Austrian allies; the Italian army was suffering from terribly bad morale and mutiny was a real danger.

But for Edward, it was much warmer and drier where they were going and another country to visit. Whilst in Italy the Battalion prepared for action in the mountains of Brenta and then moved into the line along the River Piave.

On 11th January 1918, Edward's old knee injury flared back up again and he was admitted to 15th Field Ambulance for treatment and PUO, this was a pneumonic for Pyrexia of Unknown Origin, or unknown fever. This fever was not correctly diagnosed and he was transferred to Number 81, General Hospital at Marseilles where his condition was recognised as Trench Fever. After a spell in number 2 General Hospital at Le Havre and rehabilitation in Calais, Edward recovered sufficiently to be discharged and re-joined his Battalion on 8th May 1918 when he was posted to A Company.

On 21st March 1918, Operation Michael, the first phase of the German Spring Offensive of 1918, was launched against the line held by the British Fifth Army. The objective to this offensive was to break the British line where it joined with the French, force the BEF north to the sea and destroy it there if they stood and fought, then force the French to request an Armistice. There were four phases to the offensive but the last three were ancillary to the main thrust of

Michael and this was in danger of being successful. In response to this emergency, resources were being rushed to the fighting and initially Battalions were forming a holding action with instructions to fight to the last and hold at all cost. At the same time, more reinforcements were being sent to the immediate rear of the forward British line to form a secondary front to hold firm when the German forces reached it. Edward's visit to the sunny mountains of Northern Italy were over, orders were received to mobilise immediately and entrain to North Eastern France and join the plug that was to hold back the German offensive.

On 4th April 1918, the Battalion marched from Villa Ganzerla to the railway station at Vicenza arriving there at 11.30 p.m. The trains left the station at 2.50 a.m., they arrived at their destination of Doullens North Eastern France at 7.15 p.m. 8th April 1918 and then were kept on the train in a siding for three hours before they were permitted to de-train. After forming up on the road, the Battalion marched to their designated billets at Neauvillette, five kilometres away arriving at 1 a.m. on 9th April 1918.

Initially, whilst awaiting instructions, the Battalion spent their time cleaning and preparing themselves and their equipment for the battle to come. On 11th April 1918, orders were received to entrain at Saulty for a short journey to Aire-sur-la-lys, the horses and carts went by road. At this destination, the Battalion formed up and marched to Berguette with Edward's A Company forming a precautionary advance guard, because of the rapid nature of the German offensive they did not know where and when they would meet the enemy. At various locations on the road to meet the German advance, the Battalion dug in and prepared defensive trenches only to then receive orders to move on 15th April they reached the front line at BoisMoyen and the following day 16th April 1918 they relieved the 1st Battalion Devon Regiment in the front line. There was considerable artillery fire from both sides but at this stage they did not come into contact with the enemy, the weather was dull and cold but at least it was not raining. The next few days were spent waiting for an attack, sending out patrols and avoiding the attention of snipers. One patrol recovered some useful intelligence in the form of papers and correspondence found on a dead German in No-Man's Land and the only other activity reportedwas an increase in aerial activity overhead when the weather cleared a little. On 21st April 1918, the Battalion was relieved in the front line and moved to a support position. That night they were shelled heavily with gas and spent most of the night with their respirators on. The Battalion maintained these positions until relieved on 27th April, when they retired to divisional reserve. During this period, they had endured numerous artillery bombardments including gas attacks.

The positions where the men were camped were in Nieppe Forest and they were making bivouacs to sleep and protect them from the weather; it was described as a *'wet spot'*. By Company, the men were sent to Tannay to be de-loused, bathed and issued with new clothing, after a day of cleaning the men spent the night in comfortable accommodation before returning to the forest in order that the next Company could enjoy the facilities, Edward's Company was sent last. The casualties for the month were; two officers and 13 other ranks gassed, one officer and ten other ranks killed in action and 21 other ranks wounded. Besides the gas, snipers and shelling were responsible for the other casualties.

On the day, Edward re-joined his unit, 5th May 1918, the enemy shell fire was directed on his company's section of the front line but he managed to join and greet his friends without mishap. The next few weeks were the usual routine in and out of the front line, working to improve trenches, most of the casualties were a result of shelling, sniper fire and gas. Aerial activity was a daily event and the enemy planes were not only spotting for the artillery but dropping bombs on the British positions, the art of aerial bombardment was in its infancy and the accuracy of the bombing very dependent on the aimers eye and wind conditions, but still yet another danger to be worried about. On 17th May 1918, Edward's A and B Company had the opportunity to be de-loused, take a hot bath and were issued with clean clothing, we can only imagine how good that must feel but young men playing in a hot bath and free of the stress of the war must have been a heavenly moment! The casualties for May 1918 was not high but there were some different abstractions from the establishment; three officers wounded, two officers returned to England sick, one officer posted to the divisional wing, 17 other ranks killed, 29 wounded, 13 gassed, 98 to C.C.S. (Casualty Clearing Station), one missing, one returned to base found to be underage and one man to England to receive a commission.

During the early part of June 1918, several audacious raids were carried out on the enemy trenches, the weather had been very hot and the front line now ran through fields containing a mature crop of corn. Good use was made of the corn to approach the enemy's trenches enter them kill or injure the occupants, grab anything likely to be of use and then make a dash back to the safety of the Battalion's line. There is mention of officers walking amongst the corn to the front of the line and not being shot at, rather a foolhardy thing to do and lucky that enemy snipers were taking a nap perhaps!

On the evening of 24th June 1918, the Battalion left their billets once more to go into the front line; Edward is still posted to A Company. They relieved the 16th Battalion Royal Warwickshire Regiment from trenches in the right sub-sector of Le Sart. The relief went without incident and the following day, the men set to improving and updating the trenches that they inhabited. Excavations were dug out of the parapet to create dug outs for the Royal Engineers and wire was laid in front of the trench line, the trenches were widened and made deeper and corn was cut in front of the front line which was impairing vision. On 26th June 1918, Edward was engaged in a work detail deepening the trench and he made himself a target for a German Sniper, he and one other man were hit before the sniper was put out of action by artillery. Edward was hit in the head but there were still signs of life and he was rushed to the first link in the casualty system, from here he was taken directly to 15th Field Ambulance but unfortunately the doctor's best efforts were unsuccessful and he died the same day.

Edward was buried in grave 11 of row C of plot 4, Tannay British Cemetery, Thiennes, France with 362 other young British men who gave their lives in the fight for the freedom of future generations. In accordance with his will, Edward, left £5.1s.8d supplemented by a War Gratuity of £19 to his mother Alice and this account was disposed of in September 1918. Edward was awarded the 1915 Star, British and Victory Medals and records show that these too were delivered to his mother, Alice in 1920.

Chapter 17

William Henry Eggar MM

For Helen and Robert Eggar

Bill, as he was known, was born on 5th February 1884, in Basingstoke, then in the county of Southampton. He was the second of six children born to William and Ellen Eggar (nee Miller). William Eggar was employed as a labourer but managed to elevate his profession to carter and had use of a large horse-drawn cart. By 1901, the family had relocated to 84, Holborn Hill, Nechells, Birmingham. Ellen, who was born in Warwick, still had family in that area and William's parents still resided in Basingstoke, Ellen's confinements were varied between Warwick, Leamington Spa, Basingstoke and Aston in Birmingham.

In 1901, Bill aged 17, along with his elder brother, Frederick, were working with their father as carters. They had a heavy-duty cart pulled by a team of six horses. The area of Birmingham in which they resided was industrialised and, whilst a Carter would be employed hauling any goods, it is likely that they spent most of their time carrying coal from one location to another; the type of cart and horses would support this. The coal would arrive via the canal systems and be distributed to the factories by the carters.

A local and large user of coal at the time was the Gas works, not far from the family's Nechells home and, at some stage or other, Bill sought employment there as a gas worker. At 17, it is not likely he was a skilled worker and was possibly employed with many hundreds of other men moving coal from one location to another, the gas produced at this time was a product of the destructive distillation of coal.

On Christmas day 1906, Bill married Florence Sealy at St. Mathews Church, Aston Birmingham. They set up home at 179, Cromwell Street, Nechells and subsequently produced eight children.

At the outbreak of war, Bill was one of the thousands of men who volunteered to fight for his King and country. He was 30 years and six months old, 5 feet 7 inches tall weighing 139 pounds, with a pale complexion, brown eyes and dark brown hair. These dimensions are typical of the day as working people were shorter due to poor diet. The pale complexion is probably an indicator that he was employed inside as an outside worker would have a complexion reflecting their employment regardless of the perpetual smog over industrialised areas at the time due to the widespread use of fossil fuels for energy.

Birmingham Town Hall had been turned into a recruitment station due to the massive response to the call to arms and, on19th September 1914, on attestation Bill, took the oath, signed the papers and appended a note to instruct that a third of his pay should be forwarded to his wife. He was assigned to the Royal Warwickshire Regiment, 11th(Service) Battalion, D company, number 8256, this unit was formed in September 1914 and Bill was an originating member.

Bill was sent to Ludderhall on Salisbury Plain where the Battalion had been allocated tented accommodation at Windmill Hill Camp and arrived there on 14th October 1914. Things were a little chaotic at this time, most of the men and officers had not seen previous service and training was commenced but not structured in a traditional way and discipline was not being kept to a required standard. A large problem at this early stage was men going absent without leave or returning late from authorised leave. Due to his age and experience Bill was promoted Lance Corporal, this promotion was not to last however as Bill was disciplined on three separate occasions for being AWOL. On the first two occasions, he was severely reprimanded and fined, but on the third occasion he was deprived of his lance stripe and he reverted to the rank of Private.

In March 1915 the command of the battalion, now only five months old, was passed to Lieutenant Colonel C.S. Collison, who took up residency in one of the better hotels on Brighton's seafront. Collison was a professional soldier who had retired in 1911 but had commanded a reserve battalion for the previous three years.

At this stage the battalion's strength was 1000 other ranks and 100 officers, but very few men had any previous military experience and even fewer possessed uniform or rifles. Most were dressed in a blue outfit made of serge usually referred to as Kitchener Blues and sourced from old Post Office stock. This was a temporary issue until sufficient Khaki kit could be made and distributed. (The numbers given are from Colonel Collison's memoirs and are undoubtedly accurate but reflect the disorganisation of the situation, 100 officers is a huge number, a Battalion usually having around 30 and was probably because men were waiting to be posted.) On the plus side the general morale was excellent, the men being enthusiastic and in a good state of health and fitness. Many of the officers had no idea of training and whilst they had taken part in divisional training, the basics at platoon and company level had been neglected. Collison immediately commenced a programme of training from scratch and this progressed very quickly due to the enthusiasm of all concerned.

In April, following a month of intensive training, the battalion was moved from Shoreham to Ludgershall on Salisbury Plain where they formed the 4th battalion of the 112th brigade under the command of Brigadier-General J. Marriott, D.S.O., M.V.O. The situation with regards to uniform and equipment was improving and by the end of May things were complete. The 11th now looked and behaved like a professional unit of the British army.

Training concluded with divisional operations and an inspection by the King on 25th June, preparatory to embarkation to the front.

On 29th June, the battalion's strength was swollen by 200, all other ranks, but men returning to active service from sickness and wounds. These were men who had already experienced war and the awful conditions beyond the comprehension of virgin soldiers, but they were to prove a huge asset in the days to come.

On 30th July 1915 at 01.30 hours, the advance party entrained at Ludgershall with over 70 animals, mainly mules, in a very efficient 42 minutes-the mules were surely playing the game! Embarkation from Folkestone to Le Havre was the destiny for this first group, the next two groups followed at 15.30 and 16.30 on 31st July, but disembarked at Boulogne. The Battalion regrouped after 36 hours at Pont de Brique and took a train to Audruicq arriving at 3.30pm on 1st August. The journey to the front then commenced with a short march to Zutkerque where the men were billeted around the village. It was from this point, although well away from the front, that Bill and his comrades first heard the sounds of war away to the north east - artillery gunfire. The journey to front continued by marching day after day in hot, dry and dusty conditions, along roads designed for the carriage of people and goods on a much smaller scale than 1000 men marching, plus pack animals and carts full of everything from cooking utensils to ordnance. At 2.00 p.m. on 5th August, the primary objective of Hazebrouck, (13-15 miles from the front line), was reached and the men distributed to billets in a partly built, dirty, disused hospital complex. The diary records that 25 men ‘fell out’ during this arduous march, but the Brigadier was pleased at the appearance of the Battalion as it marched into town.

The enemy were active in this area, a recent attack on trenches in the region had been successful largely due to the use of liquid fire for the first time against British troops, or as we now know the device, flame throwers. The German air force, (Die Fliegertruppe or, more formally, as Fliegertruppen des deutschenKaiserreiches.) was also active dropping bombs on the troops. Fortunately, at this stage, the art of aerial bombardment was in its infancy and extremely inaccurate.

Bill’s first visit to the front was on 10th August, when a detachment marched 13 miles for trench digging work at Lorre which was the headquarters of the 28th Division. On arrival that evening they were welcomed by the Germans who fired two artillery shells which landed nearby. The event was marked with excited cheers, no one was hurt but this wasn’t to last. Working with regular bombardments from enemy artillery would eventually bring a unpleasant result and, on 20th August, the battalion experienced its first casualty when Private

8744 Richards was severely injured by a shrapnel bullet in the right shoulder. It is interesting to note that early entries in war diaries often mention casualties by name but as time goes, on and the casualties pile up the personal touch is replaced by a note of numbers killed, wounded or missing, separately noting officers or other ranks.

Whilst Bill and his comrades were digging, the rest of the Battalion, still 13 miles to their rear, practised musketry. A rifle range had been constructed and the bill for its construction is recorded at ten Francs and 15 Centimes, just over £1!

The two parts of the Battalion were reunited on 24th August. The total strength was now recorded as 28 officers and 990 other ranks. The following day, they entrained in open cattle trucks for a journey south arriving at Doullens 02.00 on the 26th. They were met by 'English ladies' who supplied each man with hot cocoa, I am sure this greeting was a huge boost to the men's moral and the ladies probably received many offers of marriage that night! The men were then marched to Amplier arriving at 04.30 and the day was spent receiving instruction in trench warfare. The march to the front continued the following day and on arrival at Sailly-au-bois as night fell, the battalion, by company and platoon, were guided to reserve positions in the village of Hebuterne. The following week was spent learning the intricacies of the trench system; where the relevant positions were, the support and communication trenches, dug outs and the location of stores and ammunition. Without this foresight it would have been very easy to become lost in the maze of trenches.

Hebuterne was typical of front-line villages and towns, largely destroyed by artillery bombardment. In particular, the church had received serious attention as did other identifiable buildings such as hospitals, which the enemy sought to destroy as they were a focal point for potential victims and of course to seek to diminish the morale of those who would value such facilities. A large crucifix with Jesus effigy which stood proud in the churchyard and had been untouched, those with religious learnings could take solace from this apparent miracle. Bill lived in the support trenches here, which was safer than having a roof over his head in the village. During this period, he was entertained to the aerial display of a dog fight between British and German airmen; the fascination of this spectacle never diminished by familiarity.

During the night of 2nd September, the 11th took their places in the front for the first time. These changeovers were always undertaken at night in darkness and silence to avoid bringing the manoeuvre to the attention of German gunners, a well-placed shell in a communication trench would create many casualties. The men of the 11th were now the closest they had ever been to enemy troops, along their section of line the distance to the German front line varied from 250 to 800 yards. This night was the last practical exercise of the trench warfare training, again comment was made about the enthusiasm and professional approach by all ranks.

At 7pm on 4th September, the 11th left these positions and commenced a march to Humbercamps arriving their early on the 5th and were allocated to billets, barns and outhouse for the men, the officers roomed in the village but there were only four beds.

Another move was commenced on 8th September, a few miles back in the direction of the enemy lines at Berles-au-Bois where a dirty and dangerous job awaited them. The landscape in this part of France differs very much to the flat fields of Flanders where the 11th were first stationed. Here, there are rolling hill features and the job was to dig a new communication trench on a hillside but facing the enemy! The work could only be conducted at night and a line had been laid for the diggers to crawl out to from the safety of trenches, the really exposed length was about 300 yards. On the first night an attempt was made to cover the men's work with fire from the front line, unfortunately this drew attention to the situation and fire was returned with flares being used to illuminate the sky. The second night the work was conducted without covering fire and with the diggers gradually moving downwards the work became safer. It's rather remarkable that there were no casualties during this operation especially on the first night where the retaliatory fire was rifle and machine gun, this of course Colonel Collison was grateful for but it did fuel his already low estimation of the standard of German infantry.

This type of pioneering work was continued until they returned to Humbercamps on 12th September. One particular addition to the communication trenches which the 11th were making, is a system called feathers or slits. These additions were narrow, deep channels about 20 yards long cut at right angles from the trench wall, they were designed to accommodate men in the trench waiting to relieve their counterparts in the front line.

It was particularly wet at this time and written orders were drawn up to accommodate the relief operations. Many trenches were not boarded, so there was a continual slog through mud when moving. To assist with this, rubber galoshes had been made available in limited numbers and the instructions for men being relieved were to hand their galoshes tied in pairs to an NCO who would in turn hand them to a counterpart in the relieving units who would then distribute them to his men. The system of holding the front at this time was two companies holding the line with two in reserve. After six days, these companies swapped roles. The companies in reserve were responsible for taking food and beverages to the men in the fire trenches and listening posts and recovering the empty billy tins. Under no circumstances could a soldier in a fire trench leave his post. At the end of the second period of six days, all four companies were relieved and went to the rear in Divisional reserve for 12 days; this was referred to as rest period or, more commonly, out of trench period. In the evenings after dark, a transport vehicle clattered along the roads to bring provisions and the daily post. Every now and then German artillery would target the road along which the vehicle was travelling resulting in the loss of that night's treats, our artillery would retaliate of course making the German gunners think twice about their action.

This routine continued until late October, when they were sent to St. Amand for a rest period. Here, on the 25th, the battalion was marched to Acheux where they, along with a number of other battalions, were inspected by His Majesty King George V and the President of the French Republic, Raymond Poincaré. King George was born in London but his family name was Saxe-Coburg-Gotha or Brunswick or Hanover. He made many trips to visit soldiers at the front during the war and Queen Mary visited wounded men in hospitals, but by 1917 following the carnage of the war so far, there was a huge outpouring of anti-German sentiment in Britain and he saw fit to change his family name to Windsor and relinquish all ties to German titles and family.

A few days later, the Battalion was given the use of the divisional baths, this is the first mention of bathing in the diary so it is not clear how long the men had to endure each other's odours, but having been in the line for some time the air was probably a bit ripe! The bathing facilities had to cater for huge numbers of men daily and one such facility was made from a disused brewery and the beer vats were filled with hot water. At the same time lice ridden clothing could be washed and the unwanted guests expelled with Naphthalene.

Lice were a constant problem for the men of the trenches and there were 3 types, head, pubic and body. To survive the lice needed warmth and food, body heat was often shared in cold weather when the men huddled to share keep warm, this enabled the lice to move from person to person and this was how disease such as Trench Fever was spread by an inflected insect sucking blood from one person and then moving to another. The favoured method of killing them was to run a lit candle along the seam of clothing where the lice congregated but the un-hatched eggs soon replaced their parents. The insects were often known as chats and this is how the expression to chat emerged as the men gathered to delouse or chat!

During November 1915 whilst in the line, the battalion came under attack from Minenwerfer which was a short-range, heavy mortar, designed to destroy such obstacles as wire and bunkers. Requests were made for artillery retaliation until they stopped. The other notable event was the weather; it rained incessantly causing miserable conditions for the men in the trenches and continual repair work when the trench walls collapsed. The trenches became mud traps and numerous men became stuck so fast they had to be dug out by their friends. Towards the end of the month following a spell of cleaning and bathing out of the trenches, they returned to find the trenches impassable due to collapsed walls and water logging, the relief that night had to be done not only in the dark and total silence but on open ground and not in the relative safety of the communication trenches.

During December 1915, whilst in reserve a St. Amand, a divisional concert party was organised and performed in a freezing cold barn, this makeshift theatre gave the performers the name, 'The Barn Owls'. The entertainers were chosen from the men for their skills and the productions were described as, 'to London music hall standard'. Singled out for particular mention is 'the girl' who was described as particularly good looking and drew the special attentions of the officers of the transport brigade, the deprivations of life at the front had may affects!

Christmas 1915 showed no sign of the fraternisation experienced the previous year, Bill and his comrades were in the front line or company relief and all was quiet except for some artillery fire aimed at them and on Boxing Day, a British plane looped-the-loop over German lines. There is no mention of any festivities or even a special meal sent to the men in the line and on New Year's Eve the German Trench mortars targeted the 11th Battalion's positions; there was no respite from the war for Bill this year.

1916 continued with a continuous system of front-line, relief and rest at the rear until near the end of June, when the pace of the war started to take a murderous change of pace for the British. One documented incident does highlight the dangers of life at the front. At 2.30am on 4th May, the Germans launched a ferocious artillery bombardment which lasted for 45 minutes. The casualties sustained, both killed and wounded, amounted to 130 and the fact was noted that it was pointless to try to identify the casualties as they had to be collected in sandbags.

1st July this year was the commencement of the Somme offensive. On this first day, Bill was in the front line but the 11th was playing a minor role providing covering fire to the left flank of an advancing 46th Division. Even so, from their relatively safe position, there was one man killed, an officer and six other ranks wounded. By this stage, Bill had been in the trenches for 16 days and was relieved on the 3rd

July. The battalion marched in pouring rain for two days finding billets at villages enroute, they then took motorised transport on 6th July at 8.30a.m. and, at 4p.m., arrived, cold, wet and hungry, at Mellincourt. The area was flooded with troops and the situation was chaotic, foragers were sent out for food but there was none to be had.

At 7.00 a.m. on 7th July, the Battalion took up position in trenches vacated by advancing troops and provided two companies to carry bombs (hand grenades) to troops in the forward positions. At this time large numbers of Germans were being taken prisoner and surrendering, many were wounded and in a visibly shaken condition giving merit to the objective of the artillery barrage intending that effect. They were all in fear of a harsh treatment as they had been told by their officers. The British forces treated them well, but they received no friendly welcome from any Frenchmen in the area which is hardly surprising.

On 8th July, the battalion was moved to positions further forward to relieve the units that had taken this ground the day before. This now placed them in the new front line between La Boiselle and Contalmaison. The day was extremely hot but followed by a night of torrential rain. The men were expecting to be called forward to join in the fighting at any time and the tension of waiting was unrelenting. That evening at 8.45pm, the 11th moved forward and entered the area known as 'Sausage Valley', all around them were the dead marking the line of the recent attacks and movement was difficult due to the boggy terrain and the enemy's artillery constantly searching for new victims. It took most of the night to occupy the new positions but the congestion was too much so two companies were removed to reserve and Bill's D company took occupancy of an abandoned German trench.

The headquarters was established in an abandoned German bunker and its description gives a good impression of how the German forces sat out the preparatory bombardment in relative safety.

> *"Headquarters was established about 300 yards south-west of the line in an extensive dug-out, yesterday the battle centre of a*

German Regimental Commander. Two stories deep, and fitted up in the most complete and elaborate way with all modern conveniences, and the 'usual offices,' it must have been at one time a luxurious abode. It was capable of holding about eighty men; these had lived in the upper stories, and their clothing and equipment littered the rooms. Several had been captured before they were able to get out, and a large dead German was on one of the beds. The whole place was in a very dirty state, and the electric lighting apparatus had been put out of gear. Down below, the wine cupboards had evidently received a thorough overhaul, and bed clothes and French literature of a frisky nature were strewn about. One of the two entrances had been crushed in by our guns; but otherwise the building was in first-rate condition. Here we installed the first-aid post, the Headquarters Signallers and Orderlies, and a section of the Brigade Machine Gun Company".

(Reproduced as described by CS Collison in his 1928 memoir with kind permission of D P & G Military Publishers)

During the day of the 9th, patrols took more prisoners and some useful intelligence in the form of maps and plans. Some enemy artillery pieces in pits were retaken by German forces and brought to bear on the battalion's positions. The staff in the bunker enjoyed the safety designed for the enemy but casualties were experienced in the trenches. During these three days, total casualties amounted to ten officers and 160 other ranks, not considered heavy!

At 4.30pm on the 10th, a further attack was made on the town of Contalmaison which was subsequently successful and the 11th battalion's contribution was to hold the line. They successfully defeated a counter attack by elements of the elite Prussian Guard and towards the end of the attack they were required to assist with the consolidation of the town and came under heavy machinegun and rifle fire from the front and left flank. Losses for this day were three officers killed and three wounded, six other ranks killed, 34 wounded and six missing. At 6.00 a.m. on the 11th, the battalion was relieved and moved to tented accommodation but there was to be no rest as they were still receiving artillery fire and were forced back to trenches. At one point, C Company's field kitchen was hit killing three cooks. This situation continued for the next few days until, at 3.00 a.m. on 15thJuly, orders were received to return to action.

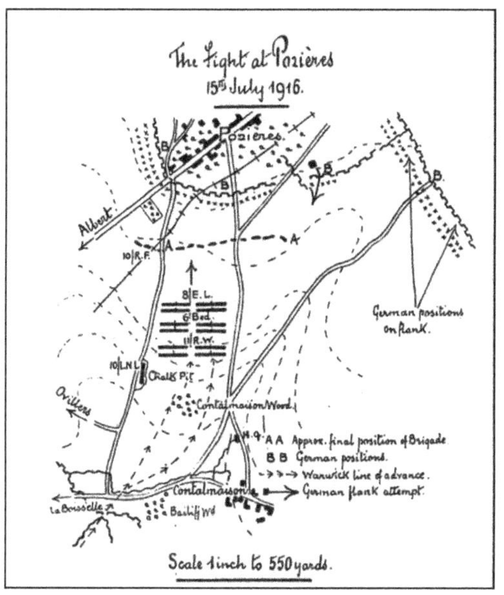

(Reproduced as described by CS Collison in his 1928 memoir with kind permission of D P & G Military Publishers)

The map shows this action involved the whole Brigade. The 8th East Lancashire took the lead, followed by 6th Bedfordshire and following on was Bill's battalion, whose role was to carry tools in order to consolidate any ground taken.

The tools involved were pickaxes, shovels and sandbags and it was usual for them to carry hand grenades in quantity along with their rifles. Consolidation of an enemy trench involved repairing any damage caused by artillery, but more importantly to create a fire step on what had been the rear face of the trench but would now be the front face and essential to create a defence against counter attack. Hand grenades were an essential tool also for repelling attacking infantry.

Diversionary attacks were to be mounted on both the left and right sides of the village and the attack was preceded by the usual artillery bombardment. At 9.20 the brigade moved forward along communication trenches but rising to open ground when these ended, after a slight rise beyond the chalk pit the enemy opened fire with heavy machine guns and the artillery continued its deadly job. The fire was accurate and sustained, the three battalions became intermixed but boldly pressed the attack which was only two companies wide, giving the machine gun crews a narrow target on which to train their guns. The attack faltered with many of the officers out of action and sergeants taking over command of companies, positions were held and consolidated. Recovery of the wounded became a priority and the regular medics were reinforced with volunteers to assist in this dangerous but necessary task. Bill readily joined men assigned to this task and under the guidance of Private 8311 B Ward, Bill set about recovering his wounded comrades whilst still braving the fire of snipers and machine gunners. Often it was impossible to use a stretcher and the wounded had to be dragged crawling back to safety, an initial rendezvous point was set at the chalk pit and there an assessment was made on the severity of a wound and in fact whether there was a chance of survival at all. Those with a chance of survival and with wounds needing immediate attention were then stretchered to a field ambulance in the rear, those whose wounds which were deemed fatal died in situation receiving the attention of chaplains. There were many wounds treated at the chalk pit and there the victims remained to await a less urgent recovery to the field ambulance.

Many of the volunteers to recover the wounded became casualties themselves and Bill was one of these. While risking his own life in an effort to save his friends he was shot through the left knee and became incapacitated, he was recovered to the chalk pit where his wound was bandaged and he became one of those waiting a less urgent moment to be evacuated.

A further artillery bombardment was called for 5.00p.m. and at 6.00 p.m., the attack was set to renew, the signal being a red flare. At the appointed time the flare was fired but fell only a few feet within the view of the Germans thus giving them plenty of warning of the infantry attack. A second flare was fired and the attack commenced but, due to the delay, it failed and the only result was further casualties. The ground gained was held by the 10th Loyal North Lancashire Battalion and survivors of the brigade retired to the positions they held before the assault had begun.

This attack was doomed to failure, the attack was committed on a narrow, two company, front, in the face of murderous rifle and machine gun fire accompanied by constant artillery bombardment, over 1000 yards of open country. The men remained under this fire from 10.00 a.m. to 6.00 p.m. and Bill's battalion alone amounted to five officers and 270 ranks (over 40%), the battalion's total losses since arriving in this sector were 15 officers and 450 other ranks.

Under cover of darkness the casualty recovery continued and Bill was eventually removed from the battle field to a field ambulance at the rear. For now, Bill's war was over. Bill arrived in England by hospital ship on 20th July 1916. They arrived in the night and were met by lady volunteers who provided the wounded and their escorts with hot food and drinks. From the ship bill was entrained with hundreds of other casualties, taken to Manchester and was admitted to the 2nd Western General Hospital. At the start of the war, the 2nd Western General Hospital was formed in Manchester and provided 520 beds, during the course of the war a total of 25,000 beds came under this single command, distributed around the Manchester area and became the largest single hospital in the UK. At the hospital Bill's old uniform was removed and following surgery, at a point he was able to get out of bed, he was issued with a convalescent blue uniform made of flannelette.

Hospital Blues Picture author's collection

Bill spent a total number of 68 days in hospital and no doubt this also included rest at one of the numerous convalescent homes in the area which had been formed in commandeered stately homes. Life wasn't too bad, taking into consideration the pain he must have experienced from this wound. The food was good and regular entertainment was laid on for the wounded men.

For his bravery under fire, Bill was awarded the Military Medal and the award was confirmed and posted in the London Gazette, dated 10th November 1916. Private Ward who coordinated the action was awarded the Distinguished Conduct Medal but was killed in the process of removing a badly wounded man from the field on 6th August.

On 7th October 1916, Bill was posted back to France where he arrived on 4th November at the 29th Infantry Base Depot. On 19th November he returned to join the 11th Battalion at a place called Station Road near Hamel. The battalion had marched to this location from reserve on 18th November and, during the course of the march, had received 40 casualties from shell fire. During the night of the 20th November, they relieved a battalion in the front line and Bill found himself back in the filth, depravation and danger of trench life which must have been so much harder to bear after the pleasantries of his life back in England. To show the situation Bill faced, it is interesting to note the casualty figures for the period when he re-joined the battalion, 14th to 27th November; officers killed three, wounded four, other ranks killed 32 wounded 153, 31 missing, 11 shell shock, sick 93. Total off the strength, nine officers, 320 other ranks. This must have been largely due to shellfire as there is no mention of operations in this period.

December 1916, was spent to the rear and training; the only noteworthy event is that on Christmas day a church parade due to be held was cancelled due to bad weather.

On 3rd January 1917, due to his leg injury, Bill was posted back to England and released to return to his pre-war occupation at the gas works near to his home in Nechells. The certificate authorising Bill's release also placed him on the Z list or army reserve and was dated 11th December 1916. On 9th January 1917, he was discharged from Budbrooke Barracks in Warwick and returned home to his family.

Bill was put to work in the retort house, this is where coal is heated and the coal gas extracted. One of the by-products of this process is a constituent part of TNT high explosive. By this time, the gas works was an important contributor to the war effort and Birmingham, being an industrialised city, had become a huge arsenal for explosives and ammunition of all types and, indeed, the production of weapons as it had a huge firearms manufacturing industry anyway.

On 5th February 1919, Bill was discharged from military service and removed from the reserve list. His wound had prevented any return to duty and his record was marked 'Discharged surplus to military requirements'. He and his family were delighted he had survived the war even though for the rest of his life his left knee was a constant reminder to him of the terrible conditions he had endured and the comrades he had lost.

Bill, in addition to his Military Medal, was awarded the 1914-15 Star, the Victory and British War Medals. He was also bestowed with two Blue Chevrons, a Gold Wound Stripe and his name entered in the Birmingham Employers Roll of Honour 1914-1918 (on behalf of the Gas Board) which is retained in the Hall of Memory in Birmingham.

Bill died on 22nd March 1949 at the age of 65, his death certificate records he was still a retort worker at the gas works living at 179, Cromwell Street, Nechells and the cause as, Chronic Bronchitis and Gastric Ulcer. A relatively young man when he died, he had survived two horrendous world wars, worked in an industry which was extremely hazardous to health and maintained him and his family at poverty level. His precious decorations would be regularly taken to the pawn shop to supplement his wages and then one day they were not recovered, on one hand it is surprising he lived as long as he did and at the same time it is hardly surprising he died when he did!

Chapter 18

Sydney William Enstone

(For Nick Enstone)

Early records of Sydney's life are elusive, but he was born in 1894, in Halford, Warwickshire, and his birth was registered in the last quarter of that year, at Shipston-on-Stour. The tenuous link to family, lies in his military file where he declared his next of kin as Mrs Enstone and brother William, both of Leamington Spa. The 1891 Census shows an Enstone family residing at 31, Avon Street, Warwick. The family head is Thomas Enstone, a 42-year-old bricklayer and his wife was Elizabeth, a 53 year old Laundress. This family had two sons, Arthur, 16, a bricklayer's labourer and William, 13, an errand boy. In 1901, the family are still in Warwick but there is no mention of Sydney. The first mention of him, is in the 1911 Census where he is found to be living at Ryon Hill, Stratford-upon-Avon, the home of John Parker Chapman, a 75 year old Farmer, Sydney, now 16 years old, is employed as a cowman.

On 8th September 1914, Sydney attended Birmingham Town Hall, which was being used as a supplementary recruitment facility due to the unexpectedly enormous response to the call to arms, where he attested and was accepted into the British Army. Private 8107 was posted to 11th (Service) Battalion of the Royal Warwickshire Regiment and joined his unit at Portslade Camp, Hove, Sussex, on 14th October 1914.

Sydney's story mirrors that of Bill Eggar in the previous chapter and to avoid unnecessary duplication we can take up Sydney's experience from where Bill was removed from the battlefield after the action at Pozières.

At 3.15 a.m. on 16th July 1916, the Battalion was relieved by 11th Northumberland Fusiliers and retired to billets in Albert. That day and the following, were spent resting, they had the opportunity of a bath and clean underclothes courtesy of the 34th Divisional Baths run by Sanitary sections of the Royal Army Medical Corps. An order to return to Pozières was received later this second day but was rescinded before the men could mobilise. The Battalion was then moved to La Houssaye for training and reinforcement. Daily route marches were undertaken as well as training new Lewis Gun crews and bombing groups. Other training included signalling and stretcher bearing. On 24th May a draft of 388 other ranks arrived to join the Battalion, very few of these men had seen previous action and many had never held a Mills Bomb. These new recruits had only 13 -14 weeks basic training which shows the desperate situation for manpower at the front following the tremendous losses in the initial days of the Somme offensive.

On the evening of 31st July 1916, the Battalion returned to duty taking up bivouac positions in Becourt Wood and formed part of the Divisional reserve. The following day their positions were subjected to an unexpected artillery bombardment of high explosive shells and before the men could get to the protection of trenches, 52 of them became casualties including; ten dead and two missing. The Battalion was moved to the Eastern edge of the wood where good defensive trenches existed but were soon required to take up front line duties at Bazentin-Le-Petite, they were subjected to heavy shelling in these positions and experienced heavy casualties. On 11 August alone, 63 men became casualties with seven of that number initially missing buried, four of the seven were dug out intact, the remainder was a collection of unidentifiable body parts. It was noted that this was a particularly trying time for the men. At 1.00 p.m. the following day, orders were received to attack a 300-yard intermediate trench in the German line, zero hour was to be 10.30 p.m. that night and the attack was to be preceded by an artillery bombardment. The artillery action advertised the intended attack and as the men climbed the parapet, they were subjected to shelling by 77mm Shrapnel fire and machine guns. The attack was pressed in the face of this devastating fire but failed a mere 20 yards from its objective, the men started to make their way back to their own trenches. The casualty count was; killed, one officer and 11 other ranks, wounded, two officers and 109 other ranks, missing, two officers and 37 other ranks. As day broke on 12th August the men were still trickling back to their trench and the Germans showed themselves and shouted that they wished a peaceful period. For some hours there was an unusual quietness which enabled the stretcher bearers to recover the wounded men who were unable to make their own way back, the rest of the day remained quiet. At 7.00 p.m., the Battalion was relieved and retired to reserve positions in Mametz Wood.

This action was the last experienced by 11th Battalion as part of the Battle of the Somme and, following a short rest, they were moved with the rest of the Brigade to billets at Maximgarbe situated between the City of Lens and Bethune where they came under the orders of 40th Division. During their commitment to the Battle of the Somme the 11th Battalion's casualty figures were; killed – six officers and 87 other ranks, wounded – 19 officers and 524 other ranks, missing – two officers and 61 other ranks, sick (here it is noted that these men were mainly suffering nervous complaints in other words Shell Shock) – five officers and 55 other ranks, total 759.

The Battalion fell into the usual routine of trench warfare, working a seven-day rotation between, at the rear, in support, and in the front line. This routine continued for several months and casualties were experienced on a frequent basis the most common cause being shell-fire. As winter set in, the trenches became very wet and muddy and men started to suffer from exposure. One particularly bad period, was 14th to 27th November 1916, where the casualties suffered were; nine officers and 320 other ranks mainly from shelling but this figure includes 11 cases of shell shock and 93 sick from other reasons, sent to a field ambulance.

Christmas 1916 came and went with little of event noted other than a church parade planned for Christmas morning was cancelled due to bad weather, however, the Battalion were out of the trenches and in billets. The rotational routine of trench warfare continued into 1917 and then, on 9th April the Battalion lined up to take their part on the first day of the Second Battle of Arras.

The breakthrough of the German lines expected of the Somme Offensive was not achieved and at the beginning of 1917 the high command was looking for a location to create the breakthrough that they foresaw would be the key to breaking the stalemate of the western Front and forcing the Germans into a more mobile war in which they could be beaten. The French City of Arras was chosen as the location to execute an offensive on a massive scale to create this breakthrough, using lessons learnt from the carnage of the Somme Offensive new tactics were deployed to make better use of the creeping barrage and mount infantry assaults on enemy strong points. The initial few days saw large areas of ground taken but then the stalemate of the Western Front prevailed when the German forces created effective defensive measures. The elusive breakthrough was not achieved but good ground was taken including the German high ground of Messines Ridge.

At 3.30 a.m. 9th April 1917, Sydney and his Battalion left their tented camp at Warlus, paraded and marched to a Brigade dump south of Dainville where a hot meal was served and equipment issued. The weather had been bad but suddenly cleared about this time allowing British aeroplanes to become active overhead, the Battalion assumed positions in a reserve trench being used as an assembly point in readiness to join in the battle. At 2.30 p.m. orders were received to go forward to the old German front line south of the Cambrai Road, this was achieved and the Battalion held onto this part of the line whilst another Battalion moved through them to press the attack, it was here that the men saw the first British tanks of the battle, three of them to their right but out of action. This was how the rest of the day progressed for the 11th, moving forward and holding positions as they were gained. At 3.40 a.m. 10thApril the Battalion retired to make ready for an attack on the German positions, at 12 noon that day the attack commenced but was received with heavy German artillery retaliation. The Battalion moved forward under the protection of a creeping barrage in artillery formation. The fighting continued until 6.00 p.m. when the Battalion took up positions at Les Fosse Farm, further advance was not immediately possible due to the Cyclists Battalion and some Bedford units adjacent to the 11th, having to fall back and no barrage available at this time. To have moved forward would have exposed the Battalions flank and made them vulnerable to counter attack.

At 3 a.m. 11th April 1917, the 11th was ordered forward to attack and occupy positions near to Monchy Le Preux. This was successfully achieved and at 3.30 p.m. that day, the Germans mounted a counter attack in force which was repulsed with very heavy casualties. The positions were consolidated and defended throughout the day, the Germans continued to fire on the 11th with machine guns and snipers. During this engagement, the 11th captured two German heavy Howitzers. At 11 p.m. on the 11th, the Battalion was relieved. They marched to Arras and were delayed due to the congestion on the road, but eventually reached rest billets at Denier on 14th April. Rest and training were the order of the days to come until further orders to return to the battle were received on 21st April 1917, two days marching brought them to their designated assembly point at 3.30 a.m. 23rd April. The Battalion moved into the front line and held awaiting orders to form an attack. At 3.50 p.m. orders came through to prepare for an attack on Greenland Hill, at 5.30 p.m. an artillery barrage commenced on the German positions consisting of 25 minutes shrapnel and five minutes high explosive shells. At 6.00 p.m., the Battalion moved forward towards the German positions on the hill. The Germans mounted a ferocious defence and the Battalion came under heavy machine gun fire from a chemical works to their right and were forced to dig in. A line was formed and defensive positions dug and consolidated. That evening the Battalion Commander, Lieutenant Colonel Francis Savage Nesbitt Savage-Armstrong, DSO, was returning to his Battalion HQ from a visit to his men in the front line when he was killed by a shell. Lieutenant Colonel Savage-Armstrong was a Dublin born poet and his death would undoubtedly be a blow to the men of the 11th, but they continued to hold the line until they were relieved at 3.00 a.m., 25th April 1917.

Despite suffering grievous casualties, the Battalion was placed in a support position behind the front line and had to create defensive positions making good use of the Lewis Gun sections and snipers. Artillery fire was intensive on both sides and, during the day, the respective air forces engaged in aerial combat overhead. Whilst holding these positions, the men not engaged in defence were put to work digging a communication trench from their support trench to the front line; this enabled a safer route for carrying parties to take ammunition and food to the front line. On numerous occasions the Battalion's positions were subjected to heavy shelling by the German artillery. At 4.20 a.m. 28th April 1917, the bruised and battered Battalion formed up to renew the attack on Greenland Hill. At 4.25 a.m. the men moved forward, they came under heavy fire from the German defenders and all the officers and senior NCO's apart from two Sergeants became casualties, either wounded or killed. Without coordinated direction, the Battalion became disoriented, eventually a ragged line was formed and defensive positions created, this line was held until the Battalion was relieved by 10th Argyle and Sutherland Highlanders at daybreak on 29th April 1917.

The Battalion were transported by bus back to billets at Denier, to clean up and take stock of the damage which had been caused to their ranks. During both actions the casualty toll was; killed, two officers and 62 other ranks, wounded 17 officers and 334 other ranks, missing one officer and 67 other ranks, a total of 483 casualties. A training programme was immediately undertaken along with reorganisation of the companies and platoons. It was not long, however, before the Battalion were required to return to the front. On 21st May 1917, the Battalion went back into the line in trenches North East of Guémappe where they were subjected to the usual artillery bombardments and subjected to a gas attack from 10 p.m. to 12 midnight on 23rd May. The gas was delivered by shells onto the support trenches and the wind was favourable for this attack, the exact locations of the enemy positions were unknown and a night patrols were sent out to locate them. The trenches occupied by the Battalion were in a very battered situation and the men were put to work repairing and improving the situation.

At the beginning of June 1917, the Battalion was moved to a rest area where they underwent training in musketry and close order drill. On 15th June Sydney left camp for a period of leave and returned to England for ten days, returning to join his unit on 25th June 1917. The Battalion were now billeted at Locre and still undergoing training; at 11 p.m. 19th July 1917 they moved back into the front line where they relieved 8th Lincolnshire Regiment. The stalemate nature of trench warfare had returned and the German air force was very active most days and they were dealt with by the Lewis Gunners and Royal Flying Corps. The Battalion were relieved on 25th July having sustained casualties; killed16 and wounded 28. This same day Sydney was removed by the Medical Officer and sent to hospital, sick. Sydney spent a short period of sick leave at the 37 Divisional Rest Station where he was treated and recovered then returned to re-join his Battalion on 7th August 1917.

The Battalion had moved to the Kemmel area in Belgium and were rotating on a four-day system between front line support and at the rear. At an unknown date following this event Sydney left the Battalion but his file does not say when and where he went. His story resurfaces when, on 4th May 1918, he arrived at D Infantry Base Depot, Rouen from Audruicq, France which was a location near to Calais where there were several receiving depots. On 13th May, 1918 Sydney was posted to 15th(Service) Battalion Royal Warwickshire Regiment and he joined them in the field on 16th May. The 15th had spent the winter in Italy and had been posted back to France in April 1918, as were many Battalions in response to the Spring Offensive launched by the German Army. The Battalion had been involved in fighting related to the offensive, but the situation had returned to the stalemate situation all too familiar to Sydney.

On the day Sydney arrived to join his new unit they had been training and billeted at Arcade Camp situated near Verviers Belgium, but on that day, they went back into the trenches and relieved 1st Cheshire Regiment in a support position. After seven days in support supplying working parties, they moved to the front line for a five day spell and were very active sending out patrols to identify enemy positions and raiding parties. On relief the Battalion moved to billets in Tannay, France from where they were again employed on the usual rotational basis.

On 26th June 1918, the Battalion was moved by light railway to front line positions from Tannay in preparation for an attack on the German lines, the following day they prepared battalion and company dumps of ammunition and supplies. At 10 p.m. that night, the men formed up in their start positions, their objectives being enemy positions West of La Plate Becque. At 1.30 a.m. 28th June 1918, parties left the trenches to cut the wire in preparation for the attack to commence, an artillery bombardment started and the infantry advanced. Each objective was reached and the occupants bayoneted or dealt with accordingly, few prisoners were sent to the rear! Bombing parties were active sending grenades into trenches to assist the storming riflemen. The fighting continued all day and, by 10.45 p.m., the positions taken had been consolidated and fields of fire created on what was now the new front line. Casualties during the day were; killed, two officers and 22 other ranks, wounded, five officers and 76 other ranks with six men missing. The positions were held throughout the day of 29th with movement difficult due to enemy snipers and machine gun fire. They were relieved during darkness that night and, whilst withdrawing came across two separate enemy working parties that were dispersed by rifle and Lewis Gun fire sustaining unknown casualties. The day's casualties for 15th Battalion were; killed two other ranks, wounded ten other ranks.

Following this action, the Battalion spent short periods in the usual rotation. Whilst in the front-line night patrols and raids were carried out with varying objectives; identifying the enemy in the trenches to the fore, capturing and destroying enemy equipment and men, and patrolling no man's land. Time spent at the rear was in various camps, training, cleaning both men and equipment and resting. On 24thJuly 1918, the battalion was relieved in the front line and were transported by light railway to Villorba Camp to form part of the Divisional Reserve. That night between 12 midnight and 3 a.m. the vicinity of the camp was subjected to an artillery bombardment. It is most likely this was part of the psychological use of artillery known as harassing fire, rather than the intended destruction of a specific target, The objective being to deprive the enemy of sleep and destroy his morale. The day was spent by everyone cleaning and resting and at 10.30 p.m. 25th July 1918, two companies were sent out to the front line to work on communication trenches, Sydney was in one of these groups. These trenches, being the main thoroughfare between support and front line, were in constant use, mainly at night for troop movement and carrying parties with food and ammunition, they were an obvious target for enemy artillery and any noise made at night would bring down artillery fire on the expectation of a concentration of men and therefore maximum possible casualties. The work Sydney and his comrades were doing was heard by the enemy who subjected the location to an artillery bombardment and no doubt the use of air burst shrapnel shells. These weapons were a canister full of lead balls designed to burst about 30 feet in the air and above the heads of the men working in the trench and were an extremely efficient anti-personnel weapon. On this occasion the balls found their intended target and one man was killed whilst seven others were wounded, Sydney was wounded when a ball hit him in the back in the area of the right kidney.

The casualties were removed to the rear to a Forward Dressing Station for immediate medical treatment and wound assessment. Sydney was then transported to 13 Field Ambulance, the next chain in the casualty system which consisted of a tented hospital system near to the front with the mobility to move if necessary. Sydney's wound was deemed too severe for his treatment to be completed at the Field Ambulance and, on 2nd August 1918, he was moved to 30 General Hospital in Calais, where surgery was performed and one lung removed. He was then returned to England on 8th September on the SS Newhaven, at that time in use as a hospital ship. On 9th September, Sydney arrived back in England was posted to the Royal Warwickshire Depot, there is no record of any duty and he was probably on convalescent leave. As part of Sydney's recovery, he was medically assessed to determine his future service and, fortunately, his wound was such that for him the war was over and on 28th November 1918 he was discharged from the army as, *'no longer fit for war service' (para 392 XVI (a) Kings Regulations'.).*

Sydney had survived the carnage of the Great War and no doubt celebrated the fact on many occasions. He had good cause to as well, having seen many of his friends wounded, killed, blown to pieces, fallen to any number of savage methods devised by a merciless enemy. He was now free to return to his civilian life, marry and have children which so many men could not. For his service he was awarded the 1914-15 Star, Victory and British War Medals, he was also entitled to wear a gold wound stripe and four blue chevrons for the years he spent in France. Sydney died in 1958.

Chapter 19

Percy Dudley and Charles Edgar Evershed

(For Francis Merton)

Percy Evershed Author's collection

Percy was born on 31st October 1895, the son of Percy Burdett Evershed (1867-1941) and Jessie Evershed (née Cheale 1870-1958) but was always known by his middle name of Dudley. The family was from the Eastbourne area of East Sussex and were established jewellers/watchmakers. In the 1901 census, they are shown living at 10, Roylestone Road, Eastbourne. He was the eldest of four children; two boys and two girls. Percy B Evershed had been ousted from the family business due to his predilection for taking a drink, so his family's destiny lay outside of the long established family business.

In 1911, at the age of fifteen, Dudley moved to 41, Kingsley Avenue, West Ealing, London and assumed employment as a draper's apprentice at a Messrs. Eldred Sayers and Son, a nearby department store. He was followed to this same employment by his younger brother Charles Edgar Evershed who, following family tradition, was known as Edgar. Eldred Sayers and Son was a long-established family firm that was a purveyor of quality goods. The training department occupied the top floor of the building and trainees were not allowed to set foot onto the sales floors until they had passed certain standards. By 1914 at the commencement of the war, at the age of 18, Dudley was a fully qualified draper.

Unfortunately, Dudley's military file was amongst the 75% destroyed by German bombers during the Blitz of London in the Second World War, but Dudley was not a professional soldier. He answered the call to arms made at the onset of war and was initially postedto the Rifle Brigade for basic training. Following the successful conclusion of his training, Dudley was then posted to the Northamptonshire Regiment, 5th (Service) Battalion, which landed in France as Pioneers to the 12thEastern Division. The 5th Service battalion was formed at Northampton in August 1914 and attached as infantry to the 12th Eastern Division. They were initially based at Shorncliffe and, in November 1914, transferred to Hythe, Kent. In January 1915 the battalion was converted to a Pioneer Unit and moved to Aldershot in February 1915 for training.

As the initial mobility of the First World War ebbed and became a static entrenched type of affair, the need for Pioneers whose main purpose was trench development and repair became more urgent. Dudley and his comrades trained in the use of pick and shovel, the filling of sandbags to make gun emplacements and the use of boarding to shore up the sides of trenches, the making of walkways and of course, dug outs built into trench walls for accommodation. Fire steps were built into the wall facing the enemy for riflemen to stand on and be at the right height to shoot at the enemy over the parapet, thus enabled the trench to be dug deep enough for men to be able to stand upright without becoming a target for snipers or artillery observation posts who would direct artillery and mortar fire when they saw any movement of troops (In some areas with a high water table the trenches were shallow and the height gained by building up the parapet with sand bags).

On 5th May 1915, orders were received for Dudley's battalion to mobilise to France. Finally, Dudley and his comrades were off to war to defend the Empire and uphold the honour of King and country. Dudley was embarking on a great adventure as were thousands of other young men of his generation, but the promise of glory and adventure was going to prove to be just words. The following day the first casualty occurred when Private Debney was accidentally shot.

The Battalion marched to the coast and were shipped to France on 30th May arriving at Boulogne the following day. The next few days were spent marching from camp to camp but on 2nd June, the second ignominious tragedy occurred when Private Bedding fell into a canal, near Arques, wearing full uniform and pack he drowned. Things were already starting to show the reality of war which is far removed from the picture painted of glorious victory and home for Christmas by the recruitment propaganda.

On 5th June, orders were received, and transport arrived, to move the battalion to Vlamertinghe where, on June 7th, they started digging trenches to the rear of Ypres for 12th Brigade ofthe Third Division. This work brought home the realities of war as whilst they were digging trenches they were exposed to enemy observation and fire. During the next nine days until June 15th, seven casualties occurred of which one 2nd Lieutenant and six NCO'S and men were wounded by shrapnel, one other casualty was from a sprained ankle.

The remainder of June was spent digging and improving trenches with also some time spent in forward positions holding the front line. A steady flow of casualties was experienced with two men killed, 12 wounded and one broken ankle. On June 30th the men were stood down for a well-deserved rest. This respite from the constant digging and danger did not last long as on 1st July it was back to work!

As trench warfare developed, so did the need for Dudley to learn new skills. Loop holes were added to the front face of the trench to provide protection from snipers, these were often made from plate steel, the loop hole being for a rifle to be fired from a protected position. The main cause of the stagnation of this war, the machine gun, was positioned in specially dug pit emplacements in front of the forward trench. At this stage in the war, the heavy machine gun in use was the water cooled, tripod mounted Vickers, which fired a belted .303calibre round as used in the standard Lee Enfield bolt action rifle. Another tactic being developed was the use of wire to create a protective barrier in front of the forward trenches; this extremely hazardous practise befell to Percy and his comrades. The hazards are well apparent in the writings of the Battalion Executive Officer, Captain A.C. Pickering who was responsible for recording the daily events in the diary.

> *Lancashire Trench 15/10/15*
>
> *Companies wiring along the front of the division (i.e. along positions gained by 35th and 37th infantry Brigades). It is found advisable where enemy's trenches are to near to use rolls of French wire intermingled with barbed wire and to fix it to the ground with staples - the noise of knocking in pickets attracting to much attention. One man wounded on 13thinst. died of his wounds – one man killed –seven NCO'S and men wounded.*
>
> *A.C.P. Capt.*

The casualty tally for the month of October 1915 was; ten killed, 73 wounded, two missing and two died of wounds. Whilst there may be a small overlap between wounded and died of wounds, the overall picture is of men being deployed in an extremely hazardous, nerve racking, filthy and exhausting work detail. There is no mention at all of any disciplinary issues and whilst I would find it hard to believe that men engaged in this work would not curse and moan about their lot, they certainly stood firm and did their duty.

December 1915 was a busy month, repairing trenches and working under the command of the Royal Engineers on a canal nicknamed

Suez. All the features of the British sector of the Western Front were given names; trenches such as Piccadilly, Oxford Street and Park Lane were all subject of repair during December.

The truce of Christmas 1914 had been a huge embarrassment to the British high command and the scale of it was such that any reprisals for offences of fraternisation with the enemy or mutiny would have only drawn attention to the event. It was thought better to keep it quiet but take measures to prevent it happening again. The diary for Christmas Day merely states, '*No work*'.

On 14th February 1916, Dudley's Battalion returned to front line duty following a short spell in the rear, the strength was recorded as;32 Officers, five Warrant Officers, 46Sergeants, 42Corporals, 980Privates, total 1068, total all ranks 1105, (I am not sure how these totals were achieved!). The men marched to Sailly-LaBourse, the destination for their next series of actions. This area was part of the Loos front and was still an active battle front following the Battle of Loos held during the autumn of 1915. The front lines in the Hohenzollern Redoubt, changed hands and due to the use of mines by both sides a constant fear existed of the ground erupting from a massive explosion beneath the feet of the men. To alleviate this constant pressure, the front was held by manned outposts, which also reduced the casualty rate when a mine was initiated. Along with mines a continual use of artillery meant there was constant trench repair and improvement work for Dudley and his comrades.

Billets were allocated in the villages of Sailly-LaBourse and Noyells and work allocated by companies repairing and making improvements by adding dog's legs, T shaped fire trenches, cleaning and sandbagging.

The 2nd March 1916 was the intended date of an offensive on the German front line trenches, the attack to be preceded by the initiation of three large mines and a fourth smaller one which had been dug underground by the 170th Tunnelling Company of the Royal Engineers. Attacking parties were to proceed immediately the debris blown into the air by the mines had returned to earth and were armed with large quantities of hand grenades to repel any counter attacks.

Supporting parties were assigned to destroy communication trenches 25 yards into the trench from the captured front line, and the Pioneers were in support to repair trenches, create a fire step on what had been the rear face of the German trench and was now the front face, lay wire to the front of attacking parties now engaged in consolidating the newly acquired position and generally reinforce the positions by sandbagging.

The attack proceeded and was successful in most of its objectives with counter attacks being repulsed. During the course of the day, the 5th experienced a variety of casualties; one lieutenant killed, two others wounded, three men killed, one man died of wounds, 11 men wounded, six men shell shocked. Dudley was one of these six men to suffer shell shock and it proved to be a life changing condition. During the course of the day Dudley and the other five men affected became buried alive under sandbags and earth whilst engaged in consolidating the position they had been assigned to. After a number of hours buried, they were dug out and taken to the casualty station allocated for this action at a place called Barts alley.

As a result of this injury Dudley shook uncontrollably for the rest of his life and every hair on his body fell out. I doubt that society would have considered Percy's wound or condition an honourable one as throughout his life he and his wife saw fit to apologise for him to guests when he was handed a cup of tea and with his hands shaking most of his beverage ended up in the saucer or on the floor. This is only worthy of note in that there was clearly a stigma associated with this and other mental conditions; a situation which clearly still persists.

September 1918 was the last active month for the 5th, they were engaged in trench works and in operations where they took substantial casualties. The last casualty of the war that the battalion took was whilst holding the line on the 26th in the region of Guyencourt, one man was killed and one wounded. The following day the battalion moved out of the line to billets in a trench situated north east of this location. The Battalion had dug its last trench and fought its last action.

October 1918 was spent repairing roads, bridges and filling in craters. For the very first time such comments as, *'some work, cleaning up and re-equipping'*, appear in the diary and the entries become much shorter, indicating a lull in offensive activity. The fact that the men were engaged in repair work of this nature out in the open and not taking casualties speaks for itself when making an assessment of the situation in the front line.

I find the diary entries for November 1918 rather sad but in keeping with the unsung nature of the work of the 5th Pioneers;

November 11th 1918
Armistice 11am.

There is then mention of the various dispositions of the companies and their work repairing roads with the Royal Engineers, but not a single indicator that this was a momentous occasion. There is no letter from General Officers praising the men as occurs in many other diaries, not even a parade held to mark the occasion. This reflects the second fiddle role played by Dudley and his comrades, they were the men used as navvies, the men running across no man's land armed with picks, shovels and sandbags to turn a wrecked captured trench into a defendable position. On these occasions their main weapons were bags of hand grenades, each man carrying twenty grenades to repel counter attacks while they consolidated the position.

In what capacity Dudley served following his injury is unclear but on 15th February 1919 he was demobilised and placed on the Z list. Class Z Reserve was authorised by an Army Order of 3 December 1918. There were fears that Germany would not accept the terms of any peace treaty and therefore the British Government decided it would be wise to be able to quickly recall trained men in the eventuality of the resumption of hostilities. Soldiers who were being demobilised, particularly those who had agreed to serve "for the duration", were at first posted to Class Z. They returned to civilian life but with an obligation to return if called upon. The Z Reserve was abolished on 31 March 1920 and Percy was able to continue with his life without the worry of a return to war.

After the war he returned to London and lived for a while at 6, Charterhouse Square, he married Maud Mary Pyatt in 1925 and they had one son Peter Bernard born in the same year. Percy did not return to his pre-war profession due to the effects of shell shock, he did however keep a wig at work for use in connection with his job, but did not wear it home. His only known profession post war was as a Tallyman or debt collector and subsequently a supervisor.

Dudley had always suffered, post war, with breathing troubles which he attributed to the gas attacks he had suffered during his time in the trenches and, in 1961, he was diagnosed with lung cancer and one lung was removed. Unfortunately, Dudley did not recover from this and died on 11th May 1962 in Worthing. To his credit, he had never recovered from his experiences in the trenches and he learnt to live with his disability and to a ripe age for his day. He did not apply for a war pension but surely would have been entitled to one; he was awarded the 1914-15 Star, British War and Victory Medals.

Charles Edgar Evershed

As previously mentioned, Charles was Dudley's younger brother and was also known by his middle name of Edgar. His antecedents prior to the war, mirrors that of Dudley even to the point of being employed as a Draper at the same London Store.

Little is known of Edgar's war service as, like his brother, he never spoke of it, but he joined the Royal Flying Corps on 2nd September 1915 and served in an unknown capacity within the UK. He was trained as a pilot in 1918 after the service had changed to be the Royal Air Force but the war ended before he could be deployed.

It is not known when Edgar was demobilised, but he returned to work for his pre service company and became skilled in watch and clock maintenance. One story about him gives a feel for how the war had affected him, even though he had none of his brother's experiences. Listening to the radio on the evening of 30th September 1938, the then Prime Minister Neville Chamberlain, returned from talks in Berlin with Hitler he brought home an agreement which had been made there, which was supposed to allay the threat of war. Standing outside 10 Downing Street he waved the paper in the air and declared;

> *"My Good Friends, for the second time in our history, A British Prime Minister has returned from Germany bringing peace with honour. I believe it is Peace for our time. We thank you from the bottom of our hearts. Go home and get a nice quiet sleep".*

On hearing this statement Edgar burst out crying saying, *"Thank god we haven't got to go through all that again"*. The fear of war was very real throughout the country and Edgar's generation feared a renewal of hostilities with Germany would again wreak havoc on the country, his relief at the announcement, short lived as it was, was very apparent.

At the outbreak of World War 2, Edgar tried to re-enlist but at the age of 41 was turned down and as his experience in the area of precision instrument making was expert, he was employed on essential war work making ships clocks and barometers. After work he also spent time as a Fire Watcher at St Paul's. Edgar was not awarded any medals for either conflict but his efforts were typical of every individuals desire to 'do their bit'.

Chapter 20

William Palmer Husselbee

(For Paul Dobinson)

The name Husselbee is very unusual and I thought it appropriate to look at its root. It is thought the origin is a mix of Norse-Viking and Old English, pre-dating the 7th Century; a combination of "Hussel" - which derives from "Hoetse-halh" - and means the place of the elf or witch, plus the Norse Bi, meaning a farmstead.

William Husselbee was born in 1895, to Florence Emma Palmer and Alexander Husselbee, who married a few months after the birth of William. William was Christened on September 24th 1897, at St Mary's Church Wolverhampton, and the family lived at 63, Wood Street, Wolverhampton.

By 1901, the family had moved to 26a, Great Hampton Street, Dunstall, Wolverhampton and William now has a younger sister; his elder brother was not living with his parents at this time. In 1911, the family were resident at 5, Dunstall Street, Wolverhampton. Florence is now head of the family and has all six surviving children living with her, three of her children having died. William at 16, was now working as a labourer at a local wood yard where his elder brother was a wood turner, the other four children were all at school.

From the few remaining records available, it is highly probable that William was conscripted to the army at the beginning of 1916 and served initially as Private 3925 of the South Staffordshire Regiment. This number will relate to his basic training and this would have been completed with the 3rd Battalion which, at the beginning of 1916, was based at Forest Hall, Newcastle. Following completion of his training, he was posted to 6th Battalion as Private 241063 and sent to join them in France. The 6th Battalion had been formed in August 1914, at Burton-on-Trent, Staffordshire and had landed at Le Havre in March 1915 as part of the 137th Brigade,` 46th (North Midland) Division. In January 1916, the Brigade was sent to Egypt and the 6th Battalion occupied tented accommodation of the banks of the Nile. There they drilled, trained and dug trenches but returned to France after only one month, disembarking at Marseille.

When William joined the Battalion, it was in the area north of Arras and taking its turn in and out of the front line there. On 15th April 1916, the 6th relieved the 5th Battalion South Staffordshire Regiment, in front line trenches at Neuville St Vaast, the changeover was completed without incident by 11.15 p.m. From dawn until noon the following day the German artillery pounded the trenches occupied by the 6th Battalion with howitzers, field guns and aerial torpedoes. An artillery duel commenced between 6 and 7 p.m. and two German mines were detonated to the Battalion's left at midnight followed by a heavy bombardment through the night.

The following day is recorded merely as 'quiet', but on 18th April 1916, William was on duty in listening post Y, forward of the Battalion's front line.

Listening posts - also known as 'Sap Heads' - were simply a place forward of the front line, manned by small groups of soldiers, whose remit was intelligence gathering about the enemy. The position of the post was usually about 30 yards forward of the front line, in No-Man's Land and could be a purpose-built trench running out at 90 degrees or a camouflaged position such as a shell hole. The men listened out for any enemy activity such as, wiring parties, tunnelling, patrols or sniper activity and any information sent back for consideration of what action to take. The information could be used to direct artillery or mortar fire or just fed to the intelligence system to create a bigger picture of what the enemy was preparing for.

At 6.55p.m. on this fateful day, the Germans exploded another mine on the left side of William's position and the Sap was blown in, killing and burying those inside. Immediate action was taken by the men of the front line to occupy the resulting crater (later known as B5) and the position was consolidated to be held against potential enemy attack. Both sides had a vested interest to take immediate action when a mine was detonated to attack and hold the position as it could then be incorporated into the front line thereby creating forward, but slow, movement of the line.

William's body was never recovered or identified and, in due course, William's name was added to the Arras Memorial. William left £3.8s.2d to his father, Alexander, this was later added to with a War Gratuity of £4 and he was also awarded the British War and Victory medals.

Chapter 21

Reuben Fell

(For Trevor Harrison)

2nd from left Reuben Fell (Pic courtesy of Trevor Harrison)

Reuben was born in the parish of Holy Trinity, Coventry, on 22 July 1872, to Thomas and Matilda (nee Hill) Fell. The first record containing Reuben's details is the 1881 Census which shows the family living in Palmer Lane, Bishop Street Ward, Coventry. Thomas Fell is working as a plasterer and Matilda as a charwoman. Both are from Coventry and, at this date there are seven children aged between one and 16, of which Reuben is the fourth eldest. By 1891, Reuben and his younger brother Edward are living with their elder brother, also Thomas Fell. Thomas is employed as a bricklayer's labourer and is married to a lady named Mary Jane, they have no children but are caring for an elderly relative, Elizabeth Croft, a widow aged 89. Reuben, now aged 18, is employed as a milling machinist, whilst his 14-year-old brother, Edward, is working as an iron turner.

On 10th August 1898, Reuben attended the Coventry recruitment facility for the Royal Warwickshire Regiment and attested as a first step to commencing a military career. The following day he returned and was subject of a thorough medical examination to determine his level of fitness, Reuben at 22 years of age, was 5'6¼" tall, blue eyed with a fresh complexion and light brown hair. He weighed 121 lbs and had a chest expansion of only ¾" when fully expanded at 34", but he was deemed fit for army service by a Dr Davidson, late of the Royal Marines and was posted to the Royal Warwickshire Regiment. On 12th August 1898, Private 6102 Fell, attended the Regiment's base at Warwick to commence his military career. He was posted to 2nd Battalion but completed basic training with 3rd (Reserve) Battalion in Warwick. On completion of training, Reuben was sent to join 2nd Battalion who were permanently based in Malta helping to protect British interests in the Mediterranean. Reuben's career was unblemished until 31st July 1901 when he was confined to barracks; he faced a Court Martial on 7th August 1901 where he was sentenced to 70 days' imprisonment with Hard Labour. The record does not tell us what Reuben's crime was but in addition to this he had a total of 77 days discounted from his pensionable service, he was not discharged from the army and the matter was probably a minor issue which was treated harshly. Reuben returned to duty on 16th October 1901 and one year later returned home to re-join 3rd Battalion at Warwick, where he was transferred to the army reserve in November 1902. His duty as a reservist would involve regular attendance at army camps for training and re-examination to determine his continued fitness for service, this reserve duty was completed on 9th August 1910 when he was formally discharged, his military service complete.

At the outbreak of World War 1, Reuben had been employed as a plasterer by Mr G. Middleton, a master plasterer, and was living at 16, Peel Street, Coventry, the home of his Sister Abigail who had married Walter Jackson. The couple had five children. Reuben's sense of pride and duty, in his Country's hour of need, took him to the recruitment facility for his old Regiment, the Royal Warwickshires, here he was medically examined, deemed fit for service overseas and attested. As Private 2841 Fell, he was sent to the Isle of Wight for training, his regiment had various units stationed at Golden Hill Fort, near Freshwater on the north coast of the island, including 3rd and 4th (Reserve) Battalions. Apart from one run in with military law where he was again subject of Court Martial proceedings, Reuben being an old hand completed his training and was posted to the 2nd Battalion who were already serving in France. The 2nd Battalion Royal Warwickshire Regiment was still stationed in Malta at the outbreak of war and returned to England in September 1914, where they joined the 22nd Brigade of 7th Division. The Battalion mobilised from its Lyndhurst Camp in the New Forest and landed at Zeebrugge at the beginning of October 1914. Between the 19th of that month and 22nd November 1914, the Battalion was engaged in the first Battle of Ypres.

Reuben completed his training and landed in France on 11th October 1915, where from the Infantry Depot, he was transported to join his Battalion in the field. He arrived on 16th October, one of 80 men sent out as a new draft. The Battalion were occupying support trenches near to the village of Cuinchy which is close to Bethune and Reuben was allocated to C Company. The following day the Battalion was relieved by 1st York and Lancaster Regiment and marched to Bethune where they were billeted for the night. At 9 a.m. on 18th October 1915, the Brigade to which 2nd Royal Warwicks belonged, paraded and marched to Cornet le Bourdois where they enjoyed some down time when the weather was fine, but were moved on yet again to billets at Les Harisois, where the weather became less than kind. On 29th October 1915, they returned to the trenches and relieved 2nd Battalion Wiltshire Regiment. The Battalion's strength is noted at a rather low total of 19 officers and 528 other ranks. Casualties started almost immediately; on their first full day, two officers and two other ranks were wounded. This first taste of trench life for Reuben lasted until 1st November 1915, when the Battalion was relieved and retired to billets, on a four day rotation. The weather was generally wet and becoming colder and the casualties were piling up daily.

On 22nd November 1915, the Battalion had just returned to billets in Bethune, when the news came in that a Victoria Cross had been awarded to one of their number.

No. 3719 L. Cpl. A. Vickers

2nd B. Warwickshire R.

Awarded the Victoria Cross for most conspicuous bravery on 25th September, 1915, during operations before Hulluch.

During an attack of the Battalion on the first line German trenches, Private Vickers on his own initiative and the utmost bravery went forward in front of his company under very heavy shell, rifle and machinegun fire, and cut the wires which were holding up a great part of the Battalion although it was broad daylight at the time he carried out this work standing up.

His gallant action attributed largely to the success of the assault. (London Gazette dated 18.11.15).

Arthur Vickers collected his medal from King George V at Buckingham Palace in 1916, survived the war and lived until 1944, he is buried in Witton Cemetery Birmingham.

This wonderful news would surely have been more than sufficient excuse to enjoy whatever hospitality existed in Bethune. This town contained a major railway junction and hospital facilities and was occupied by large numbers of British, Canadian and Indian troops. It was largely untouched by shellfire at this stage of the war and the civilian population were still in residence. Wherever these combinations existed, so did the leisure facilities for off duty soldiers. Local people and volunteers ran tea rooms, bars and snooker halls.

The Battalion now spent a period out of the trenches and entrained to camp at Amiens on 5th December 1915. Reuben's C Company formed an advance party which went ahead of the main body. The usual reason for this, was to ensure the billets at the other end of the journey were fit and, if not, to make them so. This out of the line period lasted until 10th February 1916, when the Battalion took over trenches near Morlancourt. During this rest period, the only casualty was one other rank, with a self-inflicted wound and, towards the end, when they were nearing the front again, two officers of the machinegun section were gassed. But a steady flow of replacements was arriving and the

Battalion's numbers now stood at 34 officers and 846 other ranks. During this tour in the line, the casualty count was 11 other ranks wounded and two killed, no cause stated but most likely from shellfire or snipers, the Battalion was relieved and retired to support trenches on 14th February 1916.

The periods spent in and out of the trenches was now extended to six days each. The daily routine would start an hour before dawn when the men were woken up - this was called 'Stand to' took their places on the fire step and prepared to repel any enemy attack. When stood down, breakfast and ablutions were completed and daily tasks allotted by the NCO's; rifles and equipment were cleaned, sandbags filled, trenches repaired and latrines filled in and moved when a new hole was dug. Whilst these tasks were completed, those on sentry duty remained at their posts and those off duty tried to get some sleep. This last issue was a continual problem and sleep deprivation was common. One of the objectives of artillery operations is called harassing fire which was not necessarily designed to hit a specific target but to keep the enemy from sleeping and thereby living on their nerve ends and undermining moral.

At the end of March 1916, the Battalion was housed in billets at Morlancourt and prepared for a parade where they were to be inspected by the British Secretary of State for War, Herbert Asquith. The casualty count appears to have increased around this time. In the first four days of a six-day tour in the front line at the end of April 1916, C and D Company's count were three other ranks killed and 26 wounded. On 9th May, the 2nd left the trenches and retired to Morlancourt where they went into Divisional reserve. The daily routine was forming working parties under the supervision of the Royal Engineers undertaking trench repair and improvement on the front line where any noticeable activity would draw the attention of enemy artillery spotters or snipers. The first casualties reported were not until 17th May when three men were wounded.

At the beginning of June 1916, the Battalion spent time in the front line near Bois des Tailles (near Amiens), but after one tour they retired to billets in the area to prepare for the forthcoming Battle of the

Somme. At 10.50 p.m. on 30th June 1916, the 2nd Battalion paraded and marched to their place of assembly at Lucknow Redoubt; the Battalion's strength had been reinforced during the preceding months in preparation for this action and now stood at 38 officers and 1049 other ranks. The 2nd was not a first wave unit and, at 7.30 a.m. on 1st July 1916, the whistles blew along the front line and the first wave troops went over the top and the 2nd then moved up to take the assembly positions just vacated. Reuben's C Company occupied a trench known as Lord Street. At 2.30 p.m., C and D Companies were ordered to go forward and assist a unit of the Gordon Highlanders who were held up at Mametz. This they did and, despite two officers being killed and several men wounded, they took 200 prisoners, two machineguns and one automatic rifle. The two companies, plus what was left of the Gordons, then formed a defensive line to repel a possible counter-attack between Mametz and the craters of Orchard Alley facing Fricourt Wood, which they occupied until relieved during the night of 5th July. During this action the casualties were; four officers and three other ranks killed, two officers and 98 other ranks wounded, 14 other ranks missing.

The Battalion moved back into the trenches in the Citadel line on 11th July 1916. On that day and the next, holding their positions, they suffered one officer and two other ranks killed, 13 other ranks wounded and four other ranks missing. The Germans were proving to be anything other than a beaten force and the fighting was fierce. On the 13th July, the Battalion moved forward and bivouacked in Mametz Wood ready for a Brigade attack the following day, the objective was the enemy's second defensive line. At 3.30 a.m., the following day, 14th July, the attack commenced, the 2nd Battalion led the second wave. They left Mametz Wood by the Eastern corner and crossed over the German front line, the Battalion's principal objective was Circus Trench which proved to be heavily defended, Reuben's C Company led the attack. Under very heavy fire Reuben and his comrades took the objective and were joined by D Company who went about consolidating the position. Consolidation of a captured enemy trench is important as the defensive positions of the trench are now on the rear face, it is imperative to create fire steps and machine gun positions in order that a counter attack can be repelled. Almost immediately, D

Company was ordered to assist in fighting in Bazentin-le-Petit Wood and became involved in bitter hand to hand combat. When this was successfully completed, they re-joined C Company in Circus Trench. Whilst C and D Company held their positions, B Company went forward to assist in fighting for the village of Bazentin-le-Grand but encountered heavy machinegun fire and a staunch resistance, Sergeant Poultney accounted for four machineguns, but the force was insufficient to dislodge the German defenders who counter attacked but were driven back to the village. At 8 p.m. that night, the whole Battalion took up positions on the North-East part of the village of Bazentin-le-Petit. They dug in and consolidated the positions under heavy shell fire, however, the swiftness of their actions in creating defensible positions was responsible for a reduced loss of life. They held these positions all through 15th July 1916, until they were relieved at 2 a.m. on 16th. They then retired to rest in Bazentin-le-Petit Wood, where they remained until 20th July, when they then retired to bivouacs at Dernacourt. Casualties for this action were; one officer and 219 other ranks killed, five officers and 142 other ranks wounded and 62 other ranks missing.

The 2nd Battalion Royal Warwickshire Regiment spent the rest of July and most of August 1916 out of the line, resting, re-fitting and being reinforced by drafts of officers and men. Some of them were fresh out from England; some were returnees from hospital and others, the remnants of battalions depleted by casualties. In the last week of August, the Battalion returned to the trenches in a support only role but still suffered one man killed and 14 wounded. By 1st September the Battalion's strength was recorded as 30 officers and 948 other ranks.

At 8 p.m. on 2nd September 1916, the Battalion moved back into the line. A& D Companies occupied Montauban Alley, C & D Companies occupied Folly Trench. At 7.00 a.m. the following morning, all four Companies formed up in Folly Trench which would be their start positions for the attack this day; zero hour planned for 12 noon. Whilst waiting, the German artillery targeted this assembly point, a concentration of men is a choice target for shelling and resulted in one man being killed and eight others wounded. At the appointed time the

Battalion moved steadily forward in line with D Company on the left covering the Battalions flank, then B & C Companies with A Company on the right. The objective was a line running through the West end of the village of Ginchy. By 1.40 p.m. A, B & C Companies had reached their objective and were digging in, D Company had been held up just short by machineguns and was digging-in there. All four companies had been the target of machinegun, rifle and artillery fire and had suffered large numbers of casualties. All contact with Reuben's C Company was lost at this point, but the positions were held whilst the rest of the village was taken and then a decision was made to relieve the whole Brigade because of the extent of the casualties suffered. The Battalion retired and reformed to the rear where the men started to collect in small groups, what was left of C & D Companies remained at their posts for another 36 hours and held the objectives they had fought for until they too were relieved eventually and re-joined the bulk of the Battalion. The casualty count was initially recorded as three Officers and 26 other ranks killed, seven officers (one later died) and 197 other ranks wounded, two officers and 90 other ranks missing. Reuben was originally recorded in the missing count but when the battlefield was finally cleared his body was recovered and he was buried in Delville Wood Cemetery.

Reuben left £7.10s.8d. which was supplemented by a War Gratuity of £8.10s.0d., to his sole Legatee, his sister Abigail Jackson, he was awarded the 1914-15 Star, British Victory and War Medals.

Chapter 22

Sidney Ash

Sidney Ash

Sidney's birth was registered in the first quarter of 1899 in Foleshill Coventry; he was the fifth child of Edward and Cassandra Ash. In 1901 the family were living at 164, Lockhurst Lane, Foleshill and Sidney was the youngest child aged two whilst the eldest, Alice Maud a winding machine operator in a factory, was 15. The second eldest child, Edward James at 14, was a brick worker, the rest of the children were below ten. Edward Ash was a 50-year-old man originating from Middlesex in London and employed as a waggoner at a flour mill. Whilst a waggoner with his own wagon and horses would be able to find work anywhere at this time, the Industrial Revolution had put the small local flour mills out of business in favour of large, centralised, steam-powered mills.

By 1911, Cassandra, now a widow, had moved her family to 29, Station Street, Coventry. Sydney aged 12, was still at school and the youngest person of the household. His three elder siblings were employed in either engineering or labouring whilst a boarder, John Clifford, a single man from Oldham, Lancashire was also employed in engineering.

There are no records to show when Sydney left school and to what profession he entered. His military file, which would show his employment on joining, was lost in the fires of the Blitz. What records have survived; show that he joined the army in the early part of 1917, possibly February. This date coincides with Sydney's 18th birthday and may well indicate he was answering a call up order under the conscription legislation implemented in 1916. Sydney was inducted into the Royal Warwickshire Regiment as Private 24286 but was subsequently posted to the Worcestershire Regiment as Private 41919. At this stage in the war the Royal Warwickshire Regiment boasted two training Battalions, the 3rd and 4th. Both were stationed on the Isle of Wight which is, no doubt, where Sydney was trained but the reinforcements were needed with the Worcestershire Regiment by the time he finished his training and was ready to be posted to a fighting unit. Sydney was posted to 2nd Battalion and joined them in the field in France in the autumn of 1917. As Sidney embarked on his overseas adventure in service of King and Country, his home town was being turned into a massive munitions factory. As with many industrialised towns and cities, Coventry turned much of its manufacturing industry to the war effort making guns of all sizes and shapes and, of course, motorcycles.

On 10th April 1918, 2nd Battalion were in reserve, billeted in Izel-lès-Hameau just a few miles east of Arras. They received orders to mobilise in response to rumours of a large German offensive and, by route march, train and bus the whole Brigade was transported to Méteren near to Bailleul. Here they were surprised by the huge numbers of refugees loaded with possessions and making their way away from the sounds of battle, the artillery was very active and, taking on extra small arms ammunition, they made their way to join the fight. The Battalion was still working on rumour; firm intelligence or a plan of action had not been furnished to them but when they arrived at Caëstre they were given orders to relieve the Kings own Yorkshire Light Infantry in the front line at the village of Neuve-Église. On the evening of 11th April 1918, the relief was complete. The following day was quiet until the evening time when the Germans started to mount attacks on the 2nd Battalion's line.

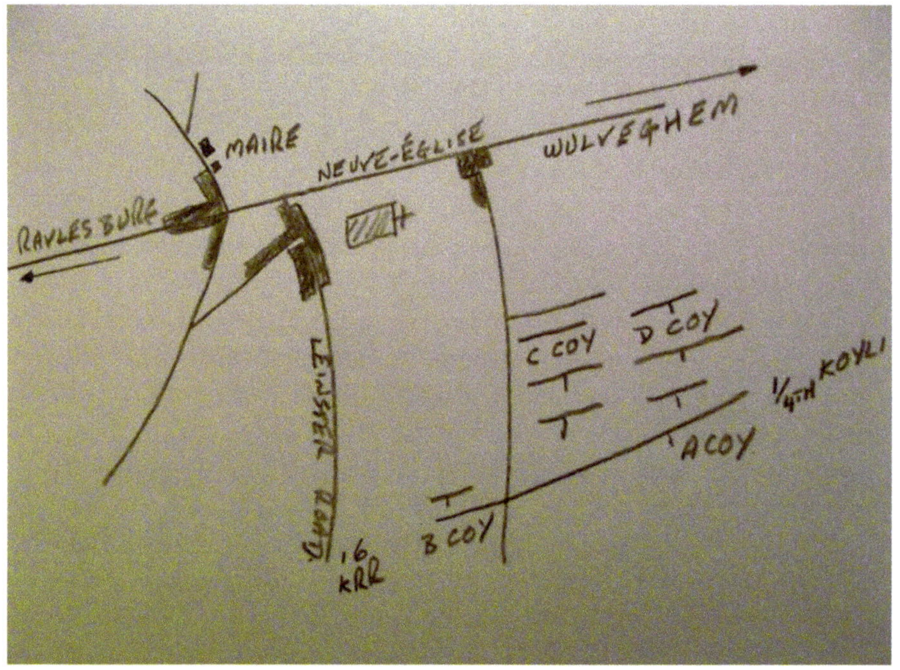

Positions of 2nd Battalion (Authors collection)

At dawn on the 12th, two patrols, each led by a 2nd Lieutenant with 25 men and supported by a Lewis Gun, were sent forward to locate the enemy, this they did and spent much of the day fighting from a forward position. Engaged by an enemy of superior number and suffering continual shelling and attention from machine guns, the patrols were forced to return to their own lines later in the day. This action was deemed a huge success as they held up the enemy forces and deceived them as to the actual location of the British line.

On the evening of the 12th, the Germans started mounting attacks on the British line with small groups of soldiers, well led by experienced NCO's. This tactic was successful but always driven back by the 2nd Battalion who were now well dug into defences which were concealed by the hedgerows adjacent to their positions. The Battalion held its positions until the 14th April 1918, when they were ordered to evacuate to Hill 70, where they were placed in Divisional Reserve.

There is no record of the casualties sustained during this period and, unusually, the diary gives no account, but Sydney was killed in the actions fought on 12th April 1918. There are no clues as to how he met his end; he may have been one of the casualties of the two raiding parties who valiantly fought to hold the Germans back; he may have been a casualty of machinegun, mortar or shell-fire whilst holding a trench position. What is certain is that every man who took part in this action played a major part in holding back the advancing German forces in order that secondary defence lines could be prepared, ensuring that the Great Spring Offensive would fail. One thing that can be said for certain, is that Sidney was a good target shooter, the better shots were selected for further training with the Lewis Gun and on the left sleeve of Sidney's uniform he proudly sported the embroidered LG badge marking him out as a Lewis Gunner. He may very well have been one the men sent forward with the two patrols to give supporting fire with his Lewis Gun.

Sidney's body was recovered, identified and laid to rest in Wulverghem-Lindenhoek Road Military Cemetery, in Belgium, alongside 657 other soldiers. He was awarded the British and Victory Medals and the records show he bequeathed £10.11s.9d to his mother who was now resident at 285, Munition Cottages, Hobbrooks Lane, Foleshill, Coventry.

Chapter 23

Thomas John Dugmore

(For Gary Dugmore)

Thomas's birth was registered in the second quarter of 1882 and, in the 1891 Census, he is recorded as nine years old and the youngest child of Thomas and Hannah Dugmore. Thomas (snr), a 46-year-old ornamental engraver and Hannah, at 40 years of age, were elderly parents for a young family and had two other children, daughters aged 12 and ten years of age. The family home was 149, Heath Street, Rotton Park, Birmingham, which was not far from father's roots in Harbourne. At the time, this was part of Staffordshire and his work was most likely in the Jewellery Quarter of Birmingham, now called Hockley. By 1901 Hannah, now a widow, has moved her family to 4, Albert Place, Brearley Street, Handsworth. There is now a fourth child, Hannah E. Dugmore, aged nine. Thomas, now aged 19, has followed his father into the Jewellery trade and is also employed as an ornamental engraver.

The following year on 11th August 1902, Thomas married Elizabeth Allibone, the daughter of a spectacle frame maker, at St. Thomas Church, Birmingham. Thomas, now employed as a tram conductor, gave the same address as his new bride, 201, Holiday Street, Birmingham; although Thomas added that he resided 'back of'. Many of these old Victorian houses in Birmingham have a side entrance to the rear giving access to what once were the servant's quarters, when no longer used as such the accommodation would be described as 'back of' 201, Holiday Street and, therefore, a separate address. The location of their home would also indicate the St. Thomas Church where they were married, was the one on Bath Row, Birmingham.

By 1911, Thomas had moved his family to 357, Camden Street, Brookfields, Birmingham; still in the area of the Jewellery Quarter which suited his return to the profession as a self-employed, jeweller's engraver. Elizabeth had given birth to four children, one of whom had since died. The surviving children were; Alfred five, Albert three, and a baby daughter, Ellen, under one. The family also had a boarder living with them, Sidney Tupman a 26-year-old single man working in the steel industry as a spectacle frame maker.

Following the outbreak of war, Thomas was one of the thousands of men who rushed to the recruitment facilities to answer the call to arms and volunteered to serve his country. The closest we can get for Thomas volunteering is mid-October 1914. Following Attestation and successfully passing the medical examination, Thomas was posted to 1/8 Battalion Royal Warwickshire Regiment. This Battalion was part of the newly raised units of the Territorial force and formed at Aston Cross, Birmingham in August 1914 as part of the Warwickshire Brigade and the South Midland Division. The Battalion was gradually equipped with uniform and equipment and at the same time trained; great reliance was put on men who had previously served to bring the novices, both other ranks and officers, to the required standard before mobilisation. This target was achieved by mid-March 1915 and by this time, the Battalion was encamped at Coggeshall in Essex and Sidney was serving with B Company. 16th to 20th March 1915, was spent ensuring that each man had the correct equipment and that the Battalion itself, was fully equipped to support the men in the field with stores, ammunition, transport, horses and mules - all had to be fed and maintained. Four mobile kitchens were allocated to each battalion. Mounted on carts and horse drawn, they needed to be able to feed and water up 1100 men. At 7.00 a.m. 22nd March 1915, Sidney paraded with the rest of B Company and, accompanied by D Company, marched to Braintree railway station where they boarded the second train of the day; the rest of the Battalion having set off at 5.00 a.m. The train's destination was Southampton where they boarded the SS Brighton bound for Le Havre; this ship was owned by the London, Brighton and South Coast Railway for channel crossings and was commandeered at the outset of war for troop transport.

The Battalion commenced a three-day march arriving at Hardifort on 26th March 1915, where they went into billets for three days. They then continued their march to billets in Bailleul where they provided working parties at night to work on trenches under the guidance of Royal Engineers. The first half of April 1915 was spent undergoing training in trench warfare and bomb throwing. At this time the Battalion's strength was 29 officers and 986 other ranks. On the night of 16th April 1915, the Battalion relieved 7th Royal Warwicks in the Steenbecque trenches, C Company were in reserve whilst Thomas's B Company under the command of Captain Davies, held the centre between A and D Companies. This first tour of duty in the front line was an introduction to the dangers of life at the front. They were relieved at 10.00 p.m. on 20th April and in that time, had been subjected to rifle, sniper and artillery fire resulting in; two Privates killed, one missing believed killed, five wounded and two Lance Corporals wounded.

Following four days in billets providing working parties to dig trenches, the Battalion returned to Steenbecque front-line trenches and experienced the same attention from the enemy, and level of casualties, as their first tour. Each man carried 150 rounds of ammunition for his rifle and a full water bottle. Carts carrying water accompanied the men and needed to be refilled on a regular basis as the water drawn from wells or pipes in this area had to be boiled before being consumed. They were relieved on 28th April and retired to billets at Jonesville where they enjoyed a single day of rest on 29th. The following day Thomas's Company, along with A Company, marched to Nieppe to take a bath; these occasions were accompanied by a change of underwear and an opportunity to de-louse and clean their uniforms.

Following a few days providing digging parties, the Battalion took over a new location in trenches at Douve, on 3rd May 1915. In two days at this location five men were killed and six wounded. They retired to billets at Courte Dreve near Petit Pont. Following time back at Jonesville providing working parties for trench work, the Battalion returned to Douve trenches on 20th May 1915. Immediately the casualties started to mount up. On the first day, a

Sergeant and one private were wounded and one private was missing. The following day, one private was killed and one wounded. Then on 22nd May, Private Hutton, who was missing on the first day, was found dead in a pool by a patrol, his body being recovered for burial. On Sunday 23rd May 1915, the diary shows that one private was killed and one wounded. It does not state the cause of these men's wounds but Thomas Dugmore was the man killed.

Thomas's body was recovered and buried in La Plus Douve Farm Cemetery. The Officer immediately in charge of Thomas, 2nd Lieutenant Oscar G. Williams, O/C No 6 Platoon "B" Company, wrote to Thomas's wife Elizabeth and enclosed letters belonging to him:

Dear Mrs Dugmore,

I am deeply grieved to have to inform you of your husband's death in action. A chance shot of the enemy's this morning (Whitsunday) at 6 a.m. when he was on duty in the trench.

I need hardly tell you how greatly we feel his loss as he was a splendid fellow, true and brave and an excellent comrade. We all mourn him deeply and unite in praying God to help you to bear this great trouble.

I know it will give you some consolation to know that he died a painless death, as death was instantaneous. He will be buried tonight at a spot a mile or so behind the trench with the other heroes of this battalion, who have already laid down their lives for their country. The ceremony will be performed by the Church of England Chaplain and I am sending his comrade, Private Cloves and his section commander, Lance Corporal Holmes to be present.

In accordance with the tradition of the army, we shall sell his personal belongings and the proceeds will be sent to you as soon as possible.

May God bless you and keep you safe is our earnest prayer.
I remain,
Yours very sincerely,
Oscar G. Williams.

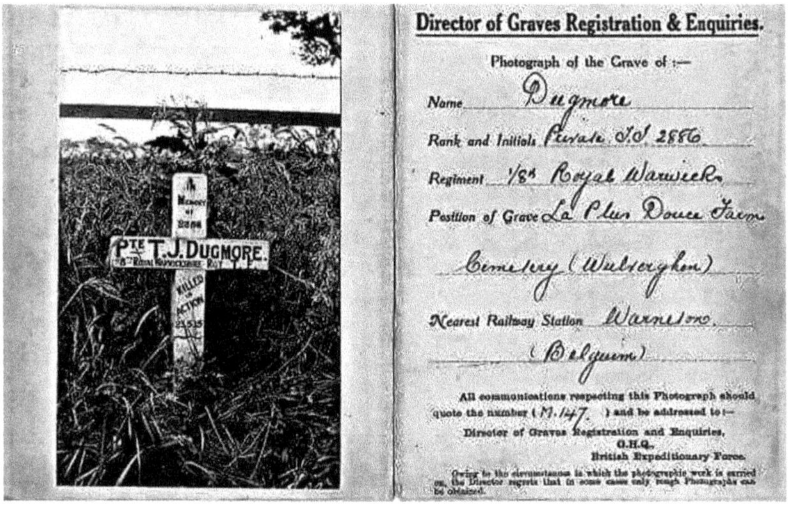

Director of Graves Registration & Enquiries.

Photograph of the Grave of :—

Name: Dugmore

Rank and Initials: Private T.J. 2886

Regiment: 1/8th Royal Warwicks

Position of Grave: La Plus Douce Farm Cemetery (Wulverghem)

Nearest Railway Station: Warneton (Belgium)

All communications respecting this Photograph should quote the number (M.147.) and be addressed to:—

Director of Graves Registration and Enquiries,
G.H.Q.
British Expeditionary Force.

Owing to the circumstances in which the photographic work is carried on, the Director regrets that in some cases only rough Photographs can be obtained.

Photo courtesy of G Dugmore

Second Lieutenant William's letter was mirrored by a letter dated the same day by the Company Commander Captain Davies; the only other detail was that the shot had entered Thomas's heart causing instantaneous death.

Thomas left £5.50 to his wife Elizabeth and the above photograph of his grave was sent to her. He was awarded 1914-15 Star, British War and Victory Medals.

Chapter 24

George Edward Dobbinson

(For Paul Dobbinson)

George Edward Dobbinson was born on 25th December 1893, at 2, Whitleigh Cottages, St Budeaux, Devon. George was also known as George William Dobbinson or William Dobbinson so for clarity, I will use the title name as on his birth certificate. George's father, David Dobbinson, was a labourer who had previously served in the British Army, His mother, Mary Jane Dobbinson, was from Dublin and by 1901 had given birth to three children; a boy aged 14, a girl aged ten and George now aged eight.

At some stage between 1901 and 1907, George volunteered for duty with 3rd Devonshire Regiment at that time a Militia unit, today what we call our Territorial Army. These volunteers attended training meetings and camps and formed a special reserve to be mobilised in times of war. This activity was probably initiated by George's father, David who had served in the Royal Artillery to the rank of Sergeant prior the Regiment's reorganisation in 1899 and may well have been a Militiaman himself. On 1st July 1899, the Royal Artillery was split into three groups; the Royal Field Artillery, Royal Horse Artillery and Royal Garrison Artillery (RGA). The first two units dressed as mounted men and the RGA as Infantry. The RGA was responsible for manning the British Empire's forts and fortresses, including the home coastal defences. This was probably why David Dobbinson, born in London, was now living in Plymouth, the home of the Devonshire Artillery units, the headquarters being at the Citadel coastal defence fort.

On 28th November 1907, George, now aged 14, standing 4'8¼" tall, weighing 86 lbs and with a chest fully expanded at 32", attested at Dover to join the RGA. He declared his previous military service with the 3rd Devonshire Militia and that his occupation was schoolboy, examples of George's handwriting at the time were similar to his father's in the accompanying note giving his consent for his son to join any unit of the British Army. David having been an NCO and knowing that to progress to Corporal would require an education, had kept his son at school beyond the legal leaving age of the day, which was 12. George's style of handwriting was clear and flowing indicating much practise and the similarities in style may well have been a result of dad's coaching.

Following Attestation and successful medical examination, George was appointed as Boy Soldier 27855 and posted to Number 1 Depot RGA Dover; he spent the next two years and 65 days at the Duke of York Military School, Dover and attained 3rd, 2nd and 1st class certificates of education. On 30th June 1908, George was playing hand ball in the ball alley at Dover depot when he slipped, fell and fractured the Radius bone of his right forearm, the injury was classed as severe and required hospital treatment. A court of enquiry was convened at Dover Castle on 6th July 1908, presided over by the commanding officer, Captain Preston, assisted by Lieutenant Pawson. Written statements were taken from other boys present at the time and the finding of the court was that the injury was not sustained in the course of military duty. This record shows that the army took seriously its responsibility as to the welfare of its boys, though we of modern times would find it abhorrent that a child as young as 14 would be subject to military discipline and values, we must judge for the times.

During 1908 and 1909 George had a number of run-ins with military discipline when he had to attend in front of officers for such offences as; stating a falsehood to an NCO, damage to government property, breaking out of barracks at night and being absent from school, the punishments on each occasion were periods of being confined to barracks, George was clearly a spirited youth with a sense of adventure.

On 1st February 1910, George was promoted to Trumpeter and posted to 77 Company, RGA, based at Katapahar, near Ghoom, Northern India. He left England on HMS Northbrook destined for Bombay and Rangoon, Burma and then an arduous overland journey to his garrison destination. On this journey, George was twice treated for health issues, in Rangoon he developed a very painful swollen foot, the cause was not known but the condition got better and in Calcutta he was treated for a mild B.T. infection (Bacillus Thuringiensis a soil dwelling bacterium). In 1911, George was again in breach of discipline for breaking out of camp after tattoo and disobedience to standing orders. This earned George ten days detention but was not sufficient to prevent his promotion to Gunner, which he achieved on 3rd August 1911. However, in November that year he was caught drunk in Darjeeling whilst under arms and given 168 hours detention.

On 20th January 1912, George was transferred for duty in Aden until 14th September 1913, when he returned to India. Whilst in Aden George attended a course in direction finding which he passed, with the comment 'Very good' placed on his file, This is the only indicator, apart with his education, that he may have followed his father on the promotion trail to NCO ranks, but he never did, choosing to remain a Gunner throughout his career. Whilst in India the war started and, by means of reorganisation on 7th November 1914, the 77th Company was renamed 77th (H) Battery, the 'H' standing for heavy and referring to the type of guns the unit used.

During the course of the war, George spent time in India, Aden and Mesopotamia with 77 Heavy Battery and, from August 1917 to July 1918, with 269 Siege Battery. Unfortunately, the surviving records for the units he served with, do not coincide with the actual dates he was there and it is only possible to talk in general terms about the roles of these units, the weaponry and tactics employed and how George fitted into the picture.

The use of heavy artillery pieces with a great range, was developed by the Boers during the Second Boer War (1899-1902) against Great Britain. European armies were impressed by the versatility of these guns in respect of their mobility, range and effectiveness and following this conflict a Heavy Battery Committee was formed to determine the future requirements of the British Army for these weapons. The wish list was for a gun with a range of 10,000 yards, weighing no more than four tons so that it could be drawn by horses and yet be able to fire the largest possible shell. After much research and experimentation, the design for the BL 60 Pounder was accepted, even though at this stage it was still half a ton overweight. When the RGA Heavy Batteries, (at the time called Companies), were first formed, they were equipped with converted 4.7 inch siege guns but by 1914 these units had been re-equipped with the BL 60 Pounder, four guns per Battery.

Looking at the diaries of those RGA (H) Batteries which are available and mobilised in 1915 as was 77th, the manpower was in the region of six officers, 200 other ranks, 140 horses. One unit, the 15th, also had 25 vehicles and a bicycle! A great deal of the manpower was committed to the welfare and working of the horses; drivers, farriers and stable staff for instance, and the army veterinary service worked closely with them.

By virtue of the great range of these guns, the batteries were sited well behind the lines but they were still in danger as the enemy forces also employed similar weapons and the diaries note a regular tally of killed and wounded. The main focus of these guns was the enemy gun positions, strong points and any target requiring the long reach. This factor placed them well out of sight of their targets and great reliance was placed in target acquisition from the information of forward spotters or Balloons and Royal Flying Corps crews. Two other methods were 'Flash Spotting' and 'Sound Ranging'. The former was an observation by a spotter of the muzzle flash of a hidden gun, who would call in fire from a battery and report correctional details until the target was hit. The latter was by use of sound directional equipment which calculated the direction and distance from the listening post.

Fine science was used in the firing of these guns, from the mathematical calculations used in target location - which made good use of such geometrical rules as laid down by Pythagoras - to the fine record keeping associated with each individual gun in the battery. A record was kept of each shot fired which inevitably caused microscopic wear to the barrel of the gun, each subsequent shot was adjusted according to a wear factor based on the record for that gun. Another science employed was meteorology, wind speed; direction and atmospheric pressure were some of the determining factors to the sighting of the gun.

The gun crews were usually eight men dependant on manpower availability, a Sergeant was in charge and referred to as number one, number two was the Limber Gunner whose job it was to open and close the guns breach mechanism whilst in action, and gun maintenance at other times. Number three was the Gun Layer who aimed the weapon on instructions passed to him, the rest of the crew were responsible for ensuring the ammunition was in the right place at the right time. The ammunition for the guns was in three main component parts, the shell itself, the charge and the fuse. The first two parts were kept separately and away from the gun, the fuse was screwed into the shell and determined when the shell exploded, either by direct or indirect action. The delayed action fuse was used against underground dugouts and allowed the shell to bury deep into the ground before it exploded. The ammunition carriers utilised a saddle type contraption which went around their necks and had pockets to carry the shells, inevitably the saddles were too long and the weight was carried on the arms, a gruelling job especially in some of the awful conditions experienced in all theatres of this war. In Mesopotamia where George served, the heat was as much an enemy as the Turks.

One of the dangers faced by the gun crews was premature explosion, shells occasionally exploded in the breach causing horrific injuries to the operators. In the early stages, there were a great many dud shells, this was a product of the rapidly raised production of ammunition to cater for the demand of the war and some of the experienced ammunition makers had joined up, causing a temporary vacuum of knowledge and skill.

In August 1917 George transferred to 269 Siege Battery, stationed in Mesopotamia. These Batteries were developed in India and differed in respect of the ammunition used as it was heavier. The guns themselves were heavier and with a longer barrel giving a greater range than the lighter gun used in India.

Each Battery was again equipped with four guns, the 6-inch, 30cwt, BL Siege Howitzer. At this time, it was semi obsolete but typical of the guns issued to these units away from the western theatre of operations and even then in short supply. The Howitzer type of gun has a high trajectory which allowed the shells to drop down on the target from a greater height unlike the flat trajectory of the guns used by the Heavy Batteries. This fact allowed the guns to be situated out of the line of sight of the enemy and could be fired from the rear side of a hill. Again, the crew operating the guns were reliant on the same 3rd parties to give details for target acquisition. Each gun fired a shell weighing 100lbs with a maximum range of 6000 yards. Each Battery had five officers, 177 other ranks, 17 riding, six draught and 80 heavy draught horses. For transport they used three two-horse carts and ten four-horse carts. Three Batteries were brought together under a Siege Brigade. Throughout the war the guns were modified and upgraded and eventually motorised transport was provided to partly replace the horses.

Mesopotamia (modern day Iraq) was important to the British which had procured the oil rights for most of the petrol deposits in Persia via the Anglo-Persian Oil Company, the oil was needed for the naval might of the British Empire. Forces were sent to the region shortly after the start of the European campaign to defend oil interests and the action featured in the area between the two great rivers, Euphrates and Tigris which contained swamplands and deserts. The enemy forces encountered were Turkish and the Allies comprised British, Anzac and Indian troops.

George's first involvement in this Campaign is likely to have been concerning the Siege of Kut which commenced on 7th January 1915, George commenced his journey to the region after this date and is most likely to have been involved in the relief of Kut. The Town of Kut was 100 miles south of Bagdad and has a population between 6000 and 7000 persons. The British forces there became encircled by the Turkish army who built defensive positions around the town and laid siege to it. Despite British attempts to lift the siege, and attempts to resupply the town from the air, the Garrison was forced to surrender on 29th April 1916. The survivors were marched to captivity at Allepo where many of them died. This has been called the worst defeat suffered by the British army.

The first attempt to relieve Kut commenced on 6th January 1916, when British forces engaged the enemy near to Sheikh Sa'ad, this became known as the Battle of Sheikh Sa'ad and over a period of three days failed to defeat the enemy completely who were able to retire, covered by particularly heavy rains, making the roads impassable for the British to follow.

On 13th January 1916, the British again attacked, this second attempt being known as the Battle of Wadi, after putting up a stiff resistance the Turkish forces retired to the West followed by the British. Enemy forces made camp amongst swamp land and defended themselves against British attack during the Battle of Hanna; the British forces sustained nearly 3000 casualties during this engagement which was a major factor in the failure to relieve Kut.

Following these failed attempts to relieve Kut, the Turkish forces brought reinforcements in excess of 20,000 men to the arena, all further attempts failed. Even attempts to resupply the besieged forces from the air by the Royal Flying Corps were only partially successful, as much of the supplies fell into the river or Turkish trenches. Attempts to end the siege by buying, (literally!), the soldiers in Kut were made by negotiators which included T.E. Lawrence but were rejected and 13000 British and Indian forces were marched into captivity. Approximately 70% of these men died of disease whilst the garrison commander, Major General Sir Charles Townshend, was kept in luxurious accommodation and seemingly amused by the plight of his men. (Source Norman Dixon's book, 'On the Psychology of Military Incompetence') Casualties sustained by the Allies amounted to 30,000 whilst the Turkish forces suffered only 10,000,

George returned to India between August 1916 and September 1917 when he returned to Mesopotamia. In March of this year, the British had captured the City of Baghdad which shows on George's file as his destination. Bad weather had curtailed the British advance and further operations were held back until February 1918 and captured the towns of H t and Khan al Baghdadi in March, then Kifri in April. Further operations in Mesopotamia ceased as British forces were urgently needed in Palestine and in June 1918, George returned to India.

George returned to England in September 1918, and was posted to Clipstone Camp Mansfield. This camp had been formed to house and train the New Armies recruited at the beginning of the war and was home to 20,000 men at its height. Following the Armistice, the camp was now being used to house men in preparation for demobilization. On 25th December 1919, George was placed on the Z List and became a civilian for the first time since 1907. This may seem like a long time for him to wait for demobilisation but following the ceasefire of November 1918, most prudent thinkers did not believe that the war had ended until the signing of the Treaty of Versailles, on 28th June 1919. Due to this the British Government had developed an army reserve for soldiers being demobilized and still fit to serve. This reserve system operated from December 1918 until it was abolished in March 1920 at which point, George finally became a permanent civilian.

Georges papers were marked, *"Character; sober, honest, hardworking"*, He appears to have stayed in the area of Clipstone Camp as, in 1920, he applied for a job with London and North Western Railway as a Porter at Nottingham station and in the same year married Hannah Wilcockson at Mansfield. He lived until he was 82 years old and died in 1976.

For his war service George was awarded the 1914-15 Star, the British War and Victory Medals.

Chapter 25

Herbert Henry Wattam

(Donated by Paul Cuddy)

Henry and fiancé (Picture courtesy Paul Cuddy)

Born on the 14thFebruary 1890, in North Reston, Lincolnshire, Herbert was the firstborn of Walls and Jane Wattam's four children. (Herbert was eventually joined by three sisters, these being Lillie in 1891, Ethel in 1897 and Edith in 1901)

By March 1891, the family were residing in the village of Belleau, where Walls was working as a farm labourer, although later that year the family moved to Bonthorpe, where Herbert's sister Lillie was born on the 6thDecember. The family remained in Bonthorpe until at least January 1901, this being the birthplace of Herbert's youngest sister Edith, before moving up to Willoughby where they were living in the vicinity of the Railway Gate House according to the 1901 Census.

A decade later, in 1911, Walls and Jane Wattam were living in Claxby, Lincolnshire with their two younger daughters Ethel and Edith May. Here, Walls was working as a farm gatherman. Herbert's sister, Lillie, was working as a domestic servant and, as such, was living away from home. Herbert was boarding with a farmer named Arthur Mason and his family, at Shaddy's Farm in nearby Candlesby, where he was working as a farm waggoner. As such, he would have worked the farm land manually, utilising heavy working horses to draw the ploughs. Aged 21, Herbert settled into a way of life, working to the requirements of the agricultural calendar. Such way of life continued for him over the following years and, at some stage, he joined the Lincolnshire Constabulary as a Police Constable. However, under pressure from his mother and sisters to 'do his duty' he enlisted into the Lincolnshire Regiment at Wainfleet for the 'duration of the war', on the 21stFebruary 1916, having received a notice to enlist. On doing so, Herbert was posted to the 3rdBattalion Lincolnshire Regiment; the regimental cap badge features the Sphinx, which honours the Lincolnshire Regiment's services in Egypt against Napoleon in 1801. The 3rd Battalion was a reserve unit based in Grimsby. It was here that Herbert underwent his basic training, which would have consisted of physical fitness, drill, march discipline and essential field craft/ and weapon skills, with the training progressing to more specific courses depending on the role assigned to the individual. Towards the end of his training Herbert would have received basic training in first aid, gas defence, wiring and other aspects, all of which would have continued after his posting to active service. Almost three months into his training, on the 26th May 1916, Herbert was promoted to the rank of Lance Corporal; his police training and career had developed his leadership potential.

On the 20thJuly 1916, just five months after signing up for service, Herbert arrived in France, and, after a period spent at an Infantry Base Depot where he received further training, he was posted to the 2ndBattalion Lincolnshire Regiment on the 4thAugust 1916 as part of a reinforcement draft. The Battalion, having been relieved from the front line by the 2ndRifle Brigade the previous day, had been moved to the trenches in Brigade Support in the Hohenzollern area of France; just south of its border with Belgium. The Battalion remained at

Hohenzollern until the 8th August where they formed working parties, transporting equipment and ammunition as required until they were relieved by the 2ndMiddlesex Regiment and moved to the Divisional Reserve at Fourquereuil, a nine-mile march which would have taken approximately three hours, where they were billeted into accommodation.

Over the following six days, 9th - 14th August, the battalion underwent training and were used as working parties. However, four days into their stay at Fourquereuil on the 12th, the battalion lined the streets where they 'cheered His Majesty the King, George V, as he drove through. The King stopped and walked up the main street then back to his car, amid the cheers of all in the village.

On the 15ththe battalion marched up into the trenches, where they relieved the 2nd East Lancashire Regiment who had been in the right subsection of the Quarries trench network. On entering this section of trench, the battalion suffered five casualties, Herbert was one of those men. Suffering a gunshot wound in the back and one in the left foot, he was taken out the line, upon which he was sent to a Casualty Clearing Station. These were small hospitals generally located at a railhead or similar transportation hub in forward areas. Their job was to provide emergency treatment and to move casualties back to the stationary and general hospitals. From here he was put aboard the Number 18 Ambulance Train which took him to Boulogne. A typical ambulance train had 14 carriages. The first carriage held the brake carriage and boiler, and depending on the number of stretcher cases, there would usually be six carriages made into bedded wards.

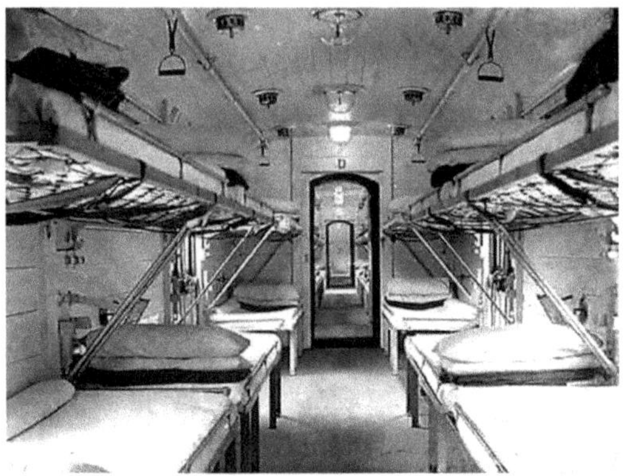

Bed ward carriage (Author's collection)

One carriage was for patients who could sit on seats and one was a combined operating theatre, pharmacy and medical store. Two of the carriages would be fitted into a cookhouse and dining room whilst two more carriages would serve as accommodation for the medical and nursing staff. The last carriage was the brake end and general store. The staff carriages were usually converted from the first-class carriages and compartments, to ensure the comfort of the nursing and medical staff that were stationed permanently on the ambulance train. As can be imagined, with so many injured men aboard, ranging from the walking wounded to those whose lives the nurses were fighting to save; the journey to Boulogne cannot have been very pleasant.

On reaching Boulogne, Herbert was admitted into the 13thGeneral Hospital. From there, Herbert was eventually transferred back to England in order to recover from his injuries. After an unknown period of time in hospital in England and subsequent period of time convalescing, Herbert appears to have been posted back to the 3rdBattalion over in Grimsby, most probably for training in order to get him fit enough to return to France. Herbert eventually returned to France, and, after initially being posted to the 9thInfantry Base Depot, he was posted to the 6thService Battalion, presumably in the opening months of 1917, although it is not possible to be certain. The 6th Battalion Lincolnshire Regiment was in the 33rd Brigade; part of the 11th (Northern) Division, alongside the 6th Border Regiment, 7th

South Staffordshire Regiment and the 9th Sherwood Foresters, all having served in France since the outbreak of the war in 1914.

Presuming that this was the case, Herbert would have experienced the Battle of Messines (Passchendaele); a British and ANZAC led operation which, following an intense and prolonged artillery bombardment commenced at 3.10a.m. on the 7thJune 1917 with the detonation of 21 massive mines. These had been placed underneath the area of the German lines in an operation that had begun almost a year prior to this. The effect of the mine explosions upon the German defenders was devastating, with some 10,000 Germans being killed during the explosion of the mines alone.

Immediately after the detonation of the mines, nine divisions of infantry advanced under the protection of a creeping artillery barrage, tanks and gas attacks. All of the initial objectives were taken within three hours, with the final objectives having been secured by mid-afternoon that day. The Germans counter-attacked the following day and continued to do so with diminishing effect until the afternoon of the 14thby which point the entire Messines Salient was in allied hands albeit devastated beyond all recognition of its former self. Although considered a decisive allied victory, it was not without cost; with almost 24,000 allied casualties and losses, against approximately 25,000 German casualties.

Having survived this battle, Herbert found himself travelling eight miles further north and further into Belgium, just north of Ypres, where on the 16thJuly, under heavy shelling from both high explosive and gas shells, they moved into the brigade reserve area; this being the eastern bank of the Yser Canal. This reserve area consisted of a cutting, some 15 feet deep with dug-outs and shelters having been burrowed into the eastern bank. The intense enemy shelling skimmed the eastern bank where Herbert was sheltering and burst on the western side. Such was the intensity of Gas shelling by the enemy that those in the reserve areas were forced to wear their box respirators often for periods of up to five hours at a time. It is hard to imagine how claustrophobic it must have been, having to wear a gas mask for such a long time, not to mention the sheer terror and mental stress of knowing that at any second they may have been killed by an incoming shell. There was heavy artillery fire from both sides for the remainder of the day, with the canal area where Herbert was in reserve being bombarded by what was a new type of gas shell (most probably Tear Gas) which, it was reported, caused violent sneezing, throat and eye irritation.

The following evening, 17th July 1917, at 8.15 p.m., 6th Battalion relieved the 9thSherwood Foresters in Hornby Trench, part of the front line which was in poor condition due to the persistent rainfall. The relief was completed by 1.20 a.m. Here they were opposed by the Germans who were in the Canadian Trench network. Gas shells were being used extensively by both sides during this period, typically comprising a combination of Blue Cross, Green Cross and Mustard gas. Usually, the bombardment would open with a mix of High Explosive and Blue Cross shells, subsequently followed by Green Cross or Mustard gas. Blue Cross gas (diphenylchloroarsine) was an asphyxiate and was fatal when encountered in concentrated amounts. Consisting of an extremely fine dust, it penetrated the filters of the soldiers' gas masks, causing intense pain to the sinuses. Desperate to ease the pain they were in, the soldiers would often remove their masks, only to then be caught in the incoming bombardment of Green Cross and Mustard gas. Green Cross gas (Phosgene) was also an asphyxiate, and it too was fatal, although it had a delayed action, with many soldiers experiencing the onset of violent coughing and choking up to forty-eight hours after inhalation. Mustard gas (dichloroethylsulphide); an almost odourless chemical, was distinguished by the serious blisters it caused both internally and externally, brought on several hours after exposure. Protection against mustard gas proved more difficult than against either chlorine or phosgene gas. The use of mustard gas also proved to have mixed benefits; while inflicting serious injury upon the enemy the chemical remained potent in soil for long periods after release, making capture of infected trenches a dangerous undertaking.

Herbert and his battalion remained in the front line for two days before being relieved back to the reserve area of the canal. This rotation of two days in and two days out continued up until the 25th

July. German shelling during this period was continuous and heavy, particularly on the 21st and 24thJuly, although in general it was quieter during the day that it was during the night.

The risk of Herbert having been exposed to lethal levels of various gases throughout his time at the front line in Ypres was extremely high. On the 26thJuly 1917, he died as a result of gas poisoning at Dozinghem, aged 27 years and five months. Dozinghem was one of three areas used to accommodate Military Clearing Stations, and was home to the 4th, 47th and 61stClearing Stations. It was located near Krombeke, just north-west of Poperinge.

'Dozinghem' was actually a humorous name given to the area by the soldiers; the humour becoming more apparent when one considers the names of all three areas together...Dozinghem, Mendinghem and Bandaghem as in dosing them fevers, mending them broken bones and bandaging them wounds.

Herbert was buried at Dozinghem, alongside 3,174 comrades who also fell prior to, and into the early months of 1918. He was awarded the British War and Victory Medals.

Chapter 26

Thomas Morris

Thomas Morris (picture courtesy of John Morris)

Thomas Morris was born in Tredegar, Monmouthshire, Wales in 1889. His father, James Morris, was an undertaker from Radnorshire and by 1891 his family were resident at 15, Market Street, Bedwelty, Monmouthshire. His mother, Ann, had given birth to seven children of which Thomas was the youngest. Thomas's family were English speakers, as were most their neighbours with only a few families being bi-lingual. By 1901, Thomas Morris had died and Ann had remarried to John Henry Mitchell, a colliery horse driver born in London. Living with Mr. and Mrs. Mitchell at 5, Powells Terrace, Tredegar, were four of Ann's children, all of whom were at school.

On 28th December 1909, Thomas, married Eva May Dare from Merthyr Tydfil and continued to live with Thomas's mother Ann. By 1911, Ann was a widow again and had reverted to her previous married name of Morris, her family consisted now of Thomas and Eva, their one-year old son, James Charles, two of her other sons and a 26-year-old Boarder, Ben Taylor. All the men were working as coal miners in the capacity of hewer; the underground job furthest from the surface hacking the coal from its seam. On 24th May 1912, Thomas and Eva were blessed with a second son, Thomas John.

On 22nd April 1915, Thomas, now resident at 20, Wood Street, Bargoed, attested at a recruitment facility in Newport to join the army. His medical examination of 21st April shows him to be an unusually tall man for both his day and profession at 5'11" tall; the coal seams Thomas worked must have been high. He was of good health with a chest expansion of 2½" but it was noted his teeth would need to be seen to. Passing the physical, he was posted to 1st Battalion, Monmouthshire Regiment as Rifleman 3923.

The Monmouthshire Regiment was unusual in that it was a Territorial Force completely, it had no Regular Battalions. Thomas was initially posted to 3/1st (Reserve) Battalion which was one of three battalions formed in February 1915 to serve as training units whilst the fighting Battalions were serving abroad. The training units remained in the UK throughout the war. Thomas attended Park Hall Camp situated in the grounds of Park Hall, Oswestry which was to become the largest military training camp of World War 1. At the time, Thomas was in attendance the camp housed 21,000 men and 4,500 officers, it also contained a military hospital with 866 beds.

On successful completion of his training, Thomas embarked from Southampton on 27th October 1915 for France and joined 1st Battalion in the field on 3rd November. Almost immediately, Thomas was attached to 173rd Company Royal Engineers, from 10th November to 3rd December 1915 and was paid 1 shilling per day extra for the 27 days he was detached. One shilling per day no doubt equates to hazardous duty pay and due to his experience of mining, meant he was working with 173rd Tunnelling Company of the Royal Engineer Regiment. The work of the tunnelling units was extremely dangerous and cost the lives of many men working below ground.

Tunnelling was used as a technique of war by both sides as early as late 1914, but was by no means a new idea. The earliest references pre-date the birth of Christ when opposing forces used tunnelling to undermine walled defences to collapse them causing a breach which could then be attacked. Post the birth of Christ, tribal forces in Germania used tunnels against Roman Forces, who learned to fear these warriors who would unexpectedly attack them from underground. The tunnelling techniques developed during the Great War, by both sides, became complex with multiple interconnected tunnels, containing galleries where stores and men could be housed. The tunnels were developed for both offensive and defensive means. The offensive tunnels had a specific objective and at its end a gallery was built to contain large quantities of explosive which could be detonated at a pre-arranged time, usually underneath the enemy's front line to precede an attack. Mines were exploded to create a crater in front of the enemy positions for the crater to then be attacked and consolidated to create an advantage in the attacker's front line. Listening posts were developed to detect enemy mining activity and defensive mines were exploded, with the objective of destroying the tunnel and to kill as many of the enemy as possible - timing the initiation was critical.

Miners were co-opted to the Royal Engineers to form Company establishment and were often transferred to the Regiment. Thomas was returned to his Battalion and I would suspect that his height was a factor. The 1st Battalion, Monmouthshire Regiment had landed in France in February 1915 and in May that year, having suffered huge losses during the Second Battle of Ypres, were amalgamated with 1/2 and 1/3 Battalions. In September 1915, having received reinforcements, they resumed their own identity and were re-designated as a Pioneer Battalion under the 46th (North Midland) Division. The Pioneers were bodies of men utilised in construction work and during the war, spent much of their time constructing, repairing and improving the trench systems and military railroads.

On the day Thomas joined the Battalion, he arrived with a draft of 60 men at Drouvin, near to Bethune. The Battalion were engaged in fatigues but this activity was cut short as the orders to move had been received. The following day the Battalion marched to billets at a location known as Les Huit Maisons, a four-hour march but still in the vicinity of Bethune. The accommodations had been left in poor order and the first job was to clean house. On 19th December 1915, the Battalion suffered the effects of a German gas attack, the gas was barely detectable but in sufficient strength to make breathing and work difficult, this was later confirmed as a German failure as the wind had changed direction blowing the gas back 18-20 miles but not until it had affected the men.

On Christmas Eve, 1915, the men were treated to an early Christmas dinner as on the following day they had been ordered to move. The Daily News had organised a collection from the people of Newport and Monmouthshire and additional rations were issued consisting of; Christmas puddings, nuts, apples, oranges, cake, dates and butter. The following day the Battalion and its transport, minus animals, entrained at Lillers and spent two days on the train arriving at Marseille on 27th December. On January 7th, the Battalion embarked on the SS Anchises, bound for Alexandria in Egypt arriving at this destination on January 13th 1916 and marched to a Camp. The Battalion was then engaged in guarding `the Suez Canal and constructing defensive positions as there had been a recent fear that enemy forces were planning to attack. The canal was an extremely important facility for the British Empire as it created a short route between the Mediterranean and the Eastern parts of the Empire. The threat was short-lived and on February 3rd 1916, they embarked at Alexandria on SS Megantic for the return journey to France. They eventually arrived at their first designated destination for work on February 11th 1916, at Brucamps in the Somme district. The next few months were spent at various locations providing working parties for trench improvement and the creation of defensive positions, the work was generally conducted at night except during periods of heavy fog which provided a protective cover.

By June 1916, the Battalion were based at Pommier near to Arras in the Nord Pas de Calais region. They were engaged daily developing four Russian Saps (a covered trench pushed towards the enemy line from the British front line, the purpose being to allow advancing troops cover to a point near to the enemy line where they could emerge and attack without advancing over open ground) at Foncquevillers, just outside the northern most point of the forthcoming offensive, the Battle of the Somme. The length of the Saps was recorded daily between 1st to 22nd June 1916, as follows; no 1 Sap, 33-410 feet, no 2 Sap, 36-399 feet, no 3 Sap 36-476 feet and no 4 Sap, 30-430 feet. 25th June was designated U day and the start of a five-day bombardment of the German lines in preparation for the infantry assault to follow, each day was a consecutive letter up to Z. On Y day, the bombardment was extended by two more days pushing Z day back to 1st July 1916. Throughout this period the men of the 1st continued to dig towards the German lines. The night before Z day, 30th June 1916, the Battalion were still digging furiously to get the Saps as close to the German lines as possible for the benefit of the men stepping out of them the following day. One of the Saps was on a slope and open to German view and the whole proceedings brought down ferocious fire causing heavy casualties, another role this night was to cut any German wire which the seven-day bombardment had not destroyed, this work also created casualties.

By 3 a.m. on Z day, the Battalion cleared the Saps and moved to designated locations for each digging party, but their job was not yet over. Their continued role was to follow the attacking waves of infantry and, using picks, shovels and sandbags, consolidate any captured enemy location to ensure it was defensible against the inevitable counter attack. The purpose for this, is that a captured trench has its defensive characteristics, such as the fire step, on what is now the rear wall, it is essential to create such defences to observe and repel any counter attack - theirs was a waiting game. At 6.25 a.m., the British and French artillery commenced a heavy bombardment on the enemy positions and at 7.30 a.m. the assault was launched. The German artillery commenced its own response aimed at the advancing troops and they also managed to man their machine gun positions and laid a raking fire down on them, one of the main objectives of the seven-day artillery action was to destroy the German front line and all in it, the German shelters were sufficiently strong and deep as to ensure this intention failed. The digging parties of the 1st Battalion never left their standby positions, the Saps were clogged with men, preventing their advance, they were however victims of the German artillery and by the time they were withdrawn to safety, late afternoon, they had suffered the following casualties; killed, 15 other ranks, wounded, two officers and 76 other ranks, wounded and missing, two other ranks and missing, four other ranks.

Two days later, the Battalion moved out of the Somme area to billets at Berles-au-Bois, and, for the next few months, the Battalion was engaged in providing working parties for trench development and improvement as well as carrying parties to bring gas cylinders to the front for attacks on the German lines when the wind was favourable. On 11th November 1916, the Battalion was on the move to Caours, near to Abbeville, 41 London Buses were used and, following a 30 mile ride on bumpy roads, the men then had to march the last five miles. This was followed shortly after by a move to Lucheux, where parades and training took place. A regular feature of the work at this location was working parties, sometimes 500 men strong; to Lucheux Forest where, under the guidance of Royal Engineers, the men were put to making hurdles and facines (the latter being bundles of sticks used in road improvement).

On Christmas day 1916, no working parties were sent out and a dinner of roast beef, vegetables, beer and Christmas pudding was enjoyed by all. Following this single day of rest the men were put to improvement of communication trenches which, due to the heavy rainfall were collapsing and, in places, three to four feet deep in water and mud. The next day off the whole Battalion were to enjoy was on 8th May 1917, in commemoration of the heavy losses they had suffered at the second battle of Ypres. The intention to do this was read out on parade on 7th May and it would appear this generated some celebration as on 26th May 1917, a General Court Marshal was held for 2nd lieutenant H.C. Morris (no relation of course!) for the offence of being drunk. The officer was found guilty and ordered to be dismissed from His Majesty's service. The same day five other ranks were gassed and one man died of wounds at a casualty clearing station.

During the early part of 1917, the soldiers' numbers were reorganised due to the expanding nature of the army and a need for greater efficiency, Thomas's number was changed from 3923 to 226627. From 23rd June to 3rd July 1917, Thomas enjoyed a spell of leave back in the UK which proved productive and nine months later, Ivor Albert Joseph Morris was born! In July 1917, the system of rest was changed and each platoon worked 12 days with four off, however the rest days were to be utilised for rest and training. At the end of July 1917, Thomas received the tragic news that his 18-month-old son, Rees, had died of measles, bronchitis and convulsions, at the family home, 67, West Street, Bargoed. Unfortunately, due to his recent period of leave, he was not permitted to return to console his family.

On 5th August 1917, the Battalion were at work during the night on trenches in the Sailly-Labourse area when the alarm was raised for a gas attack. Small box respirators were worn and the work continued. The Germans had released a gas cloud from cylinders and this had drifted across to where the 1st were working. In addition, they also sent over a heavy bombardment of gas shells. Casualties sustained this night were one officer and 23 other ranks wounded by gas and hospitalised. These gas attacks were happening on a regular basis; 6th August - one officer and four men wounded, 8th August- 21 other ranks wounded and so life went on for Thomas and his comrades. The daily life of hard work, filthy, muddy and insanitary conditions, infrequent baths, lice and rats became the norm. Not to be outdone though, retaliatory gas attacks were made on the Germans, on 9th August the Battalion assisted in the transportation and placement of 270 gas cylinders at 50 different locations which had been chosen for their deployment.

From 15th to 25th August 1917, the Battalion worked extremely hard, mainly at night, supporting the successful attack on hill 70 near to Lens, a strategically important piece of high ground which the German forces did not want to give up and fought fiercely to recover once lost. Thomas was only present in this action for the first few days as on 18th August 1917 he was admitted to a Field Ambulance with a dental problem, his teeth was an issue raised at his initial medical examination and it had now become a debilitating issue. From the Field Ambulance, he was transported to a Casualty Clearing Station, neither of which could deal with the problem and he was then evacuated to No 4 (Canadian) Stationary Hospital at St Omer where he was admitted and the necessary treatment administered. Thomas re-joined his unit on 3rd September. It may seem to us, with our modern medical services, that this hospitalisation for a dental issue to be a little extreme but in the filthy conditions these men were working and living, open wounds of any sort could well be a death sentence. With no antibiotics, open wounds became infected and sepsis soon killed the individual.

Life at the front wasn't all bad though as every effort was made for recreation facilities, football being a popular sport for most men and leagues were formed, On 11th October, the 1st Battalion's football team beat 139th Brigade HQ staff team, 13 goals to one. The Battalion was not quite so successful at a much more appropriate sport for Welshmen, Rugby, when, later in the month, they lost 11-0 to 6th South Wales Borderers. Well at least they lost to fellow Welshmen!

The remainder of 1917, was spent on trench improvements including development of defensive positions such as machinegun posts, road repairs, miniature railway development and laying of a water pipeline. Christmas 1917 was a special affair this year, the Honourable Colonel of the Regiment, Lord Tredegar, had commissioned the making of one solid silver and 24 silver plated bugles. Each bugle was engraved with the Battalion Crest and Battle Honours of South Africa 1900-1902 and the words, *"Presented by the honorary Colonel Lord Tredegar, October 1917"*. The presentation of these bugles was made at a morning parade by Brigadier General Campbell to each bugler in turn, the parade then marched off to Church Parade. Dinner that day was roast pork, potatoes and carrots followed by plum pudding, apples, nuts, oranges, cigarettes and beer, cake was also provided at tea time. This feast had been paid for with the generosity of the High Sheriff of Monmouthshire, J.W. Benyon who donated £150, £30 by other Monmouthshire friends and 800 Francs from the 46th Divisional Canteen accumulated profits. The following day a Smoking Concert was held for the men with more beer and rum punch served. This type of concert was popular in Victorian times and for the sole entertainment of men who would smoke and talk about politics, I am sure these men of the 1st could think of better things to talk about than politics, some of them having not seen home for a long time! There was no work on Boxing day but the following day working parties were found and the work schedule for January 1918 proved to be gruelling.

As the Battalion were billeted in the village of Sailly Labourse, work on the defences were ongoing. A Company was permanently employed in laying wire, whilst the other companies were building machinegun emplacements and repairing and improving trenches. The weather had been very cold, but frost and heavy snow did not prevent the work from being continued, the men were never out of danger as enemy shelling was a constant feature of life at work and in the village and this took a steady toll on the Battalion's strength. On 23rd January, the Battalion was withdrawn from the front line and retired to billets at Bethune, where many of the men occupied an old tobacco factory. A few days later they moved by route march to Bellerive, where they were billeted in barns which were in fairly good condition and here they were attached to 138 Brigade for training purposes. A training schedule was set for a six-week period and involved bayonet and musketry practice on the rifle ranges, platoon and section drill, parades and physical exercise. At the end of January, the Battalion were visited by member of a War Savings Scheme who delivered several presentations on the merits of saving surplus army pay; as a result, 61.39% of the Battalion subscribed an amount totalling £2,922.5s.0d.

Following this period of training the Battalion returned to billets in Bethune where two companies returned to work, burying cables, and the other two continued training in musketry on the ranges, bayonet practice and physical exercise. The realities of war were again realised when on one day, eight men were injured by shell fire with one Rifleman subsequently dying of his wounds. Towards the end of February, orders were received to reorganise the Battalion in compliance with instructions to all Pioneer units and reduce the number of Companies to three. One piece of construction work which was completed at this time was on several fortified dugouts, on their completion the work was inspected by senior army commanders who were so pleased with the result they instructed them to be named Monmouth Castles and set a standard for future constructions. The Battalion returned to billets at Sailly Labourse where they returned to the usual routine of front-line work.

On 21st March 1918, the German army launched its Spring Offensive resulting in a large portion of the British line being pushed back. Battalions were rushed to hold the advance and ordered to hold to the last man whilst a second defensive line was built behind the front. A few days later, on 24th March, the 1st Monmouths were addressed by their Commanding Officer, Lieutenant Colonel C. A. Evill D.S.O., he informed the men of the grave situation facing the Brigade, (in fact it was a situation seriously affecting the whole B.E.F.).The German offensive was expected near the La Bassee Canal and that the Battalion must be ready to defend any piece of ground they were given, at all costs and to the last man. Excitement reigned; the Battalion had not been involved in any front-line battle since 1915 but had been on the receiving end of countless enemy attempts to kill them with no opportunity to settle the score for those they had lost. The organisers of the Battalion began frenzied activity to be ready, the command staff attended Brigade conferences, whilst the Transport and Quartermaster staff reconnoitred the ground leading to the front line that they expected to occupy, with a view to ironing out in advance supply issues. The British artillery were busy laying down barrages on the German lines to disrupt any build-up of forces and in the meantime the men were still forming working parties as normal. Towards the end of March, the Battalion had to surrender its billets as Sailly Labourse was required as a staging post for battalions being relieved from the front line. There was a further move before the end of the month, but the men continued to work despite very heavy rainfall and the impending action they had been warned for.

On 12th April 1918, the Battalion was stood down and moved to Hersin, where they rested but continued to provide working parties. 90 men were found to have lost their voices because of a recent gas attack and they were isolated in a nearby hut to recover, a few days later a further 90 men were affected by the recent gas attack and were also removed from the work schedule, four of these men were subsequently reported as casualties; the staff of the Casualty Clearing Station monitoring their condition. On 18th April, the Battalion were put on a one-hour notice to move due to a further alert of the possibility of an attack around the La Bassee Canal. Early in May, C Company, which was the unit worst affected by the recent gas attacks could only field 50 men for work details, by 9th May, the M.O. had reported the whole Company unfit for work. Due to the state of readiness and the Battalions continued commitment to developing the secondary defensive line, one company was allotted to work detail and the other active company was kept in reserve in billets with orders to sleep with their boots on! On 25th May 1918, two companies were assigned front line duties with the 5th and 6th South Staffordshire Regiment, and left for the front. The following day 51 men of A Company were also found to be suffering the delayed reactions of the recent gas shell attack and removed from duties to join those still sick from C Company. These men were joined on 31st May by a further 16 men of A Company similarly affected by the same gas attack. During all this mayhem, the Battalion continued to provide men for work and play, a small Brass Band was formed from the Battalions Buglers who could play a band instrument, they performed their first public concert on 29th May 1918, in the public gardens of Bethune; a town continually the target of shelling!

At the beginning of June 1918, the reorganisation plan for Pioneer Battalions was implemented and D Company was dissolved, the manpower being absorbed by the three remaining Companies. The remainder of June was spent providing working parties and half way through the month those recently affected by gas started to return to duty. This work routine continued throughout July and, on 18th, the German Offensive was ended and the situation at the front stabilised. On 24th July 1918, Thomas returned to England for a period of leave until re-joining his unit on 7th August, the day before the British and French Forces of the Western Front commenced what became known as the 100-day Offensive. The German offensive having petered out, had left their line in such a way that it was necessary for them to start retiring actions to straighten their line and give up positions which were untenable due to the difficulties with supplying the forces holding those areas. This created an opportunity for the Allied forces to mount their own offensive designed to destroy the Germans and commenced on 8th August 1918 with the Battle of Amiens in the Somme region. At 2.00 a.m. on 12th September 1918, the 1st Battalion formed up to commence movement to a location from where they could take part in the offensive. They marched in pouring rain until they reached Calonne Ricouart railway station at 5.00 a.m. The train was late, the rain continued to pour and it was not until 10.30 a.m. that all the men were aboard and out of the rain. The Battalion then marched to La Houssoye where billets awaited them.

A new form of Platoon attack had been devised and the companies took turns over the next few days to practise this technique on a range. It was a rundown commencing at 300 yards from the targets, double time to 200 yards, fire two rounds prone, advance at the double another 100 yards, fire one round prone, finally double to 50 yards and fire two rounds standing. On 18th September 1918, the Battalion joined the 139th Brigade transport column of 150 London busses, they debussed at 2 a.m. and bivouacked at the side of the road to Vermand, at dawn they started to dig in, in a nearby wood. This wood was constantly bombed by enemy aircraft so the men dug deep and covered their fox holes in corrugated metal sheeting, the previous night 150 bombs had been dropped, this was sufficient incentive to dig deep! The men were put to work repairing roads and received orders to relieve 4th Australian Pioneer Battalion and take over their billets at Vendelles. On arrival the Australians' orders had been cancelled and the 1stMonmouths had to find an alternative home in trenches. The work on road repair continued and casualties started to occur, the first man killed was Rifleman Morse on 22nd September 1918.

On 28th September 1918, the Battalion received orders to take part in the forthcoming assault on the St Quentin Canal, this was part of the main assault on the centre sector of the Hindenburg Line which was the main German defence which they had commenced building in 1916. Z day was 29th September and Zero-hour, 5.50 a.m. At this time the Battalion formed up in their allotted location. Their job was to follow the 137th Brigade who were to lead the assault, they were carrying Cork Pier Bridges (cork floats on which a wooden surface was laid) and super structures to bridge the canal on behalf of the assaulting infantry. At Zero hour, an artillery barrage was commenced and a dense fog swept in over the battleground, visibility was but a few yards ahead. At Zero plus 15, the Battalion moved forward and, despite the fog, managed to find the right place and commenced placing the bridges, whilst the German machineguns started to account for casualties. After lunch, the Battalion crossed the bridges and commenced work repairing roads damaged by the artillery barrage, the fog started to lift and German prisoners were captured. The casualties taken this first day were surprisingly not severe; one other rank killed, two officers and 19 other ranks wounded, five other ranks victims of gas, five other ranks wounded but remained at duty. This last statistic gives a measure of the men's commitment and morale. Any wound, especially an open wound, was treated very seriously due to the real danger of infection and with no antibiotics, an infected wound was a potential death sentence from sepsis; even boils were treated in hospital. Having worked continuously for 48 hours, on 30th September the men were only required to work for four hours!

This road work continued until orders were received on 2ndOctober, for the Battalion to take part in an attack on the villages of Ramicourt and Montbrehain. At 4 a.m. the following morning the men were in their start positions. At 11.15 a.m., they moved to take up positions in a railway cutting near to Joncourt, their role to repel any counter attack on that position. At 3.00 p.m., B and C Companies formed up in extended order and moved forward to do just that. The Battalion came under heavy artillery fire consisting of both gas and high explosive shells, the fighting lasted all day and after dark they dug in and by sending out patrols, contacted the units on their flanks. On 4th October, a strong fighting patrol was sent, under cover of a barrage, to establish a post in Montbrehain. The patrol found that the location was heavily defended and returned with only two men not wounded. The fighting continued all day and heavy casualties were inflicted on the enemy by the Lewis Guns and snipers, nine prisoners were taken and sent to the rear. At dusk on the 4th, the Battalion were relieved and retired to trenches away from the fighting, to rest and resupply for two days.

On the night of 7th October 1918, the Battalion relieved 8th Sherwood Foresters in the front line, at the village of Sequehart and held the line whilst a converging attack was made on the village by British and French troops. During the early hours of the 8th October, orders were received for an attack to be made on two German machine gun nests situated on the Sequehart to Mericourt Road about 150 yards in front of the Battalion's positions. Under cover of a barrage, which commenced at 5.00 a.m., two platoons of B Company commenced their attack which was repulsed with heavy casualties. At 6.00 a.m., a second attack was mounted by the remaining two platoons of B Company under the command of the Battalion Adjutant, Captain W.M. James. This attack also failed with heavy casualties, including the Adjutant who was killed. C Company took over the positions vacated by B Company and an order was received to cease the attack. At 6.35 a.m., the Battalion's commanding officer, Lieutenant Colonel J. Jenkins MC, was mortally wounded and command was passed to Major F.G. Phillips. Even though the machinegun nests were captured at 1.30 p.m., the Battalion suffered continuous heavy artillery and machinegun fire all day until 8.00 p.m. that night. The German forces commenced a retreat and the 1st Monmouth continued to hold their positions until 4 p.m. the following day when the gruesome task of body recovery and burial took place. The casualties for this engagement were heavy by comparison with what the Battalion had experienced since their big losses of 1915; killed, three officers and 30 other ranks, wounded, two officers and 40 other ranks, two other ranks were wounded but remained at duty. Some of the wounded were to die of their wounds over the next few days including the Commanding Officer, but Thomas was amongst those killed outright.

Thomas was buried alongside many of his fallen comrades in grave A.7. Sequehart British Cemetery No.1. and he was subsequently awarded the 1915 Star, British War and Victory Medals. His widow, Eva and three children, continued to receive a proportion of his pay whilst a pension was determined. On 9th January 1919, Thomas's son, Ivor aged 9 months, died of Acute Bronchitis (six days), but then Eva was awarded a War Pension of 29s.7d per week based on three children, this may have been later reduced due to the death of Ivor.

Chapter 27

Walter James Allen

(For Phil Christie)

The first record we have of Walter, is the 1891 census when he was seven years old, the second son of William and Ada Allen, living at 8, Lavinia Terrace, off Ada Street, Rotton Park (now part of Edgbaston Birmingham). William, a carter by profession, was born in Sutton Coldfield which is also where all five of their children were born, perhaps Ada spent her pregnancy confinements with her in-laws. Walter had an elder brother, a younger sister and two younger brothers and of course at this time all the children were recorded as at school.

On 5th October 1902, Walter, now resident at 94, Downing Street, Smethwick and working as a carter, married Edith Maude Legge (20), of 6, Downing Street, at St. James Church, Handsworth.

The next surviving record of Walter is in 1911, where we find him living at 40, Monument Road, Birmingham (now part of Edgbaston but no district was given on the census form). He is 27 years of age, as is his wife Edith and an unemployed labourer. Times were tough for a man with no skills, who probably left school at the age of 12. Walter and Edith have three children; a son, also Walter, aged eight and two younger daughters. They were born at differing locations; Bilston, Erdington, Handsworth and Smethwick. There is also a record of an 18-year-old boarder living with the family, William Allen - an ironworker in the engineering industry. This is, no doubt, a younger brother of Walter's not born for the 1891 census and not wishing to remain at home, or perhaps Walter's address was more convenient for work, this part of Birmingham was highly industrialised at this time.

On 15th June 1914, Walter, now resident at 35, Mornington Road, Smethwick, was arrested and charged with attempted highway robbery with violence. He appeared at Smethwick Police court on 25th June and had very likely been in custody since his arrest, along with James Clewley a 62-year-old man from 133, Spon Lane, Smethwick and John Cooper (34) of 15, Middlemore Road, Smethwick. The allegation against the three men had been made by George Henry Glover, a man of nearly 70 years of age, residing in Marshall Street, Smethwick. It was alleged that Mr Glover, a seller of boots and clothing, had popped into the Old Navigation Inn to have a drink and had engaged the three men in conversation, he further alleged that they had asked him to stand them a drink whereby he declined and left to walk home. On a local canal tow path, he became aware that the men from the pub had followed him, they then accosted him demanding a shilling, manhandling him in the process. They searched his pockets unsuccessfully and he was then thrown into the canal. The defence denied any aspect of the incident involving violence or attempted theft and counter alleged that Mr Glover had made indecent propositions to Cooper who then told Walter Allen to throw him in the canal, which he did. The Magistrate took the attitude that this incident was high jinks fuelled by beer and reduced the charge to one of Common Assault and fined the three defendants 10 shillings each, plus unspecified costs.

On 26th August 1914, Walter Allen attended Smethwick Town Hall, one of the ancillary recruitment offices, and completed the Attestation process in application to join the army. The paperwork for this application and period of his service, has survived and shows that he was 29 years and eight months old, resident at 35, Mornington Terrace, Mornington Road, Smethwick and was employed as a riveter. Depending on the accuracy of the information given to the person recording the details, which is the same handwriting as the person witnessing the application, then Walter's birth date is somewhere around 26th December 1886. His medical record shows him to be a fit man, 5'5 ¾" tall with a chest expansion of 3½", the minimum height being 5'3". Although Walter had at least one minor brush with the law, which if taken more seriously would have led to a lengthy incarceration, he was able to declare that he had never been to prison. On signing the attestation, Walter indicated that he wished one third of his pay to be deducted and forwarded to his wife and children and assigned the number A3164 of the King's Royal Rifle Corps (KRR).

On 1st September 1914 Walter received a posting as a Rifleman with the 7th Service Battalion K.R.R. Corps. This battalion of the New Armies had been formed on 19th August 1914 at Winchester and moved to Aldershot as part of 41st Brigade in the 14th (light) Division; Walter arrived at Aldershot on 2nd September. Walter's military career was not destined to last very long, at this stage, for on 15th September, he hit Lance Corporal Stewart, for which the following day, he was brought before the commanding officer, Lieutenant Colonel Rennie DSO, on a charge of misconduct and sentenced to 21 days detention. It was also recorded that he was to be discharged from the army, clearly at this early stage of the war there was no lack of available manpower for them to deal with Walter's case in such a manner. Walter's service is noted as 42 days with 21 days eligible for pension and he was discharged from North Camp Aldershot on the authority of the G.O.C. (General Officer Commanding) 41st Infantry Brigade.

Walter returned home and to civilian life but for how long is uncertain as the rest of his military record has not survived. What is certain that at some later date he re-joined the army and was posted to a unit of the Royal Garrison Artillery (RGA). It is most probable that on re-enlistment, a separate military file was created which was later destroyed by fire in the Blitz of London during World War 2. There is a record which survived which shows his unit on his death as 1st Battalion Royal Warwickshire Regiment, formerly 53145 RGA, which related to the Royal Garrison Artillery. This part of the Royal Artillery forces was formed to deal with the issues of heavy artillery in the defence of Britain and the Empire. Many of the Heavy Battery units were transferred to the conflict in the Balkans from India in 1915 and it is likely that Walter, on re-joining the army, had been posted with one of these. His medal card shows his entitlement to the 1914/15 Star as 31.10.1915 and the qualifying theatre as the Balkans.

What is certain was that at the time of his death on 25th June 1916, he was serving with 1st Battalion, Royal Warwickshire Regiment. The most likely explanation is that he was serving with the RGA in the Balkans in 1915 and, at some stage, he was wounded, injured or became sick and returned to England for hospital treatment. On his return to fitness, he was posted to France with the huge numbers of soldiers deemed necessary for the Battle of the Somme.

On being posted to the 1st Battalion, he was given a new service number, 12278 and his rank changed from Gunner to Private. The 1st Battalion was a Regular Army unit and had been posted to France in August 1914 as part of the 10th Brigade in the 4th Division.

On 1st June 1916, the 1st Battalion was in reserve at Gapennes near Abbeville, France, training and, in particular, practising attacks at Battalion and Brigade level, for the great push planned for the end of the month. On 4th June, the Battalion, along with the rest of the Brigade, began a march back to the front. On this day they marched to Fienvillers, stopping for a two-hour lunch and they completed the journey at 2.00 p.m. The following day they again marched as a Brigade, setting off at 7.00 a.m., arriving at Warnimont Woods at 2.00p.m. where they went into billets of huts and tents in the woods. They remained at this location until 11th June, spending the time providing working parties to assist the Royal Engineers. At 8.30p.m. that day, the Battalion moved to Bertrancourt arriving at 9.00p.m.where they were billeted in huts and the following morning, 150 of the men were given the opportunity to bath at Bus nearby. Following a day of rest, the journey continued arriving at MaillyMaillet at 12.30p.m. where they were placed in tented accommodation in woods. There the men spent time on working parties improving and repairing trenches or cleaning when not and then on 18th June 1916, the Battalion went into the front line at Auchonvillers, relieving the 2nd Battalion, Royal Dublin Fusiliers at 5.30p.m.

This first night was very quiet and two patrols were sent out to bomb a crater but no Germans were seen. This quiet did not last long and on the following afternoon, between 2.45 and 3.30p.m., A and B companies received a heavy artillery bombardment from German 4.2 guns and ten men were wounded including Walter. The wounded were removed from the front line by stretcher bearers and taken to the nearest field ambulance where they received immediate medical attention prior to being taken to a safer hospital facility. Walter's injuries were severe and for six days he fought his final battle; on 25th June 1916 he succumbed to his wounds and died.

Walter was buried at Auchonvillers Military Cemetery. The record shows he left £1.4s.4d to his sole legatee, his wife Edith, this was later supplemented with a war gratuity of £7 and no doubt with children to support, a war pension.

Walter was clearly a man with a natural fighting spirit, often these types of men are drawn to boxing or martial arts. Sometimes men like this never have the opportunity to express their desire to fight through acceptable or legal means and satiate the fighting spirit in behaviour which becomes illegal or unsociable. Walter, however, had World War 1 in his lifetime, which gave him the opportunity to experience the ultimate form of fighting - one of life or death. His readiness to volunteer, followed by the bitter disappointment of being jailed and thrown out for a moment of ill-discipline on his part, before military training had taught him self-control, did not stop him from the driving force to fight. He volunteered again and we know from his medal card, that he was awarded for the 1914-15 Star, British War and Victory medals.

Chapter 28

William Matthew Smart

(My Somme Poppy)

Author's Picture

In 2016 to commemorate the 100th anniversary of the Battle of the Somme, The Royal British Legion presented a very special metal poppy, the component parts were made from things recovered from the battlefield including metal from shell fuses. Each poppy came in a presentation box and was dedicated to an individual soldier who had died during this battle. Mine commemorated Gunner 4318 William Smart of the Royal Field Artillery who died on 11th October 1916. This is William's story.

William was born in 1892, the eldest son of John and Isabella Smart of 39, Albion Street, Aberdeen, Scotland. John Smart was a foreman in an Aberdeen chemical works. William married Nancy Wood and the marriage produced a daughter, Georgina, born on 10th November 1913.

William's military file has not survived and there is little information about his life, but in an obituary in the Aberdeen Weekly Journal of 20th October 1916, his wife had stated that William had been a time served soldier prior to the start of World War 1 with the 2nd Highland Brigade, Royal Garrison Artillery (RGA) as Gunner 1087. At the outbreak of war, William was employed at the chemical factory where his father was foreman, but he immediately re-joined the army at Aberdeen recruitment offices and was posted to Royal Field Artillery (RFA) as Gunner 4318. William arrived in France on 2nd May 1915 with his new unit the 1st Highland Brigade RFA Territorial Force.

The War Diary for the 1st Highland Brigade RFA Territorial Force commences on 1st June 1915 and merely states that they were, 'In the field', no location is given but they were posted to the 51st Division of the British Expeditionary Force (BEF). During May 1915, there was some reorganisation. The Brigade was initially equipped with old 15-Pounder Field Guns. These guns were problematic and, on 18th June, a battery was withdrawn from the action they were engaged in as they were described as ineffective. This situation was not rectified until August 1915 when these obsolete guns were replaced with up-to-date18-Pounders. On 15th May the Brigade was renamed 255th Brigade of RFA Territorial Force; the batteries were cut from four to three and named A, B and C Batteries.

July 1915 was spent alternating between being in the field, with only two Batteries, or at rest until 26th July when the whole Brigade entrained to a different location on the front and detrained at their destination on 30th July. Still no locations given but on 5th August, they relieved the 35th Regiment of Artillery of the French 1st Groupe and took over their positions and zones. On 24th August 1915, the Brigade took delivery of new 18-Pounder Guns and equipment, the following day the new guns were fired registering the individual fire zones for each gun and the old 15-Pounder guns and equipment were packed up and sent back to base. On 31st August, the Brigade HQ took possession of a wireless installation from the Royal Flying Corps for use; '*between batteries and flying machines*'. One of the most dangerous jobs undertaken by the artillery was to provide a 'Spotter' who would take a position within view of the targets and report back by telephone to the batteries to report the accuracy of guns. Dependant of the lie of the land would mean just how close the Spotter had to get to the enemy, these men were the target of snipers, artillery and anyone else who could stop his reports. The Royal Flying Corps started to act in this capacity from the air and consequently drew some of the attention from enemy guns away from the spotters.

The diary for October 1915, gives the first details of the Brigades locations. The HQ was in Albert and the wagon lines for the batteries in the field were from Bresle, with the wagon line for the ammunition at Bazieux (now spelt Baizieux). The wagon lines were where horse drawn wagons were located and carried ammunition, food, water and other supplies to the batteries in their firing positions. For rest and meals, the men could travel back with the empty wagons to the start locations. The wagon lines were a prime target for enemy artillery and movement was often done under the cover of darkness. At 8.00 p.m. 26th February 1916, the Brigade's wagon lines were subjected to a heavy bombardment; seven horses and three men were killed, whilst four men were wounded.

By June 1916, the Brigade were situated in the Arras area and the wagon lines were at Frévin-Capelle. The guns had been used on several occasions in conjunction with mines being exploded and raids on the enemy lines, but on 25th June 1916, all batteries were involved in a four-day bombardment of the enemy trenches. This coincided with the initial phase of the Battle of the Somme and, whilst there is no mention of an extension to this bombardment, there was in the area of the battle and the start date of the infantry attack was pushed back until 1st July 1916.

At the beginning of August 1916, the Brigade was moved to assist in the Battle of the Somme and relieved the 2nd Field Artillery Brigade of the New Zealand Division. By now, a D Battery had been added to the Brigade, armed with four18-Pounder guns whilst A, B and C Batteries each had six18-pounders. Wagon lines for each Battery were set at Jesus Farm and the Brigades role was to support the 154th Infantry Brigade.

At some stage prior to the 11th October 1916, William was involved in an accident with a gun, there are no details of how and when, but he was removed to either the 3rd or 44th Casualty Clearing Stations situated at Puchevillers where he died of his injuries on 11th October. William was buried in Puchevillers British Cemetery, he left £27.9s.5d. which was supplemented with a War Gratuity of £9.10s. to his wife, Nancy and his daughter Georgina. William was awarded the 1914-15 Star, British War and Victory medals.

Chapter 29

Frank Short

(For Patricia Wright)

Frank's family were from West Hartlepool, resident at either 17, or 19, Alfred Street. Both these numbers are taken from the 1901 and 1911 census records and, as the family was quite large, they may have occupied both. Frank's dad George was a shipyard worker employed as a riveter, whilst his mum, Jane Ann, was a housewife. In 1901, the family comprised the parents and six children, aged from 13 years to six months, Frank is number four, aged four, having been born in the first quarter of 1896. In 1911, the family had expanded by two more children at home. In all Jane had successfully given birth to 12 children of whom three had subsequently died; there was no requirement to register still born children at this time. Frank aged 15, had left school and was employed as greengrocer's assistant but later on joined his dad at the shipyard.

The local ship building industry was a major employer for this area; in fact, almost every shown occupation on the 1901 census forms for Alfred Street is related to that industry. The men responsible for securing the steel plate to the ships framework were called riveting gangs and comprised of four men. The most experienced were the riveters who sat on a plank suspended over the ships side, they were supported by a holder-up, a heater and a boy. The rivet heater worked on a coke brazier inside the hull, his job was to take a red hot rivet in long tongs, throw it up to the boy whose job it was to catch the rivet with his own tongs, pass it to the holder-up who placed it in the hole for the riveter to beat it into place. The gang were paid on performance and each finished rivet was inspected by tapping it, any that rang a hollow sound were re-done at the gang's cost.

The whole industry was very hierarchical and it was a five-year apprenticeship to become a riveter, starting with labouring and progressing via the various jobs. The riveting gangs were seen as extremely important and particularly strong men; in 1913 the average pay per gang was £5-6 per week.

At the outbreak of the war, there was a massive response to the call to arms and the expected response of 200,000 men was approximately doubled in the first few months. The height limit of 5' 3" was one of the means of sifting through the eager applicants, shorter men were rejected. Towards the end of the year, however, this was reviewed and the regulatory height reduced to five feet. The static nature of trench warfare had commenced and short stature was an asset, tall men often had to crouch to avoid becoming the target of a sniper or machine gunner. Many Regiments were now forming Bantam Battalions specifically to cater for men between 5' and 5' 3" tall. One such Regiment was the Durham Light Infantry which formed the 19th (Service) Battalion, in Durham on 13 January 1915, by the Durham Parliamentary Recruiting Committee. The Battalion was moved to Cocken Hall, Durham in May 1915, then in June 1915, moved to Masham, North Yorkshire and came under orders of 106th Brigade in 35th Division.

On 16th March 1915 Frank made a successful application to join the Army and following attestation and medical examination was posted to 19th (Service) Battalion. We have no way of knowing if Frank had made previous attempts to join up and been rejected but the date would indicate his willingness to join and serve his country and not wait for the inevitable conscription which was being considered at this time. Frank had been working at the Shipyards as a rivet heater so had commenced an apprenticeship and was working his way up through the jobs in the footsteps of his dad. Private 19/761 Short aged 19 years and one month old, was 5' 1" tall, with a 34" chest boasting a 3" expansion and weighed 118 pounds. The examining officer marked his development as good and passed him fit for service; he was assigned to Y Company and commenced basic training.

By January 1916, 19th Battalion were housed in billets at Perham Down Wiltshire. Mobilisation orders were received and there then followed frenetic activity to get ready to move. At 3.00 a.m. on January 31st, the Battalion left camp and entrained to Southampton where they boarded ships and sailed to Le Havre. On arrival the following day, 1st February, they went to number 1 rest camp. The rest of this month was spent in training with a selection of officers and NCOs sent for instruction in trench duties with the Guards Division. From Frank's Y Company Captain Washington, Sergeant Johnson and Corporal Thorley spent 8th to 15th February in the front line. At the end of the month the whole Battalion was divided between various elements of 57th Brigade to receive trench instruction, they rotated between front line, support and reserve until 11th March when they went into the line at Tilloloy, Somme district as a complete Battalion. The first casualties were two men injured at 11.20 a.m. on 13th March by enemy artillery. This was, of course, the daily routine of artillery exchanges and during this tour the casualty count was 17 men wounded and one who later died.

Over the next few months, the Battalion settled into the routine of front line, support and reserve, usually four days in each. Whilst not manning the front line, men were assigned to working parties both day and night and training schedules were drawn up. Regular specialist training, such as machine gun, sniper, trench mortar and bombing were attended by selected men to enhance the fighting capacity of the Battalion, they were not to know at this stage but planning and preparation was underway for a large-scale offensive in the Somme district.

Trench routine continued until 18th July 1916, when the Battalion was finally committed to the Somme battle. On this occasion they were committed to the final taking of Delville Wood, with orders to hold at all cost, this they did but the casualty figure was 12 officers and 250 other ranks. The Battalion's next big commitment was in the line on the Eastern slope of Malz Horn Ridge; here they lost another three officers and 110 other ranks. Towards the end of 1916 the Battalion was transferred to the Arras sector.

During May 1917 the Battalion was engaged in the routine of front line, support and reserve, now having transferred back to the Somme sector. When not in the front line, working parties were formed mainly repairing roads, a hazardous duty attracting the attention of enemy artillery. There was also a training schedule to adhere to, practising new attacking formations, musketry and specialist skills. On 28th May 1917, the Battalion relieved the 17th West Yorkshire Regiment in the line, East of the village of Villers Guislain. The relief went without incident and the men settled down to their duties aware that carelessness or a random shell might lead to tragedy.

Unfortunately, the diary makes no mention of incidents during this spell, the entry for 30th May 1917 merely reiterates the previous day's entry, *"Bn in front line situation normal"*. Frank's file and other relevant records such as Commonwealth War Graves Commission and Register of Soldier's effects, state he was killed in action on this day; the only other clue is his body was recovered and buried. The greatest hazards during these quiet spells in the front line were from snipers or random enemy shelling with high explosive or shrapnel. Frank's stature gave him a distinct advantage over a tall man in a trench and a sniper would only have an opportunity from a careless peep over the parapet. A direct hit of high explosive would likely leave nothing left to bury but indirect hit would kill someone without apparent damage by concussive force; the explosive concussion causing huge trauma to internal organs. The most likely cause of Frank's death would be a shrapnel shell, these were designed to explode about 30 feet in the air raining a shower of lead or steel balls down on unfortunates below.

We only know that Frank was killed this day and he was buried at Heudicourt Communal Cemetery Extention. Frank is the only recorded casualty killed from 19th Battalion that day, but of course, someone may have been injured and removed to hospital dying at a later date or, hopefully surviving.

Frank had made a will and left his estate of £12.2s.6d., supplemented by a war gratuity of £9.10s.0d., to his mother Jane. The usual scroll, death plaque and the British War and Victory medals were also forwarded to Frank's family.

Chapter 30

George Bamber

(For Martin and Louise Bamber)

Picture Courtesy Martin Bamber

George was born on 27th February 1891, and baptised at the parish church of St. Clement, Ordsall-in-Salford, on 18th March the same year. His father Henry, by trade a carpenter, was born in Penrith in Cumberland and had married Maria Holiday on 18th January 1878. They set up home in the Salford area of Manchester and commenced a family. George was the fifth of seven children and, at the time of his birth, the family were resident at 8, Rock Street, Salford. By 1901 the family had moved to 22, Pickering Street, Hulme and had expanded by one more son, who was now seven years old, George, aged nine, was still in school. In 1911 George, now aged 20, had moved away from home and was living as a boarder at 21, Albert Street, Rusholme;

the home of James and Ellen Murphy. James worked on the railways as did the other four boarders but George was now employed as a clerk at the Broughton Copper Company.

With the outbreak of war, George volunteered to join the army and, for an unknown reason, decided to join the Northamptonshire Regiment who had opened a recruitment facility at Salford in Manchester. A number of local Regiments had been forming Pals Battalions which enabled men with common interest, either professional or sporting, to join up, train and serve together. This included the Manchester Regiment which formed a total of 12 Service or Reserve Battalions based on the Pals model. George attested on 2nd September 1914 and was medically examined on the same day for his suitability for military service. There were two options at this stage and the volunteer did still have a choice, home service was available to men who did not wish to serve abroad and also for those whose fitness level was not high. Service abroad was available for those fit for war service and who wished it. George, who was now 23 years and seven months old, and was still employed as a Clerk at the Broughton Copper Company. He was 5' 7" tall, weighing 130 lbs with a fully expanded chest measurement of 35 inches, the medical officer conducting the examination noted that George was of good physical development and fit for service. He was issued with a document explaining his options for service and he signed willing to go abroad to join the fight and signed on for the duration of the war. Accepting his King's shilling, a long-standing tradition dating back to the naval press gangs, George was assigned the number 47086 and posted to 3rd (Reserve) Battalion, Northamptonshire Regiment. This unit was a training Battalion which had been formed at Ashton-under-Lyne in August 1914 but moved to Cleethorpes, Lincolnshire, in October of that year to form part of the Humber defences, where it remained throughout the war.

Whilst undergoing training George contracted bronchitis and suffered a burst lung. This condition is normally associated with diving decompression but can also be caused when severe coughing causes a breach in the lung wall and air escapes to form a cavity between the lung and chest wall. He was treated at the Plank House Red Cross

Hospital Gillingham Dorset. This injury effectively put an end to George's aspirations to join the fight in France and he was retained with 3rd Battalion on training and defence duties. George had shown that he had leadership qualities and had been promoted to Lance Corporal on 29th September 1914 and then acting Corporal on 1st October.

The Humber Estuary had long been recognised as a potential invasion of England point and in fact been used for just that by the Saxons. In 1860 due to the very real danger of the invasion by the French the Coastal Defences Act was passed which enabled the building of fort and artillery bases on both north and south banks of the Humber to defend against hostile action. During World War 1, the danger was seen as German naval or submarine attack and during 1915 two large forts were built to accommodate hundreds of troops and artillery in the Cleethorpes area. These were called Haile Sand and Bull Sand Forts but were not fully completed until 1919; there is however a good chance that George was familiar with these two projects.

On 28th May 1917, George finally achieved his military aim and was shipped from Folkestone to Boulogne on a transport ship as a replacement/reinforcement and initially posted to 17th Infantry Base Depot (IBD) at Calais. Here he reverted to the substantive rank of Lance Corporal and spent a gruelling few months undergoing further training whilst awaiting a transfer to a front-line battalion. On 3rd August 1917 his ambition finally realised, he joined 6th (Service) Battalion Northamptonshire Regiment in the field and his number was changed to 15063.

6th Battalion had been formed at Northampton in September 1914 and landed in France on 26th July 1915. At the time when George joined his new comrades, they were in a reserve camp in the Zillebeke area of Belgium in preparation to take part in the major British offensive of 1917; the Third Battle of Ypres otherwise known as Passchendaele. At 4.30 p.m. that day the Battalion marched to take up reserve positions in or near to Sanctuary Wood, this location was used as a place soldiers could go to in the heat of battle, be fed and re-equipped and sent back to join their units, hence the name.

Throughout the time this wood was occupied it drew the attention of enemy artillery and was by no means a safe location, on his first day with the Battalion George experienced the dangers of life in the trenches. In this area the water table was near the surface making deep dugouts impossible to create, in wet weather conditions life in the trenches became a battle to keep feet dry and out of the blue clay for which the area is famed for, many men and much equipment were lost trapped in the mud.

Sanctuary Wood 16/7/1917 (M. Bamber)

Sanctuary wood 2018 (Author's collection)

The City of Ypres was strategically important to both sides as it was a junction point for rail and road networks which were necessary for the resupply of armies in the field. The City had been denied the Germans by the British in 1914 and survived two attempts to take it. The result had been that the German forces occupied high ground on two sides of the city and had created a salient which they could target with heavy artillery. By 1917 this historic city had been reduced largely to rubble and the Allies attitude was now that to relinquish control would be a betrayal to all those men, women and children who had sacrificed their lives to keep it from enemy hands. The offensive planned for 1917 was to gain control of the high ground controlled by the German army and to push them out of the rail systems from which they were resupplying their army. The joint British Commonwealth and French Offensive commenced on 31st July 1917, preceded by a 3,000-gun artillery bombardment. The infantry stage involved nine British and six French Divisions and finished on 10th November the same year. The first stage of the offensive, known as the Battle of Pilckem Ridge, was met with initial mixed results, the northern flank led by British and French forces were successful advancing 2,500 – 3000 yards. The area, which George and his comrades now faced, had met with the strongest of German defences, artillery and counter attacks and they had been pushed back to the start line. The second stage of the offensive known as, the Capture of Westhoek had been postponed from 2nd August 1917 due to torrential rain and was rescheduled for 10th August 1917.

By 4.35 a.m., the designated zero hour, the infantry were all in position and a rolling artillery bombardment was commenced, behind which the infantry advanced. The ground over which the men moved forward had been churned up by bad weather and artillery and was now an extreme obstacle course of flooded shell holes, mud, fallen trees and barbed wire. Again, success was mixed. On the left flank of the attack, the objectives were easily taken but in front of George's Battalion, the Germans had managed to man strong points with heavy machine guns in Glencourse Wood and the main assaulting parties were held up. Two Lewis gunners very bravely rushed the German position killed the occupants and the trench was occupied. The Germans counter attacked from behind a smoke screen and during the course of the day and night pushed the British back and reoccupied most of Glencourse Wood. This exposed the flank of the line of attack adjacent to the wood and allowed German snipers to take advantage, the British artillery was very effective in dealing with the Germans in these positions and preventing further units from coming forward. Total casualties for the day incurred by 6th Battalion were; one officer and 27 other ranks killed, six officers and 123 other ranks wounded, three officers and 23 other ranks missing.

The following day, the 6th were holding the line in Chateau Wood, Artillery was very active on both sides as was aerial activity. At 7.00 a.m., a German aeroplane was brought down in flames, much to the applause of George and his comrades. Later that day the 6th came out of the line and retired to camps from where they continued training. On 1st September the men were treated to a seaside outing.

On the afternoon of 18th October 1917, 6th Battalion returned to front line duties near to the town of Poelcapelle. The tour was short, just two days, but during that time there was heavy shelling by both sides which also included the use of gas. There followed a period of routine trench duties in this area, a few days in the front line or support then to a camp for cleaning and equipment maintenance. The conditions in the trenches were very wet creating a quagmire of mud, the high water-table made it difficult to keep trenches in good order and continual maintenance was required to repair weather damage and create dry standing areas in the forward posts. There was continual vigilance necessary to monitor enemy activity who was likewise engaged in attempts to create conditions where they could keep their feet dry and avert the dangers of trench foot. The main activities during this period apart from trench work were night patrols to locate and monitor enemy activity; these were dangerous activities as the slightest sound would be followed by a flare in the sky and machine gun fire. Aerial activity was a daily occurrence by now, both sides gleaning intelligence about their opponent's locations and activity and at the same time trying to keep the enemy from doing the same, resulting in dog fights over the trenches. Each short tour in the front line produced a steady flow of men killed, wounded or missing. Christmas 1917 was a better time as the whole Battalion were out of the line from 16th December until 3rd January 1918 in Bapaume Camp the diary notes the duties as; *"Parades, training, general holiday"*.

On 10th January 1918, the holiday over, 6th Battalion re-entered the front line at Pascal Farm near to Boesinghe. The winter freeze was beginning to thaw resulting in the return of the mud. The Battalion was working a system of self-relief whereby two companies were in the front line at any one time, with a Company in close support and the fourth in reserve. After two days the Companies rotated duties and were relieved in the early hours of 15th January. This tour had at least created no casualties, but everyone's feet were soaked and the priority after getting to dry accommodation was to dry out and inspect for damage, having a bath being a lower priority, this was not done until the following day. Bathing on the scale required for a Battalion of men was usually done in a facility such as an old brewery where the brewing vats were filled with hot water. The whole enterprise was supervised by sanitary sections of the Royal Army Medical Corps and clean underwear was issued and the opportunity to de-louse afforded. Lice were the ever-present fellow occupiers of the trenches and the process of killing them called 'chitting', one method was to run the seam of clothing over a candle but the reproductive cycle of these insects was such that cleaned clothing was very soon re-inhabited.

There followed a period of routine trench rotation; front line, support and reserve. This was during a quiet period and much work was done on trench repair, reinforcing the defensive wire and carrying ammunition in support of the ammunition columns. On 21st March 1918, the Battalion went back into the line between Ly-Fontaine and Gibercourt. On this day the Germans launched their last great offensive of the war - now known as the 1918 Spring Offensive or Kaiserschlacht. At 10.30 p.m. that night the Battalion retired to a position on the San Quentin Canal at La Montagne Bridge to await the arrival of the German forces.

The Battalion was positioned on a railway embankment with orders to prevent the Germans crossing the San Quentin Canal; an attempt to blow the La Montagne Bridge was made with limited success on 22nd March and German attempts to cross the canal were thwarted despite the men being attacked from the air and by heavy artillery bombardment. On the morning of 23rd March, the battalions on both flanks of the 6th were successfully attacked pushing them back, this exposed the vulnerable sides of the Battalion and a withdrawal became necessary at 11.30 a.m.. At 12 noon, the Battalion retired to positions at Bois de Frieres where they were subjected to violent artillery shelling and enfilade machinegun fire. At 3.00 p.m. the Battalion withdrew from the line into billets.

The tactics used by the German army during the early stages of this offensive were extremely successful. Small groups of experienced well trained and lightly armed men punched through the British lines leaving strong points to be dealt with by follow up groups. Armed with small arms, grenades and flame throwers these Storm troopers created havoc and panic and huge numbers of men were cut off and then either systematically destroyed or taken prisoner. The situation on these few days is best described by someone who was there; Ross Morris was a Sergeant with the 6th Battalion which was occupying a

200-yard front on the railway embankment on 22nd March and very likely to be in the same place as George. Ross Morris had joined up early on in the war and joined the 6th in the field on 22nd December 1915, he was interviewed by Imperial War Museum staff in 1992 and the audio recording is available online.

"1918, the German's big advance came then. It was very misty. They took all the big guns back; we had no artillery at all. We were told 'you're there ... sacrifice'. You've got to stop them as best you can.

It was very misty and we all had to go in an extended line like that. Over the country, try to find the Germans. We got to the canal and it was dusk then ... dusk, and they told us to retire to a railway embankment 300 yards back. And in the morning, the 2nd Lieutenant and the platoon and me, I was a Sergeant then, just one trench and we had to hold at the sluice gate of the canal. Then they told us to retire to the embankment again, still misty. Then they told us to go forward again, and as we were going forward the mist cleared as if like a curtain. There was thousands of Germans in front, over the canal. We dropped into this trench and they tried to get over and we shot some of them. And they came around the back of us like and sideways and they hit me through the wrist, and they took a bit of my knee and a bit of my thumb there. And they hit me sideways; a machine gun bullet must have got me like that. When I stood up as best I could, and Germans came over then, one chap had got a spade; he was going to hit me over the head with it. A German Under Officer came over and knocked it away with his stick like that. Comrade he said."

Ross Morris was a very lucky man as was George, who had no doubt become isolated by the fast movement of the Storm troopers and was suffering the explosive effects of a hand grenade when his trench was overrun, both men were taken prisoner.

George was transported to Darmstadt Prisoner of War Camp. His journey was most likely by train in cramped conditions, with wounded men amongst them and this was largely due to the vast numbers of men being taken prisoner at this time. His journey would have been via a transit camp or Durchgangslager where wounded men would be taken to a medical facility and the others transported to a *Stammlager* or Parent Camp. Darmstadt was a parent camp and was situated four miles from the town of that name. The original camp was a cavalry exercise ground with some brick buildings but had been extended with wooden huts to accommodate 10,000 men largely Russian and French. The camp was split into compounds where prisoners were divided by nationality; each compound with barracks housed 1,000 to 2,000 men and the wooden barrack buildings accommodated 250 prisoners. On arrival George, along with all new arrivals, was housed in a separate compound which was used as an isolation unit for six weeks - the incubation period for most infectious diseases. Following registration, newcomers visited the Entläusunganstalten or delousing plant where they were freed from the detestable pest which was the bane of the men's life in the trenches and one type, the carrier of the disease, Typhus. On entry to the delousing unit, the men entered an anteroom where they removed all their clothing, men and clothes were given a corresponding tag the latter hung on hangers and sterilised in either a steamer or hot dry air unit. The naked prisoners then went to a shower and soaping room where head and face were shaved; they then thoroughly washed with a creosote soapy mixture and other hairy areas of the body rubbed with a powder which removed all other hair. Total removal of body hair was necessary to remove any nests of louse eggs of which one type was the carrier of Spotted Fever. The nests were extremely difficult to remove any other way. Many of the men were very reluctant to leave the showers as it was probably the first time many of them had ever seen such a luxury let alone used one! The men then moved on to a dressing room where in return for the tag they were given their sterilised clothing back, they were also issued with a second set of clean clothes.

Following the period of isolation George was transferred to the British compound and allocated to a barracks room. Each compound was equipped with its own washing facilities, for small items of clothing but larger items were sent to a central washing facility which contained large clothes boilers and wash tubs with a drying facility on an upper floor. The compound contained its own kitchen, canteen, reading room, playground, theatre and workshops such as shoe, tailor or carpentry.

The Germans had a strong belief that spinach was very nutritious and contained healing properties and this was grown in large quantities around the camp along with other foods, such as pigs, which were utilised to dispose of the scraps and leftovers from the kitchens. Also grown in quantity were apples which were dried and stored for the winter months.

Darmstadt was the mother camp to a number of work camps which provided labour to local factories and agricultural farms. Convention dictated that officers did not work and they were usually housed in better conditions than enlisted men, such as George, who were not afforded the same protection. George was sent out to work in a Salt Mine but details are not known as post-war the matter was a taboo subject in the Bamber household. This POW camp was regularly inspected by the Young Men's Christian Association who had formed a War Prisoners Aid Section they called the Flying Squadron in 1915 and although American, was able to operate from Berlin throughout the war unhindered. The reports sent back from inspections rated Darmstadt very highly as the standard there was not enjoyed by prisoners in camps elsewhere.

George spent the rest of the war at Darmstadt and after 11th November 1918 when the guns fell silent, he was repatriated back to England. Still a serving soldier with an impeccable conduct record, he was most likely transferred for administrative purposes to a home-based reserve battalion. However he wasn't far from Northampton as on 8th February 1919, he was admitted to Northampton Military Hospital and treated for tonsillitis but was transferred to Duston War Hospital from 19th February, until 4th April 1919. Following discharge from Hospital George was sent to Heaton Park dispersal camp in Manchester. Here he was medically examined due to his burst lung and incarceration, he was classified fit and placed on the Z reserve list. On 23rd April 1919, George walked out of camp and went home to his family at 14, Ivy Grove, Hulme, Manchester.

George returned to his Job with the Broughton Copper Company, married his sweetheart from Kent, Marjorie, who bore 14 children. The family relocated to Birmingham at a later date as the copper works was taken over by Kynochs and his job relocated to the factory there. He was awarded the British War and Victory medals and whilst he never spoke about the war very much, he did not hate the Germans but actually admired them as soldiers. George died in 1963 of natural causes.

Chapter 31

Stanley Broughton (Sandy)

On 19th November 1914, Stanley Broughton, a 23-year-old man from Burnley, Lancashire, answered his country's call to arms and attested to join the Royal Army Medical Corps. Following a medical examination, where he was found to be of good health, Stanley, a weaver by trade for a company called Preston's of Burnley, was accepted, given the King's Shilling and became Private 373 Broughton, posted to 2/2nd East Lancashire Field Ambulance. This unit was part of 66th (East Lancashire) Division which was a second-line reserve unit based in England. These formations were manned by men who had joined up but did not wish to serve abroad; at this stage; there was still a choice. In 1916, the Division was moved to the South Coast of England to form part of the coastal defences and Stanley's Field Ambulance were stationed at Crowborough, East Sussex.

Whilst stationed here, the unit was called on for various duties. As well as providing hospital staff, men were trained in some of the skills needed to look after transport horses such as cold shoeing and they even provided men for munitions work. The main drain on strength was providing officers and men as replacements for 1st line units which were serving abroad. In February 1916, the establishment was ten officers and 182 other ranks, with 37 Army Service Corps (ASC) personnel attached to provide transport. In this month the actual strength was only one officer and one ASC man short of the establishment figure.

On 11th February 1917, the Division was given orders to mobilise to the Western Front and by 16th March the last units arrived in France. Stanley arrived in France on 13th March and joined with his Field Ambulance at Bethune. The newcomers to the Western Front were given instruction in batches of three officers and 40 - 50 men by 13th Field Ambulance (FA). The familiarisation training which newly arrived men undertook involved living, survival and the dangers of trench work. At five feet three and a half inches tall, Stanley had just made the minimum height limit to join but was much better suited for trench life than a very tall person who, to avoid the attention of snipers, were often forced to move about stooped over. As well as manning aid stations, providing stretcher bearers and transport for wounded soldiers, 2/2nd FA supervised the bathing provisions in the area. The facility provided could accommodate 50 men per hour or three officers. Clearly the facilities provided for the latter were a personal bath with fresh water whilst that provided for the men were much larger, quite often beer brewing tanks. Whilst the men were very grateful for the opportunity to bath, de-louse and obtain clean clothes, the beer vats emptied of a favoured tipple must have caused some regret but much opportunity for jocularity! The 2/2nd FA provided the staff, one NCO and six men, to man the baths and keep the boilers stoked.

By April 1918, the now war seasoned 2/2nd FA, was based at Roisel in the Somme area of France. On 21st of that month, the German army launched Operation Michael which was the first stage in their Spring Offensive known as Kaiserschlacht (Kaiser battle). The battle commenced at 4.40 a.m. with the largest artillery barrage of the war, the targets for this barrage were spread over an area of 150 square miles and approximately 1,100,000 shells were fired in five hours. The intention of this offensive was to split the allied forces, destroy the British army and force the French to seek an armistice. The German army on the Western Front had been reinforced by 50 Divisions released from the Eastern Front as a result of the collapse of the Russian forces due to the revolution. Chaos reigned during the initial stages of this offensive and desperate battles commenced by battalions ordered to hold the line at all cost whilst a secondary defensive line was constructed and manned by Australian forces.

On the morning of the 21st while the artillery roared, the commanding officer of 2/2nd FA, Lieutenant Colonel Baxter, received instruction to man battle stations and remove the wounded. Very soon the walking wounded post and the emergency gas centre started to receive the first of many men needing treatment that day. All available stretcher bearers, including Stanley, were sent to report to the officer commanding the advanced dressing station at Templeux and evacuation plans were brought into action before positions were overrun by the enemy infantry. The walking wounded were placed on lorries and the more serious cases and gas victims were rescued by motor ambulance convoy and divisional cars, a Daimler ambulance was put out of action and two horses killed by shell fire.

Tirelessly the unit worked to relieve the suffering of wounded men and to save as many lives as possible. On a daily basis, the facilities created became dangerously close to being overrun and had to be moved to safer locations. By the end of the month the 2/2nd were in facilities created near to Pont de Metz near to Amien, here they were able to take stock of their situation and assess their losses. During the period 21st to 29th March 1918 the following statistical return was recorded; seven men evacuated to casualty clearing station due to sickness, nine men wounded one of whom later died. In addition to casualties and due to positions being overrun, 35 men were reported missing presumed prisoners of war. Initially Stanley was listed in this last category but eventually he was reported missing presumed dead and his family informed accordingly. There was a considerable time in which the family waited hoping for good news. The report of him missing presumed POW was reported in the Burnley Express on 25th May 1918, but it wasn't until 21st June 1919 that the paper ran the sad truth of the matter. Stanley's elder brother Richard had been killed in August 1917 serving with the Loyal North Lancashire Regiment in France, we can only imagine the terrible suffering this awful conflict had placed on this family and thousands like it.

Stanley's body was never recovered and identified and we can only assume he was a casualty of the artillery bombardment. His name was subsequently carved onto the memorial at Pozzieres and he was awarded the British War and Victory medals. Stanley left £7.7s.7d. to his mother, Mrs Nancy Broughton of 15, Trout Street, Burnley, and the same sum less a penny to each of his two sisters, Lizzie and Emily and his brother John.

Chapter 32

Herbert and William Wilkins

(For Terry Wilkins)

In 1911 Thomas, from Kent, and Rosina Wilkins resided at 59, Cromwell Street, Coventry. Thomas was a labourer in a gas works and Rosina, a local girl, kept home for her husband and the ten of her 12 children who had survived to this date. 59 Cromwell Street had five rooms including a kitchen so life was a bit of a squeeze when everyone was at home. The children's ages ranged from one to 25 years of age and the eldest four were in employment.

Herbert Musgrave Wilkins was born on Bonfire Night 1893 and baptised on 29th November the same year. He was the second child for Thomas and Rosina who had a daughter from a previous relationship; she was the eldest child in the family. In April 1896, Rosina gave birth to her third (surviving) child and he was Christened William on 15th April.

Prior to the outbreak of the war, Herbert had been employed as a butcher and William as a van boy for a laundry business, however, these records are from 1911 and do not reflect what the two men were doing in 1914 onwards.

From the available records William, the younger of the two men, joined the army in the winter of 1914 and was posted to the 1st Battalion Warwickshire Regiment. This was a regular army unit and at the outbreak of war was mobilised from its base in Shorncliffe Folkestone and landed in France as part of the original British

Expeditionary Force on 22nd August 1914. William was no doubt initially allocated to a training Battalion either 3rd (Reserve) or 4th (Special Reserve), both were raised at Warwick in August 1914 and at the time William joined them, they were based on the Isle of Wight.

William completed his training and embarked to France, landing there on 23rd February 1915. His first base would be an Infantry Base Depot near to his place of disembarkation to await assignment to a Battalion in the field. Whilst waiting could be a variable length of time, the life was often tough; training continued and every day involved physical exercise, route marches and assault courses. Further instruction to trench construction was not classed as work, but it involved a lot of digging and hard graft.

During the middle of March 1915 which is likely to have been about the time William arrived in the field, 1st Battalion were in the Armentières area near to the Belgian border. On 16th March 1915, the Battalion having been relieved from trenches the night before, were billeted at a location referred to as PT 63 or the Piggeries and that day, a draft of one officer and 43 men arrived as replacements. The Battalion were providing working parties to operate under the guidance of the Royal Engineers. This could have been all sorts of work from trench improvement and repair to removing spoil for tunnelling operations or carrying stores. On the evening of 21st March, the Battalion returned to the trenches at Wulverghem. That night, one man was killed and two others wounded, most likely during the relief - any movement or noise detected by the enemy would attract artillery fire onto the communication trenches being used. The Battalion spent the next few days with two Companies in the front-line trenches and two Companies in the second line support. They relieved each other daily and the main dangers at this time were enemy artillery and snipers. During this tour of duty, three men were killed and ten were wounded. Apart from night patrols which did not prove very productive, the main cause for excitement was when a noise was heard originally identified as a tunnelling operation. This of course was extremely worrying for men in the trenches as at any moment an underground mine may have been detonated beneath their feet causing numerous deaths and destruction. An investigation revealed the cause to be a Bull Frog heralding the first sign of spring; a few sighs of relief were no doubt exhaled and much made of the incident at the expense of the originator of the alarm no doubt!

The Battalion continued in this routine of four-day trench relief where the duties were manning the front line and being in support, followed by a period in reserve training and providing working parties. It is evident that William had been promoted to Lance Corporal as a letter from him bearing that rank appeared in the Coventry Evening Telegraph on 12th April 1915, thanking the people of Coventry for sending him some games on behalf of his C Company. It may well be that he was working in an unpaid capacity, which meant it was a temporary rank to determine his suitability for permanent promotion. It would have appeared on his file but his status in reality was Private. Other notable events were German aeroplanes dropping bombs on support trenches and a Zeppelin airship dropping 15 bombs one of which destroyed two farm buildings and killed two women and one baby.

On 22nd April 1915 the Second Battle of Ypres commenced, this was an offensive action by the Germans who had been denied the City of Ypres by the BEF in 1914 which would have been an important location for the resupply of their armies by rail networks converging there. The result had been the creation of a salient held by the British and French armies which was overlooked on high ground on two sides by German forces that made good use of artillery. Life in the salient was in constant danger from artillery fire and the German forces that were in places, just a few yards from the Allied front line. The area is renowned for its blue clay and high water-table creating a continual fight to keep water out of the shallow trenches which were reinforced and made higher by sandbagging. On the first day of this battle the German forces released chlorine gas for the first time resulting in 6,000 French casualties, protection against gas at this stage of the war was primitive and often was merely a mask soaked in urine.

The Battalion went into action at 4.30 a.m. on 25th April 1915. The day before, they had marched through the City of Ypres to get to their start positions; the City had been heavily shelled that day and was on fire. The Battalion were attacking a wood on the German line near to Vielje but were unsuccessful, largely because the artillery had not done sufficient destruction and they met fierce resistance also the supporting units could not get to them. They retired at 7.00 a.m. to the reserve line and dug in to count the losses. In that one action, the Battalion had 17 officers and 500 other ranks killed, wounded or missing; by any standards a high price to pay. The rest of April was spent in these positions and on two days, assisted in repelling German assaults on the British line, but during these last few days only two other casualties occurred, both men wounded.

For the first three days of May, the Battalion was brought forward to support the front line and suffered heavy casualties from shelling. They were relieved on 4th May 1915. At one point during these last few days William was wounded, removed from the field and entered the casualty chain. This involved being taken to a Forward Aid Post, then a Field Ambulance and a Casualty Clearing Station. He was then taken by train to a Base Hospital at Wimereux near to Boulogne where he died of his wounds on 4th May 1915. It is most likely, due to the time period involved, that he received his wounds on the two days in April where casualties are noted, but the first few days in May cannot be discounted, there is insufficient detail, such as type of wound or actual cause of death, to determine accurately what happened.

William was buried in Wimereux Communal Cemetery. He left £5.6s.11d which was supplemented by a War Gratuity of £5 to his father, he was subsequently awarded the 1914-15 Star, British War and Victory Medals.

In the Spring of 1916, Herbert Wilkins attested to join the army and was also posted to 1st Battalion, Royal Warwickshire Regiment. The Battalion had not left France and Herbert was also trained in one of the Reserve units before being sent to France. Whilst no records to confirm how he came to being in the army exist, it is most likely that he was either conscripted under the new legislation which came into force that year, as voluntary methods were not producing sufficient manpower for the army's needs, or he had reacted to the Derby Scheme of 1915, and elected to volunteer but have his enlistment deferred to a later date. Herbert is not likely to have joined his Battalion in the field for the preparatory period, or even the start of the offensive of that year known as the Battle of the Somme, but more likely to have arrived as a replacement for the horrendous losses which were experienced during that battle.

At the beginning of October 1916, 1st Battalion was out of the front line having played an active part in the early stages of the offensive. They were training and taking part in Brigade exercises in readiness for their next participation in the battle. On 9th October the Battalion marched from their tented camp at Mametz and took over a section of front-line trenches East of Les Boeufs. The usual system of two companies in the front line and two in support was adopted and the relief was over by 10.00 p.m. The next two days were quiet with the artillery of both sides reacting to each other's shelling activity, snipers were active and casualties were taken on each day - the highest being on the 11th, with 12 men injured. The Battalion received orders to take part in the stage of the offensive known as the Battle of Le Transloy. This was a town now just inside the German front line, which was heavily defended and the attempts to take it started on 1st October 1916 and by the end of the offensive, 18th November had still not fallen. The Battalion's objective for this assault was the brown line; Le Transloy is just beyond this point.

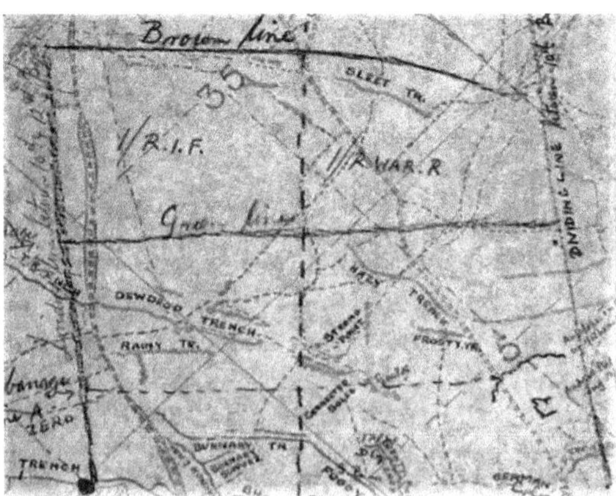

Trench map indicating the boundaries and objective of 1st Battalion (Author's collecton)

At 2.05 p.m. 12th October 1916, the men taking part in the attack stood ready in their assembly trenches, a creeping barrage opened up from the British artillery and the infantry advanced behind its cover. The fighting to gain the objectives lasted until nightfall that same day. Two German strong points covering the units on the left and right flanks of the Battalion, held the line back at this point causing the whole attack to stop and consolidate new positions after gaining approximately 500 yards. During the course of the day, artillery and machine gun fire accounted for the following casualties from 1st Battalion; five officers killed, one wounded, 259 other ranks killed, wounded and missing. Herbert was counted in this last category.

Herbert's body was never recovered or identified and, eventually, he was listed as killed in action. How long his family had to wait for this dreadful news cannot be ascertained accurately but having lost another son the previous year, it must have been an agonising wait. The family posted a missing report in the Coventry Evening Telegraph asking for news of their son but the report of his death appeared in the same paper on 17th November, stating that Herbert had been killed by the 'bursting of a shell'. When William died, a telegram would have been sent, possibly the same day, to England for his family to be informed but on this occasion the 'missing' report would have been sent after the Battalion were relieved from the battle on the night of 13th October. The change of status from missing to KIA would have been by means of a telegram and the information about him being killed by a shell sent in a letter of condolence by a member of his Company.

Herbert's name was included on the pillars of the Thiepval Memorial along with the 72,333 other men killed during the Somme Offensive but having no known grave. He left £2.3s.11d which was supplemented by a War Gratuity of £3, indicating just over six months of service, to his father and he was awarded the British War and Victory Medals. The family received the medals for both sons lost and a Scroll and Death Plaque for each of them also.

Chapter 33

George Albert Hunter

(For Denise McNulty)

George was born in 1898, at Chilvers Coton, Warwickshire. His parents, Joseph Hunter and Frances Mary Hunter, nee Pratt, were great believers in a large family producing a total of seventeen babies, of which seven survived childhood. Joseph was a fishmonger but had served in the British army in India and Ireland where some of the children were born. The numbers involved here are reflective of the high mortality rate in general due to lack of sanitary medical services, medicines and poor diet but mostly the plight of poor families. In fact, it is remarkable that Frances survived this number of births herself and lived until 1928.

The tough conditions people lived with, is reflected in an entry from the Tamworth Herald on 11th June 1904, which reported on a court action taken by George's father Joseph. At this time the family were resident at 38, Bolebridge Street, Tamworth and Joseph had been employed as a miner at the Pooley Hall Colliery, Polesworth. Joseph had been dismissed from his job whilst he was on sick leave and was not in a position therefore to work his 14 days' notice. Joseph had been involved in an underground incident in May of that year when he was hit by a piece of fallingroof, he was then unable to work due to his injury. He wasn't claiming unfair dismissal nor any liability on behalf of the mine owners for neglect, he was merely asking for a small consideration of £1.14s.8d to which he considered he was entitled in lieu of notice not worked. The Chairman of the bench apologetically found in favour of the employer, dismissing the claim. Tough times Indeed!

The 1911 census shows George at the age of 12, still at school. It is likely that he left school soon after that to work in the local mining industry as a pit boy as the compulsory school age at the time was five to12 years of age.

In 1917, George was employed by Messrs George Skey and Company Ltd, of Wilnecote, Tamworth, as a miner at the Tame Valley Colliery, when he received his call up papers to join the army. Conscription had started in 1916 to replace the grievous losses of the start of the war and 1915 and 1916 had also seen incredible losses in manpower during the course of the failed Battle of the Somme.

On 25th July 1917, George, standing 5'7¼" tall, weighing 143 pounds, of 41, Bolebridge Street, Tamworth, took the oath in Lichfield and was assigned as Private 203787 to 5th Battalion North Staffordshire Regiment. On 28th July he was sent to the base infantry depot for basic training with 12th Battalion which was a reserve unit used for training purposes throughout the war and was formed at Parkhurst on the Isle of Wight.

Following training with the 12th, George was then posted firstly to 1/6th and then on 18th November, to 2/5th battalion and commenced his journey to France to join his new unit. He arrived in the field at Gouy-Servins, between Bethune and Arras on 2nd November and was posted to D company.

On the day he arrived, the Battalion had recently withdrawn from the line and the day before paraded for the presentation of medals and awards. His first few days were spent training with both company and platoon. On 6th November, all companies spent the day on the rifle ranges which was an indicator of a return to the front. In the afternoon, the Divisional General inspected the battalion's transport. At 5.30p.m.the same day, the Battalion entrained from Gouy-Servins railway station in light rolling stock to an assembly area, known as Red Trench, to prepare to relieve the 2/8th Sherwood Foresters in their front-line location which had the Souchez River on their left flank. These change-over operations were conducted under the cover of darkness, unit by unit, using the communication trenches from Red

Trench to the reserve and front line positions. The movement was conducted without light and with as little noise as possible, as to attract enemy attention was to court the danger of artillery attack. The relief was completed at 1.30a.m.with no casualties reported.

The first few days of George's war were spent in Avion Trench in support of C Company who held a section of the front line. The twoCompanies swapped duties, whilst one rested in readiness the other had eyes and rifles pointed towards the enemy positions.

On 13th November 1917, the Battalion was relieved after dark by 2/6th North Staffordshire Regiment and returned to Red Trench assembly area. The casualty total for this period in the front was no officers killed or injured, whilst the other ranks experienced seven wounded, two self-inflicted wounds and 47 wounded from gas shell attack. George had obviously taken note of his gas mask training and escaped being a statistic at this point. The next few days were spent supporting the front with carrying parties, transporting ammunition, food and water.

On 16th November, the Battalion was relieved by the 15th Canadian Battalion and preceded to Souchez Camp arriving at 1.00a.m. on the 17th. That day they marched in Battalion order to Gouy Servins arriving at 2.00 p.m. where they assumed the role of Divisional reserve.

There was to be no rest for the men as on the 18th, they route-marched to Petit Servins and were then transferred from 1st Corps, 1st Army to 5th Corps 3rd Army and moved by route march to Berneville, situated east of Arras. Here they were placed in army reserve under orders to move at half an hour's notice. Movement continued with another transfer to 3rdCorps 3rd army, route marches being broken up with parades and inspections.

On 24th November, the men arrived at Heudicourt, south east of Cambrai where they commenced training in preparation for their move to the front line again. On 27th November, the Battalion moved forward to relieve the 2nd Canadian Guards in reserve trenches in the

Hindenburg Line. That night the whole brigade moved forward to relieve the front line. 2/5th battalion relieved the 1st Battalion Coldstream Guards in the Fontaine Notre Dame sector.

Between 12 noon and 1.00 p.m. on 30th November 1917, the Battalion was subjected to a very heavy attack by German infantry which was beaten back with extremely effective defensive fire. The ferocity of the attack can be judged by the casualty toll for this single hour, one officer killed, one wounded, 16 other ranks killed, 32 wounded and two injuries judged self-inflicted

On 1st December 1917, the Battalion was subjected to a further attack, but by night this time and with effective rifle and Lewis Gun fire some 90 to 100 casualties were inflicted on the enemy, with only one casualty reported. The following day they were relieved by the 2/5th Lincolns and proceeded to the Hindenburg support line and were employed on night time working parties digging defensive positions.

On 5th December the battalion proceeded by route march to Metz and then on to Pioneer Camp near Ytres, further south west of Cambrai. Total casualties for the period in the front were, one officer killed, one wounded, 16 other ranks killed, 53 wounded, three self-inflicted injuries, one missing and one accidental injury. No gas attacks during this tour and the majority of the casualties were experienced in one engagement. For the next few days the men were engaged in platoon training, parades for interior economy (all beds and bedding taken outside, weather permitting, shaken, aired and all floors scrubbed) and bathing.

On the night of 9th December, the Battalion moved with the whole division to relieve the 177th Infantry Brigade in the front line at Flesquires. The relief started at the Hindenburg Support line and took two nights to complete with the 2/5th relieved the 2/4th Battalion, Lincoln Regiment. Georges immediate duties were night time carrying parties and, on 13th December, the Battalion relieved 2/8th Sherwood Foresters in the front line at Flesquieres.

During the night of 14thDecember 1917 an assault was planned on the German front line trench. The attack involved two platoons of D company, including George, and was led by Lieutenants Aked and Belcher. The objective of the mission is not stated but was likely to involve collating intelligence on enemy dispositions, capturing prisoners or just killing a few of the enemy. At 10.20 p.m. under the cover of darkness, the attackers moved to a position in front of their own lines ready to move forward protected by artillery fire. The artillery fire finished at 11.00 p.m. and the men commenced the attack, entering abandoned trenches which the Germans had run away from in the face of the shelling. The diary records the casualties, Lieutenant Belcher, severely wounded and one other rank killed, this fatality was, unfortunately, George Hunter.

It is not clear how George was killed, but the clues point to his death being caused by the British artillery as opposed to enemy fire. The Germans were seen fleeing the trench by the light of the artillery guns flashes and there is no mention of encountering enemy fire or counter attack of any form. In a later letter to the family by Lieutenant Emery who expressed the sorrow of the whole company at the loss he said;

> *"Private Hunter was one of the most popular men, was loved by all his comrades and was killed while fighting with them – taking part in a raid against the Germans. During the whole operation Pte. Hunter showed coolness and bravery and it was rank poor luck that he was hit."*

The significant part of this is the last sentence about bad luck and all clues considered it was most likely a shell falling short and exploding which killed George rather than enemy fire.

George was later buried in Ribecourt Road Cemetery, Trescault, France. Notification of his death was sent to his family and reported in the Tamworth Herald on 5th January 1918. He was subsequently, but posthumously, awarded both the Victory and British War Medals

In 1922 George's former employers, Messrs. George Skey& Co., Wilnecote Tamworth, commissioned a memorial to those of the company's former employees who had fallen during World War One. The memorial was originally situated on the outer wall of their offices on Watling Street and the unveiling attended by a large crowd of local people. The office buildings have long gone but the memorial is still there for all to see in what is now a supermarket car park.

Author's Picture.

Chapter 34

Bertie John Biddle

(For Jane Selby)

Bertie was christened on 6th February 1898, at Erdington Parish Church, Birmingham, having been born on 26th November 1897; the family lived at 276, Short Heath Road at that time. His father Henry was a gardener and his mum's name was Emma (Nee Townsend). Bertie's siblings were three brothers and two sisters, with an age range from seven to 18; the eldest two in employment. In 1911, the family were still living at Short Heath Road but was reduced to four sons all in employment except Bertie, who at 13, was still in school.

On 11th December 1915, Bertie, now a works clerk living with his Mum at Sunnyside, Jerry's Lane, Erdington, attended a Birmingham army recruitment centre and attested to join up. Bertie was answering to a voluntary system developed in 1915, called the Derby Scheme, so named after its founder Lord Derby. The eagerness with which men and boys has answered the call to arms at the beginning of the war was waning. The myth that it would all be over by Christmas had been exposed and the sustainability of the static nature of trench warfare, a war of attrition, was dependent on a steady flow of replacements for the grievous losses experienced so far. The scheme involved door to door canvassing to identify men of eligible age and their occupations, each man was issued with a numbered card to be taken to a recruitment centre where he could be medically examined and attest, for this the individual received his King's Shilling and a day's pay. The scheme had two options for the individual. Option A was to attest and enrol immediately to a Regiment or option B, was to Attest and return home as an army reservist to await mobilisation.

(With this option came an armband bearing the initial D, to be worn in an effort to avoid accusations of duty dodging and cowardice). Bertie chose option B. The Derby Scheme was replaced with conscription in 1916.

Bertie who is recorded as 5' 5" tall with a fully expanded chest measurement of 35", was mobilised on 6th March 1917 and posted as Driver 214742 to 7th Reserve Battery, Royal Field Artillery RFA. On 30th June, he was transferred to the Royal Horse Artillery, 8th Reserve Brigade, then, on 8th December, as a Pioneer to 8th Provisional Company, Royal Engineers. On 9th January 1918, Bertie was then given a permanent home when he was again transferred, this time to the newly formed 15th Battalion Tank Corps, based at Bovington Camp in Dorset and was assigned the number Private 307200.

Bovington pre-dated the First World War as a military camp and, due to its remoteness, had been used in the development of the latest weapon of war, the tank. As the Tank Corps grew, this camp became its home and is still so today. The machine gun had largely been responsible for the static nature of the war and the armouring of vehicles was seen as a way of breaking this stalemate. The tank had made its debut on the Battlefield in the Battle of Flers-Courcelette on 15 September 1916, a stage of the large-scale Somme Offensive. The tanks were organised into groups of two or three and were sent in action ahead of the infantry. Open lanes were left in the British artillery barrage, through which the tanks could pass. It was realised that the tanks would draw enemy fire and the infantry followed at a cautious distance, this left the tanks undefended by infantry and vulnerable to attack. Whilst the tank's appearance created surprise and initial panic due solely to the secrecy with which they were developed and transported, it was not the great success it could have been if they had been technically more reliable and tactically supported.

Bertie had been posted as a driver with the Royal Artillery but there is no indication he had previous experience of horses. His employment on enlistment was as a works clerk. Both the units he was posted to, were reserve/training Batteries based in England and in the time he was with them, he would have received some training in the operation of artillery. The volume of tanks being produced at this time was such that a proportionate number of crews would be required and training at Bovington was stepped up to accommodate the numbers. Bertie, like many others, was compulsorily transferred to the Tank Corps on 21st January 1918 and attended Bovington Camp to commence training.

Following the introduction to the battlefield of the tank during the Battle of the Somme in 1916, a training school for recruits to the Corps had been developed. The training programme had been devised to produce sufficient trainers to accommodate the predicted volume of recruits. Initial recruitment had benefited from the men of such units as the Motor Machine Gun Service whose original purpose - to provide a mobile heavily armed service on the battlefield - had become redundant as the vehicles concerned were not of use on the Western Front by virtue of the damage to the terrain. These men had been largely recruited from technically based industries and understood mechanical maintenance. Men of this experience were now also sought after by the Royal Flying and Army Service Corps and men with little experience such as Bertie were now being recruited.

The training programme developed, was designed to create small teams of men able to specialise in a role but also able to understand and stand in, on other areas of the team if needed. The programme included; driving, maintenance, gunnery, signalling, reconnaissance, bombing and the care of pigeons. A driving school had been developed and training delivered on driving tanks; originally over a 40-acre site. By the time Bertie arrived, it had been considerably enlarged. This facility consisting of areas of trenches, woodland, obstacles made from tree logs, craters and bogs created by explosives, this was intended to give the trainees a variety of experience to benefit them for service on the Western Front. The bog areas were used to train men how to recover from the tank becoming stuck in a bog, the lessons being called 'unditching'. A lecture theatre was available with a cinema facility to teach lantern techniques and this also contained a cut away four-cylinder Daimler engine to teach how it and the differential worked. Before being allowed to drive on the tracks, students learned from the display engine and a jacked-up tank to get practice of the lever mechanisms used to control the vehicle. The full training schedule is described in the memoir of Colonel G H Brooks who at the time was a 19-year-old Subaltern;

> *"My first course was Driving and Maintenance and I found it was really good fun. The tanks, although very slow, had a magnificent cross-country performance and as four of the eight members of the crew were required solely to manoeuvre the vehicle, good team work was required to get the best performance. There was no tactical driving and the main object was to get the tank over the most impossible places and when stuck to get going again with the aid of pick, shovel, crow-bar and brute strength. This training was essential as each tank had to be self-supporting and recovery was in its infancy.*
>
> *Maintenance was very heavy, especially greasing up, as there were nearly sixty points on the outside of each tank alone which required the grease gun at the end of a day's run.*
>
> *The Gunnery Courses were also carried out at Bovington. These courses included indoor instruction in the huts below "G" Battalion lines and firing with the Lewis guns into the butts on the training ground north of the camp either from the ground or from gun sponsons removed from the driving and maintenance tanks. The six-pounder sub-calibre shooting was carried out in this area from a standing battery firing across a valley.*
>
> *My most vivid memory is of the so-called battle practice which took place shortly before the Battalion proceeded overseas. 18 Company marched in the early morning to Lulworth, where they found two or three store tents for the ammunition, a standing Battery of about half a dozen six-pounder guns and a couple of tanks. After the whole company had fired their first live shells and a few machine gun rounds from the Battery and from a slowly moving tank, they marched back to Bovington in the evening.*
>
> *Somewhat apprehensively after tales from my more experienced companions about the kick of the .45 revolver, I was next sent*

on a Revolver Course which was run by Captain Bill Watkins on a range he had built near "I" Battalion lines.

The last two courses were mild ones – a Compass Course and a Pigeon Course. The latter was necessary as each tank carried a basket of two pigeons into action. I cannot recall any incident when they proved of much use as either the tank had to be evacuated in a hurry, the pigeons were stupefied by the fumes or they were used up as an emergency ration."

At each stage of the training the students were subject to examination and assessment, the course lasted from three to four months and in Bertie's case he was transferred to the Tank Corps in January 1918 and travelled to France in the July of that year as a sponson-gun operator. The Mark V tank now available for use, was either male or female by description. The male was armed with the QF6-pounder, six-CWT gun of naval origin but shortened for use in the sponson turrets, whilst the female version was armed only with machine guns. The gun was designed by American designer Benjamin Hotchkiss, in France but adopted by many nations and manufactured under license in Britain by Armstrong Whitworth at Newcastle upon Tyne. The gun was a rapid firing weapon capable of firing 25 rounds per minute each round weighing six pounds, the complete unfired round weighed 9.7 pounds. The gun's muzzle velocity was 1,350 feet per second giving it an effective range of 7,300 yards and ammunition was available in high explosive or shrapnel types.

Pigeon release hole in the side of a tank

At the beginning of July 1918 an advance party consisting of four officers and 25 other ranks left Bovington camp and embarked to France to organise in advance accommodation for the main body of the Battalion. On 8th July at 10.00 a.m. that main body marched proudly out of Bovington under the command of Commander W.G. Ramsay Fairfax DSO RN, their initial destination being Wool Railway Station, here they entrained under the watchful eye of Brigadier General W.G. Glasgow CB the officer in charge of the Bovington Tank Corps training centre. The train's destination was Southampton Docks where they detrained and boarded in two parties on two ships the SS Siptah and Marguerite, all the other passengers were American soldiers, for all these young men it was most likely the first time they had the opportunity to experience what was later to be described as two peoples divided by a common language.

On arrival at Le Havre at 7.00 a.m. the following morning, the Battalion formed up and marched to number two rest camp to spend a night recovering from the journey. The following morning all the men were given a short gas course and put through two gas chambers to experience the feeling of wearing a mask in a gas environment and give them confidence that the mask would save their lives. It is likely that the gas was a harmless irritant in which case Bertie and his comrades would have been ordered to remove the mask and recite their name rank and number until they inhaled and felt the effects for themselves. This can only be described as a horrifying experience the lungs feel as though they are bursting and with no oxygen a choking sensation, all the facial orifices stream with fluid and they would have been led out to the fresh air on their hands and knees to cough and splutter with water to wash the face until eyesight returned. Seemingly cruel, but whenever the alarm went up for gas in the future, there was never any complacency in seeking the sanctity of a gas mask!

That same day the Battalion entrained to the destination area 2 Corps was to operate from and a tented encampment at Bermicourt France, arriving there on 13th July 1918. For the next few days the men continued to drill and train with gas masks and revolver. On 17th July, the Battalion fetched its first 12 Mk V Star tanks followed by a further 12 the following day and then the emphasis was changed to maintenance and tank training. Towards the end of the month the Battalion moved to Simencourt a forward position nearer to the front and prepared for action.

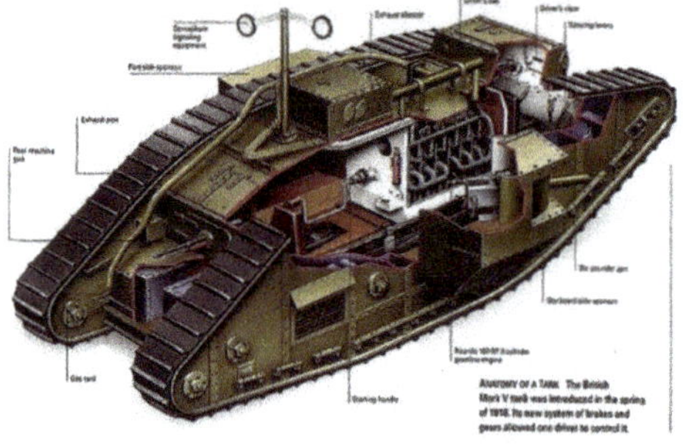

Mk V Tank Bovington Museum (Authors Pic)
Mk V tank cutaway showing side sponson gun (Great Military Battles.com)

The main events of 1918 had been the German Spring Offensive, reinforced by huge resources transferred from the Eastern front due to the 1917 Russian Revolution, this offensive was designed by the German High Command to drive a huge wedge between the French and British armies, destroy the British and force the French to an Armistice. This was seen as a last attempt to win the war before the might of the American forces could be organised to an effective standard at which point the war would be lost. The desperate defence put up by the Allied forces was, despite tremendous losses in casualties and prisoners, successful and the German offensive finally petered out. It was now the Allied turn to drive the German armies back and bring the war to a successful conclusion. This is now known as the 100 day Offensive and lasted from 8th August, to 11th November 1918, commencing with the Battle of Amien, the French attack on the Southern flank of the British, Australian and Canadian forces was called the Battle of Montdidier. On this first day, ten Allied Divisions supported by 500 tanks made a complete surprise attack of the

German lines and forced a gap 15 miles wide and over the next three days pushed forward 12 miles. 30,000 casualties were inflicted on the German army to a mere 6,500 Allied; 17,500 prisoners and 330 artillery pieces were also captured leading to a huge loss of morale and the first day being dubbed by General Ludendorff, 'the black day for the German army'.

By this stage of the war, 15th Battalion consisted of three Companies. Each Company was divided into three Sections of four tanks each, one training Section and Company headquarters. Each Section had four crews of eight men plus a Commander, one Section Commander and three Batmen to service the officer's needs. The total compliment of the Battalion was 32 officers and 374 other ranks. We do not know where Bertie was placed within this structure but there are some clues in the battle reports from the War Diary.

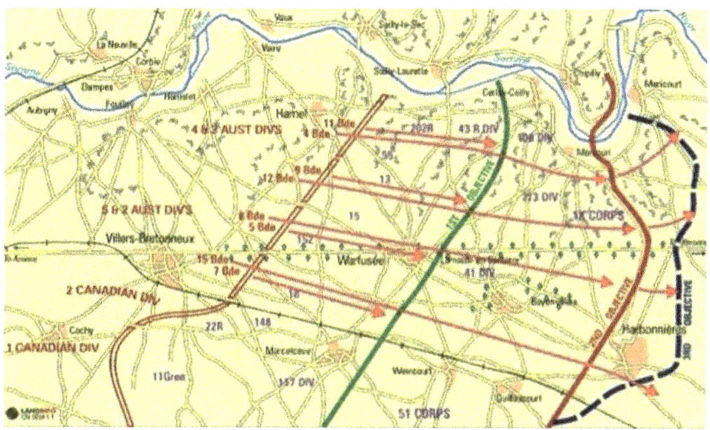

Attack plan for 8th August showing all three objectives (Authors Collection)

15th Battalion were positioned on the right flank of the Australian sector with the Canadian forces on their right. Their role on the first day was to carry machine gunners, their guns and ammunition with the advancing infantry to the Blue line where they would set up a defensive holding line against counter attack. The first phase of the plan was an attack by the 2nd and 3rd Australian Divisions to capture the first objective shown as the green line, this was to be followed by the 4th and 5th Divisions attack to take control of the second objective shown as the red line. The third objective was the blue line where the tanks were to deposit their machine gun passengers. Training experimentation in the days leading to the attack showed that the Mk4 Star tank could accommodate one of the following combinations;

- Three Lewis guns, one officer and eight other ranks, two men per gun, total personnel 15 men plus 16 magazines per man.
- Or
- Two Vickers guns, one officer, ten other ranks plus two men per gun, total personnel 15 and ammunition.

On the night of 3rd to 4th August, the Battalion moved to Querriers Wood, a point on route to the start positions for the forthcoming battle. The movement of tanks was conducted at night as secrecy for the operation was being preserved. During this movement an officer, 2nd Lieutenant Lakeman, tripped over some wire and was accidentally killed, a second officer, 2nd Lieutenant Jones, was injured in the same incident. The following night the Battalion again moved this time to Fouilly where the tanks were camouflaged again to keep the operation secret for the enemy. From this date to Y Day (7th August), the time was spent preparing the tanks for battle and allotting the Australian machine gun crews and support infantry to each group. The Australians joined the Battalion on Y Day and, at 11.30 p.m. that night, the Allied forces moved to their assembly positions to await the attack scheduled for X Day, 8th August. The noise of the tanks moving to these positions had been disguised by RAF aircraft flying overhead and a deep fog covered the movements of tanks and infantry.

Despite a large attack on the British 18th Division on 6thAugust, Zero hour, 04.20 a.m. on X Day, the Allied artillery commenced a creeping barrage of high explosive shells falling 200 yards in front of the advancing Allied forces. The tanks of 13th Tank Battalion moved through to lead the advancing infantry. After three minutes, the barrage moved forward in timed 100-yard advances. No preparatory barrage had been used to maintain the element of surprise and the German defenders were totally unaware of the attack. Little retaliatory action was experienced as the infantry and tanks emerged from the fog and the tanks' guns dealt effectively with strong points and machine gun posts. Germans started to surrender in large numbers and the Green Line was taken by 7.30 a.m. and, at 8.20 a.m., the second wave commenced the attack on the Red Line. This second objective was taken on schedule and then the 36 tanks of 15th Battalion followed through ahead of the infantry to achieve their objective, delivering the machine gun crews to the Blue Line. This was a new untested tactic and was only possible as the new Mk V Star tanks were much bigger and capable of carrying this considerable amount of men and equipment. It proved a successful move and the Blue line, some 10,000 yards from the start positions was taken on schedule. To measure the success of this first day, in total, the Allied forces captured 29,144 prisoners, 338 guns, and liberated 116 towns and villages. The cost to the Allies however was high, total casualties of all ranks, 21,243 of which one in four was killed.

Of the 36 tanks of Bertie's Battalion which started out that day, 29 reached the Blue Line and fulfilled their mission, six tanks received direct hits, six tanks failed to reach the objective due to mechanical failure. Five other ranks were killed in action, four officers and 12 other ranks were wounded, two officers and ten other ranks were reported missing in action.

The following day, 9th August, the battalion were called on to provide tank support for infantry assigned to attack the villages of Vauxvillers and Framerville. The attack was scheduled for 4.30 p.m. and was not preceded by artillery barrage. 14 tanks were available for this operation and split into three groups of five, five and four tanks, the attack was over a frontage of 3,000 yards and each group was allotted a 1,000-yard front. At 2.30 p.m. the Australian Infantry and the allotted tanks were moving to the start positions, the German artillery fired gas shells and a large flight of enemy aeroplanes flew over firing machine guns at the troops on the ground, they took to their heels when the RAF arrived and the practice Bertie had undertaken with gas procedures was put to good use. The Germans had recovered from their surprise of the day before and had arranged for field artillery to be positioned and used against tanks

The tanks moved forward in line with scouts sent ahead to guide them, the infantry followed, of the group of four machines, one broke down on route to the target and one received a direct hit and all the crew killed it was not recovered until 13th August. The other two tanks survived the barrage and reached their objective inflicting large casualties on the enemy. The second group attacking Framerville from two sides, their attack destroyed three machine gun posts and operated in this area until 6.40 p.m. and on the way back one of them received a direct hit. The third group all achieved the objective and inflicted heavy casualties on the enemy, on the way back three of this group received direct hits and only one returned. Casualties were again heavy, one officer and 12 other ranks killed, three officers and eight other ranks wounded and three other ranks missing, Bertie was in the second statistic.

Bertie received a shrapnel wound to his right arm on this day and recalled how he was helped out of the tank by Australian infantry and placed out of harm's way in a shell hole from where he was rescued and taken to a dressing station. The wound was most likely caused as a result of a direct hit on the tank's armour causing metal fragments to break off the armour on the inside face of the steel directly opposite the point of impact; he was certainly a lucky man that day! The wound was not to be a 'Blighty one' and he was taken to 61 Casualty Clearing Station from where he was transferred to 22nd General Hospital at Camiers. Following seven days medical treatment, he was transferred to the Convalescent Depot at Etaples where he spent a further ten days, before being discharged to the Tank Depot from where he was posted back to 15th Battalion, arriving back with them on 3rd September 1918.

The post action report by the 15th Battalion's commanding officer contains some remarks about the men and the machines. He pays homage to the leadership and the men emphasising that the Battalion arrived in France on 9th July and was issued with tanks on 31st, giving them only seven days to train before going into battle for the first time. A remarkable achievement on behalf of all concerned. He also notes that the condition of some of the crews and their passengers was seriously marred by the atmosphere inside the tanks due to the fumes from the petrol engines, a situation made much worse if the tank's exhaust was shot off which did happen to Bertie at one point and they were forced to were their gas masks which misted over from the heat of the engine. This was also an issue raised also in the training memoir previously quoted. He suggests that certain improvements could be made. The atmosphere and speed of the tank could be vastly improved and there were no ammunition racks for the 6-pounder ammunition causing great inconvenience - an understatement for sure.

When Bertie arrived back with his unit, he had missed further operations conducted against the enemy which had caused further losses to the Battalion but had pushed the German army further back towards Germany. They were camped at Courcelles and were resting from the latest battles and engaged in cleaning and maintenance of the tanks. During the course of the month the Battalion made moves to keep it near to the front as that moved in a slow advance. The fast gains of the beginning of the offensive were not being replicated but were sufficient to convince the German High Command that the war could not be won. From mid-August, 15th Battalion commenced training with various Brigades of the 3rd Guards Division in preparation for their next involvement in the fighting.

On 27th September 1918, the Battle of the Canal du Nord commenced. Zero hour being 5.20 a.m., this was one of four battles to commence at this time as a continuance of the offensive. 15th Battalion was committed, and their three Companies split between two separate Australian Infantry units with different objectives. Whist we have no definitive proof that Bertie was in action, I do believe he was, but not specifically where. One of Bertie's memories was being in a tank when machine guns were trained on it was like there was a thousand maniacs with a hammer in each hand banging the outside of the tank. They were issued with chain mail masks to protect their faces from the tiny red-hot shards of metal which flew through the air during the course of the action. The post action report submitted from the Commanding Officer makes a point of the intensity of the machine gun fire trained on the tanks; an observation not made about the action of 8th to 9th August in which we know Bertie was involved. This was probably due to the Germans being ill-prepared on the first action of this offensive but by now, had learned tactics to counter the tank threat.

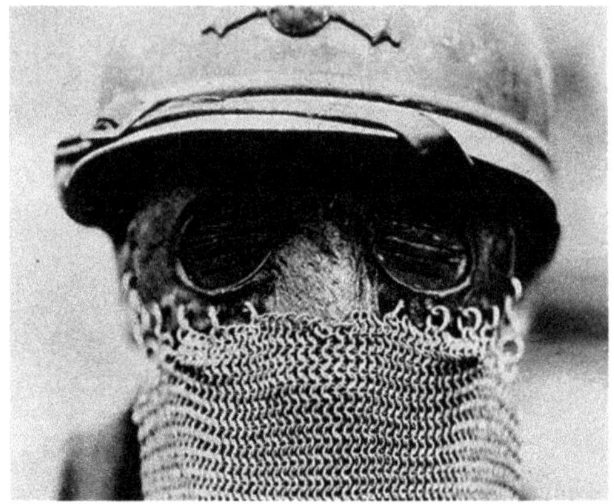

Chain mail face mask (French)

On the night of Y day (26th September 1918), 15th Battalion deployed a total of 24 tanks of either Mk V or Mk 5 Star type, on route to the assembly positions. Two of vehicles broke down with mechanical trouble. In position and waiting Zero hour on Z day, the German artillery pounded their positions with high explosive and gas shells, this resulted in the deaths of one officer and two other ranks and five other ranks wounded, the element of surprise as experienced on 8th August was never achieved again.

There is an interesting note about communications in this brief, radio for tanks had been developed but it is not known whether it was ever used, on this occasion the communication used was; at forward positions, runners, pigeons and wireless telegraphy and at back positions, airline, wireless telegraphy and despatch riders. A later comment about the success of communications forward allowed the Company Commanders to supervise their tanks going forward effectively. The report does not say who had the radios, so whether they were in each tank is still a mystery.

The action of that day was varied but in each case, there were huge losses for the Germans. The tanks brought all guns to bear whenever they had a target and particular use of case-shot (shrapnel) was made - often at point blank range. In one objective, the village of Plesquieres,

German infantry was encountered but shot down when they were leaving a house. One tank was lost in this village when it received a direct hit. The final objective for this group was a brown line 1000 yards beyond this village, it was defensively manned by riflemen and machine guns which manage to hold up the infantry. The tanks supporting at this point went forward and subdued the resistance inflicting heavy losses which were later confirmed by the body count.

Another section was supporting an attack on the Hindenburg Line - a heavily defended and reinforced line which guarded Germany itself. The tanks assisted in breaking the defensive wire, an objective which the artillery had repeatedly failed to do throughout the war, leaving men trapped in the open, unable to proceed and at the mercy of machine guns. The three tanks involved in this action breached the defences and proceeded along the line dealing with the defences. To keep in touch with their support infantry, they turned repeatedly and continued to destroy the enemy. Field guns and other artillery targeted the tanks and one received a direct hit early in the operation wounding all the crew. The tank commander chose to keep the machine in action until only he and one other crew member were able to stand, it then received another hit and was put out of action. All three tanks were eventually put out of action receiving between them, eight direct hits. Of the three officers and 19 crew members involved, one was killed and 19 wounded. This gives us an idea of the ferocity of the fighting and the priority the defenders were giving to neutralising the tank threat.

The section of the Canal du Nord where tanks could be used, was heavily defended by machine gun crews who were in the open sat on top of the parapet, the tanks were targeted and caused injuries from the 'splash' which refers to the splinters sent flying inside the tank when the outer armour is hit. The machine gun crews were effectively dealt with and one crew destroyed when the tank drove over their position.

By 4.30 p.m. that day, the tanks had been in action all day and those that had survived to this point were running low on fuel. This was brought to the attention of the Brigadier General in charge who was told there was a risk of the tanks being stranded in a forward position. He chose to take responsibility for this eventuality and pressed the tanks forward. The action continued with the help of petrol scavenged for tanks put out of commission and into the night, eventually they were withdrawn the survivors exhausted beyond our comprehension.

The total all ranks casualties for this day's fighting was; 17 killed and 53 wounded; over 30 percent of the men who started that day. That night, of the 24 tanks which had started only ten rallied and two managed to return the following day, the Battalion remained on standby in the event of them being needed.

On 1st October, the Battalion was situated at Graincourt, the work of cleaning and maintenance was started but orders issued in the event of an attack, which never came. The Battalion was kept out of the remaining fighting, occupied by providing tanks for reconnaissance and supply. The time was filled with cleaning, maintenance, training and the occasional Church Parade. The failure of the German Spring Offensive, the success of the Allied 100 day Offensive and the addition of the American Expeditionary Force, convinced the German High Command that the war was lost and they sued for an Armistice. At 11 a.m. on 11th November 1918, the guns fell silent. Bertie had survived. At 10.22 a.m. that day, the Battalion diarist noted, "Official confirmation received Armistice signed". At 10.45 a.m. the Battalion was paraded and informed of the news and then given the rest of the day off as a holiday. The following day it was business as usual, Company training and the first mention of a bath for a while!

Bertie returned to England in 1919 and was demobilised on 11th March that year from a camp at Chisledon. He returned to the family home in Erdington, Birmingham. As well as the entitlement to wear a gold wound stripe he was also awarded the British War and Victory Medals.

Bertie married Bernice Green at Erdington Parish Church, on 30th July 1921, the very church he was christened in. He worked as an electric welder until retirement and died of natural causes on 10th May 1976, at his home, 281, Marsh Lane, Erdington, Birmingham.

Chapter 35

John Berry, Beatrice Kirby & Lawrence Diamond

(For Carole Brabrooke)

John Berry was born in 1890 and baptised at St Andrews Church, Leyland on 23rd November that year. John's father, Edmund, was a Medical Doctor and Physician. His mother Ellen,formerly Ellen Ackroyd, but widowed previously and whose maiden name was Culshaw, was a local girl and daughter of Joiner/Wheelwright, James Culshaw.

In 1891 the family were resident at Prospect House, Sandy lane, Leyland. At this time John was six months old and he had an elder sister, Evelyn, aged one. The family enjoyed the trappings of middle class life and employed two servants, Annie Bell as a domestic and Elizabeth Owen nurse to the children.

At school age John was sent as a boarder to Hutton School, Liverpool Road, Hutton. This Grammar school was affiliated to the Church of England and formed in 1517 with the permission of Henry VIII. Aged 11, John is on the 1901 census as resident at this school and on leaving he was sent to medical school in Edinburgh where he was shown in 1911 aged 20. This census shows that his family were still resident at Prospect House. Ellen had given birth to three children, but the last one had since died. Also resident were Margaret Berry, sister of John senior and a woman of private means, a medical student, Cyril Wilmot (no doubt studying under the guidance of Edmund) and two servants.

On 6th October 1914 John, still a medical student, attended an army recruitment facility at Dunkeld, Scotland. Following medical examination and attestation he was accepted as Private 97 in the Field Ambulance of the Scottish Horse Brigade. John had given up his medical education to serve his country in its hour of need and this meant that serving as a Private soldier, he would be employed in the various capacities of the RAMC for his rank. This could be stretcher bearer, hospital orderly, in the sanitation unit giving soldiers baths and new underwear. This very patriotic but naïve move was not in the best interests of both country and John. Very soon after joining, in fact 11 days, John was discharged and returned to medical school. Whether the intervention was family, university, the army itself or a combination is not known, but by resuming his studies meant he would join the army in a much more important role.

John finished his medical training in 1917 his qualifications being LRCP Edin, LRCS Edin and LFPS Glas. This was known as the Triple Qualification which meant that, as well as being an MD, he was also a Surgeon. He then rejoined the army and was accepted by the Royal Army Medical Corps as a Lieutenant. This second part of John's army record was lost and the only clue as to his service is his medal card, which shows that he landed in France on 29th October 1917 and at some stage was promoted to Captain. Hours of research through countless files and dairies has failed to unlock the secrets of John's war, but the probability is that he served in one of the many hospitals in the Pay de Calais area, operating on an endless line of casualties from the front.

Surviving the war and of course the 'flu Pandemic, which hit the hospitals hard killing medical staff and patients alike, John returned to England and in July 1919 John married Beatrice Kirby in a civil ceremony in Amesbury Wiltshire. The records do not include details of whether family attended. John's fatherhad died that year and Beatrice was considered to be of an unsuitable class for John by his family and did not approve of her. In 1920, following the death of his father, John resigned his commission and returned to Leyland to take over the practice. In 1923 the couple had a child who tragically died in 1924, but in 1925 Beatrice gave birth to a son, Oswald (Carole's dad).

John was awarded the British War and Victory medals for his army service, but he died of kidney failure in 1927 aged 36 and was buried in Leyland parish church cemetery on 5thSeptember that year.

Beatrice Kirby was born in Grandborough Buckinghamshire on 24thMarch 1901, but wasn't christened until 25th May the following year at Grandborough Parish Church. She was the sixth child of Mary and Amos Kirby, a Domestic Groom for the local Lord of the manor. By 1911 Mary had given birth to four more children, all who had survived to this point and was a remarkable achievement for the day. In this census Amos is noted as working away and it is known that he accompanied an expedition to the Antarctic, in his capacity of groom to the horses and the famous Scott expeditions were undertaken between 1910 and 1913.

Schooled locally to the age of 14, Beatrice left school and gained employment as an Armature Winder for Electric Motors. On reaching the age of 17, in 1918, she applied to the Women's Army Auxiliary Corps (WAAC), which was shortly after renamed Queen Mary's Army Auxiliary Corps (QMAAC) and she gave her date of birth as 1900 to appear 18 years old, the required minimum.

The WAAC was established in 1917 and employed women in many capacities to assist with the war effort. The first women sent to France was in March that year, when 14 cooks and waitresses embarked.

During the course of the war 57,000 women served with the QMAAC, which was disbanded on 27th November 1921.

Beatrice volunteered for the duration of the war in any capacity, but due to her employment requested a role in electrical engineering. She was employed as an Orderly, sent to the school of cookery and housed in a hostel in Saltley, Birmingham. Following completion of her training she was posted to a military camp in Dorset and from there to Rollestone Camp, Larkhill, Wiltshire, arriving there on 7th July 1918. She fell foul of the strict disciple at the camp and was twice fined two shillings and sixpence for fraternising with an officer. The officer in question is not named, but on 2nd August following a whirlwind romance, she married Captain John Berry at Amesbury. Her treatment and the disapproval by John's family gives a clear picture of societies expectations of keeping a respectful distance between working class folk and their 'betters'.

Following the death of her father-in-law, Dr Edmund Berry in December 1919, Beatrice was discharged from service on compassionate grounds and with her husband moved home to Leyland to take up the life of a Doctor's wife. The couple developed a story about Betty, as she preferred to be known and again this demonstrates prejudicial thinking of the day, as instead of telling family she had been a lowly cook during the war, they were told she was a nurse and drove an ambulance.

Little is known of Betty's life following the death of John, but in 1932 she married Lawrence Diamond and in the 1939 census the couple were living in Preston Lancashire. Betty died in October 1952.

Lawrence Bannister Diamond was born 22nd May 1898 in Preston Lancashire. His mother Catherine was a single woman who worked as a Confectioner/Baker. In 1901 she was living with Lawrence at 61, New Hall Lane, Preston and was purveying her produce from home. Lawrence's father was Charles Bannister, hence his middle name. Charles was a married travelling salesman who had two children with his wife. It is likely that Charles maintained a relationship with Catherine and Lawrence as at the time of the 1911 census he was living as a boarder with them at 11 Walpole Street Preston. The form had been filled in by Catherine who declared herself head of the household.

On 3rd December 1914, Lawrence now working as a Fitter's Apprentice, volunteered at Preston recruitment office and was accepted as Driver 1738 in the Royal Field Artillery. Very little record remains about Lawrence's service, but we know he was sent abroad and arrived in Egypt on 4th June 1915. At this time he was part of the Mediterranean Expeditionary Force, which supplied the forces to protect the interests of the British Empire, in particular the Suez Canal and the operations in Gallipoli. There is no mention of Gallipoli and it is likely he was retained in Egypt protecting the Suez Canal. In March 1916 the MEF became the Egyptian Expeditionary Force and concentrated its efforts in that country. A great deal of the forces efforts were put to building a series of interlocking defensive posts east of the canal. The intention was to push out into the Sinai thereby reducing the length of the defensive line and reducing the numbers of troops committed to this front.

Whatever Lawrence's involvement, his war did not last long and on 7th August 1916 he had an accident involving an ammunition box and his right lower leg. The injury was clearly severe and the ammunition box referred to is more likely to be a caisson or ammunition wagon, which weighed 37 cwt, possibly plus its 24 rounds at 18.5 lbs, (assuming the usual 18 pounder field gun was in use), considerably heavier than an ammunition box which could be carried by a man.

Lawrence was treated for his wound in Egypt as the skin over the right tibia on the shin had been punctured, very likely to the bone and had taken too long to heal thus exposing the bone to germs causing necrosis. Three operations were conductedwhich involved scraping bone away,leaving a cavity in the shin 2½" x ½" x ¼" deep. Eventually he was shipped back to England, where he was admitted to 2nd Western General Hospital Manchester. By now the wound was healing but Periostitis had developed causing considerable pain. This condition causes the tissue around the bone to inflame and it would appear that the treatment at the time was rest and he remained in hospital until 16th June 1917, a total of 177 days. On 30th October the same year, Lawrence was re-admitted to 2nd Western and radical operations performed to treat the cavity in his shin. On this occasion he remained in hospital until 30th May 1919 when he was discharged to Oswestry Military Hospital.

On 18th July 1919 Lawrence was discharged from the army and awarded a silver war badge to be worn on his right lapel, indicating he was an injured veteran and he was also awarded the 1914-15 Star, British War and Victory medals. His injury was assessed by the discharging medical board and he was probably awarded a pension, but this is not mentioned in the file. The treatment to his leg was ongoing, including a stay in hospital from November 1920 to February 1921, where an ulcer was treated over the wound. That same year he was again admitted to Preston Royal Infirmary with sinus (white puss) exuding from the scar tissue on his leg. Clearlythe infection was still there and most likely his condition very painful. His pension was re-assessed on numerous occasions, until 1927 when he was judged to be fit and finally discharged.

In 1932 Lawrence married Beatrice Berry and this was a second marriage for Laurence, who in 1922 had wed a woman named Kate Annie Jaques. This match ended in divorce and the cause given as adultery. John's marriageto Betty produced one child and in 1939 the family were living in Preston, Lancashire with Betty's mother, Catherine. Lawrence was employed as a car and commercial vehicle salesman and he died in 1983. He was buried in the parish church of St Mary, Preston on 9th February that year.

Chapter 36

Arthur Grove Earp

Arthur is the final story in this volume, I have chosen this as a sobering reminder of the brutality of war. Brutality is expected from the enemy, but it doesn't get any worse than the treatment meted out to this man and many more like him under the expediency of maintaining discipline.

On a balmy summer morning at dawn 22nd July 1916, Private 2676 Arthur Grove Earp, of the 1/5 Battalion, Royal Warwickshire Regiment, was led from his place of incarceration and tied to a stake. A white patch was pinned to his clothing over his heart whilst he was blindfolded, and a priest prayed throughout this horrendous procedure. Arthur could only have been terrified but resigned to his fate as he stood facing his executioners with the courage he had been accused of not possessing. Six of his former comrades lined up in front of him and following the orders of the officer in charge, raised their rifles, took aim and fired on the command. Arthur was hit by up to five .303 bullets and died instantly. One of the rifles had been loaded with a blank cartridge, a nicety to allow the members of the firing squad the comfort that they might not have killed a friend. What terrible crime did this young man commit to deserve such an ignominious end; murder, treason, rape? No, nothing of the sort, this is Arthur's story.

Arthur was born in Moseley Street, Birmingham in 1902, his exact date of birth is not known as any records giving this date are missing. In 1911, his family were living at Lodge, Rookery Road, Handsworth, Birmingham, which at that time was part of Warwickshire. His family consisted of his parents, Thomas Grove and Jane Earp, and five children; three girls and two boys, all of school age or below. Thomas Grove was a self-employed gardener.

By 1911, Thomas had passed away and Jane has moved her family, now six children, to 1, back of 102, Sherbourne Street, Ladywood, Birmingham. Jane is not employed, the youngest of her children are still at school, but the elder four have a variety of jobs; cardboard box maker, florist's assistant, printers clerk and Arthur was a bedstead polisher.

Arthur's military file has not survived but his medal card shows he arrived in France on 23rd March 1915, and was serving as Private 2676 of the Royal Warwickshire Regiment, later accounts state he was a member of 1/5 Battalion. This Battalion was formed in Thorp Street, Birmingham in August 1914, one of the many battalions of the New Army raised in response to the outbreak of the war. Thorp Street was the location of a military barracks and the Royal Warwickshire Regiment had set up a recruitment office there to assist with the overwhelming response to the country's call to arms. Given the time scale between the raising of Arthur's Battalion and the coincidental date of both him and the Battalion lading in France, it is safe to assume that Arthur was an immediate volunteer and that he trained with the fledgling Battalion until the whole unit was ready for mobilisation on 22nd March 1915. The Battalion's war diary paints a picture of what Arthur's life was like during his short service for his country.

At 4.00 p.m. on 22nd March, 1/5 Battalion, consisting of 30 officers, 1003 other ranks and 78 horses, embarked for France from Southampton to join the British Expeditionary Force (BEF) there. They landed at 8.00 a.m. the following morning and disembarked at Le Havre and marched to a rest camp. On 24th March, they entrained to Cassel and commenced a two day march which took them to their first operational base at Bailleul where they spent the rest of the month digging trenches.

At the beginning of April, the Battalion received training and instruction on trench warfare and, on 12th April 1915, went into the line for the first time in Douve Trenches. Every day until relieved on 16th March, the diary records five men killed and seven wounded. The diary records no action, nor attack by the enemy or snipers, so the casualties were most likely the result of enemy artillery. This first taste of what was to come, must have shaken all those who had never experienced war before and started to dismantle the propaganda of glory and easy victory for which many young men had signed up. By the end of May 1915, the Battalion strength had been reduced to 22 officers and 889 other ranks by only five visits to the trenches for purely holding-the-line duty. The usual pattern of front line, reserve and out of the trenches, continued in the following months with a constant similar record of men being killed and wounded mainly from shelling.

The winter months of 1915 into 1916 were subjected to heavy rainfall, which with the cold weather led to miserable conditions in the trenches. In the front line the men were issued with waders but movement through the mud was slow and arduous, a demoralising situation with only one respite at Christmas 1915, the Battalion were out of the trenches but returned a few days later.

On 1st June 1916, Arthur's Battalion went back into the line in the Couin Trenches, this being a location approximately half way between Amiens and Arras in the Somme district. They were relieved on 8th June and, in that time, they had 23 casualties from enemy shelling. Following a short respite in huts in Couin, they returned to the trenches. The casualties commenced immediately and then, on 24th June 1916, U day, the British artillery commenced a continuous and intensive bombardment of the German lines preceding the planned great offensive of 1916, the Battle of the Somme. This bombardment, originally planned for four days, was extended until the end of June and the infantry attack delayed as a result, until 1st July 1916. During this bombardment, over 1,700,000 artillery shells were fired by the British alone. On commencement of the bombardment, the Germans responded with an artillery barrage of their own on the British lines. Arthur was described during his Court Martial as, "a man normally of a nervous disposition but during this period he was especially affected". It doesn't take too much imagination to realise what was happening to Arthur and the likelihood that he was suffering from the effects of Shell Shock is extremely high. In 1916, Shell Shock was a recognised medical condition, but it was believed to be a result of physical damage to the nervous system. It was later in 1917 that it was accepted the condition could be present in someone who had not been at the front. Before this, it was necessary for a soldier to have either been buried alive or subjected to heavy artillery bombardment to be suffering this condition. Arthur fitted the criteria perfectly.

At 4.00 a.m. on 26th June 1916, Arthur's Platoon Sergeant, Williams, had placed him and the platoon in a trench position and left a Corporal in charge. Both NCO's gave evidence at Arthur's Court Martial that they had told him he must remain at his post until told he could leave, as they had with all the men. Arthur was still at his post at 12.30 p.m. that day, but at 1.00 p.m. it was noticed he was missing. It was also reported to the court that the conditions at the time were extreme. The men had been completing 24 hour duties in the front line for four days without a break, the artillery bombardment had been ongoing for over two days and the retaliatory artillery fire was fierce - 20 casualties are reported in these first days. Gas was also discharged on the day Arthur went missing; this was a stressful time as a wind change could blow the gas back into British trenches. Sergeant Williams made an unsuccessful search for Arthur, who turned up at a dugout behind the front line at 2.30 a.m. on 27th June 1916 and reported to the Corporal in charge there. Corporal Golby, who had reported him missing, went to the dugout and saw that Arthur was in a highly agitated state and said that he couldn't stand the shelling anymore. Arthur was reported for leaving his post without permission.

At 7.30 a.m. on 1st July 1916, the infantry attack commenced in the first phase of the offensive, the Battle of Albert; 12 hours later 29,000 people lay dead. What was intended as an infantry advance into German positions through barbed wire, both of which should have been destroyed by the artillery bombardment, without any opposition was an unmitigated disaster. The wire was not cut and the enemy positions had not been destroyed. They had simply built their defences too well and on the sound of the whistles and the cessation of the guns, they came out of their deep bunkers and manned the line with machine guns and riflemen, who then proceeded to decimate the advancing infantry. It was an embarrassment to the high command who then proceeded to press the attacks and send more and more men to their deaths, to overcome the fear subsequent waves of men had about advancing it was necessary to make them more fearful of the retribution likely if they failed to obey orders. On 8th July 1916, a Field General Court Martial was convened to try Arthur for the offence of leaving his post, the Judges were all officers of the Royal Warwickshire Regiment, the President being Major Hanson of the 1/7th Battalion.

The only defence was from Arthur himself who said that during the heavy shelling he became giddy and did not know what he was doing, he went to the dugout and when he tried to return to his post he couldn't because the shelling had re-started. The only other defence evidence was from the main prosecution witness, Sergeant Williams, who described the nervous state that Arthur was continually in, particularly on the date of the alleged offence. No medical evidence or opinion was solicited as to whether he was suffering the effects of shell shock and Arthur had a good record as a soldier and no disciplinary measures had been taken against him, Arthur was found guilty but with a recommendation that mercy be shown. The Brigade Commander recommended the death penalty as he had for three men from the same Battalion only three weeks earlier but, significantly, before the disaster of 1stJuly. These men had had their sentences reduced to two years imprisonment. The Divisional Commander disagreed and recommended as per the Court Martial, the Corps Commander made the same recommendation. The next stage was General Hubert Gough who disagreed with the plea for clemency and stated that an example was necessary but the final decision rested with the Commander-in-Chief of the British Forces on the Western Front, General Haig (later to be Field Marshal Lord Haig). Haig confirmed the death penalty and openly stated his opinion that victory was impossible if cases like this were dealt with leniently.

On the morning of 21st July 1916, the whole brigade was paraded around a small group of officers, NCO's, drummers and Private

Arthur Earp, the findings of the court and the sentence was read out and Earp was then stripped of all buttons and badges giving any identity of military status, he was then marched away, his humiliation complete and the message sent out to every man in attendance. At dawn on the morning of 22nd July 1916, the sentence of Death by Shooting was carried out, Arthur was buried in grave I.C. 25 of Bouzincourt Communal Cemetery Extension.

Arthur left £6.10s.6d which was divided amongst his family as per his will. No War Gratuity was granted, he was awarded the 1914-15 Star but not the British War or Victory Medals.

Chapter 37

Life at the Front

Following an opportunity to sleep off the journey from mobilization point to the rest camp, the Battalion formed up and travelled by route march ondouble decker open topped buses and trains, which were often open goods wagons, to a camp in their designated area of operations. This journey couldlastfor days,often camping overnight at the side of the road in all weather, stopping for meals that were prepared by Battalion kitchen units, who had been sent ahead, to have the meal ready at a given time and location.

At their destination the officers and men received instruction in trench making and repair. Then,in groups, they were taken to front line positions, for instruction in trench life under the guidance of an experienced Battalion. On completion of this part of their education they then went into the rotation system of front line, support and reserve. The turnaroundperiod was designed as a fixed number of days, but research indicates this was variable and no doubt dependant on need. It also varied on location. The awful conditions and dangers of the Salient at Ypresdictated that the time in the front line was reduced from four to two days. The experience in the trenches was dependant on location and time of year. The Somme area has a chalk base,whereas the fields of Flanders have a blue clay below the topsoil and a high water table making living conditions wet and muddy. In Italy the main fronts were either in low swamp land or in mountains often constituting rocky flint. The swamp land was a breeding ground for disease, whilst mountain life was in caves or trenches made by explosives and many of the shrapnel injuries were flint chips as well as metal. The seasons created different difficulties, winter was often a wet and freezing experience, but fog and difficult visibility would give respite from snipers and spotters. In summer the necessity to cut grass exposed those tasked to do so to the attention of snipers, but living conditions were better.

The common denominator for life in the front line was danger, be it from bullets, shells, gas or infantry attack it was the constant fear of injury or death that the men lived with. Anotherfeature of life,whether in front line, support or reserve was hard manual labour. The trench system was constantly in need of development, maintenance and repair. Bad weather, explosions and ground movement caused trench walls tocollapse whilst new ideas to overcome logistical problems would create work. One such example, designed to ease the passage of troops travelling in opposite directions in narrow communication trenches, were side alleys dug into the trench wall. Men supposedly resting, following a spell in the line, were put to work at night labouring or forming carrying parties for front line trenches or in support of Royal Engineers. Those not engaged in these duties continued to train, drill, play sport or attend church parades of one denomination or another.

When a Battalion took over a section of trench the changeover was completed at night and as discreetly as possible, as enemy listening posts could pinpoint troop movement and direct artillery fire accordingly. From an assembly area the men were led through the complex system of trenches by guides, to manthe front line and support trenches, often two companies in each. During the hours of darkness sentries were posted one man out of every three stood on the fire step, head and shoulders above the parapet for one hour at a time. Bayonets fixed, eyes and ears uncovered, the sentries stood and tried to identify enemy movement. Whether it be a trench raid, working party or an intelligence gathering mission, their observations were duly reported to their NCO and action determined accordingly. Dependant on moonlight determined the quality of sightings. Anyone who has worked at night can say howan object can be seen as something sinister, but hearing was a more reliable sense.

The danger of enemy offensive action was always more likely as dawn broke and just before first light each day 'stand to' was called and every man came to the fire step, rifle at the ready and bayonet fixed. Sun rise was a dangerous time for the Allies as they faced East and snipers made good opportunity of this advantage. When the danger of attack was over the men were 'stood down, the guard ratio was reduced to one in ten,a rum ration was handed out and breakfast commenced. Anenemy watch activity was maintained throughout the dayby use of periscope, forward listening posts and aerial observation. Throughout the hours of darkness working parties worked on the trench system and carrying parties from the reserve companies brought the necessary stores and ammunition to the front line.

Anyone wishing to report sick removed themselves with permission to an aid post to report to the Medical Officer (MO), who had a team of Royal Army Medical Corps staff at his disposal. The MO and his staff had duties throughout the day dealing with anything,which if ignored, could result in a deteriorating condition for the men. Trench Foot was an ongoing problem in wet conditions and we must remember that without antibiotics, the tiniest cuts could result in death from blood poisoning due to the unsanitary conditions which prevailed. The duties of the day commenced with weapon cleaning as grit and water cause havoc with finely machined armsand a jammed gun in a fight is a liability not an asset. Magazines are unloaded not just for safety purposes, but to relieve pressure on magazine springs, as without regular relief springs lose their memory and can fail to cycle the next round to breach level, causing a jam.

Whilst not undergoing their two-hour spell on guard duty the men are free to relax, smoke and chatter. Any movement is restricted by the danger of becoming a target and the need to be in constant touch with a weapon. The call of nature is one reason to move to a latrine dug into the wall of a trench, but was kept to bare minimum in daytime due to the danger. At noon lunch is served, often a stew carried forward in the night in thermal containers. Letters and parcels from home were handed out and often contained food, sweets, cigarettes and clothing. More importantly news from home was a link to life outside of war and an escape from the constant danger of trench life.

The afternoons were spent resting and taking the opportunity to catch up on lost sleep. Men would create a funk hole in the trench wall in which they could lie down, with some protection from the elements and shell fire. Whatever the activity the men fought a continual battle with vermin and clothes and bodies were infested with lice and a time-consuming activity was 'chitting'. The lice were squashed whilst in the seams of the clothes or the items were held over a candle, but no matter how thorough the hunt was, the life cycle of the lice was so prolific it was an unfair fight. The other main vermin were rats, bloated by the feast of human and animal flesh on the battlefield and were described as "rats as big as cats" Private Thomas McIndoe, 12th Battalion Middlesex Regiment wrote in his memoirs;

"Rats! Oh crikey! If they were put in a harness, they could have done a milk round, they were that big, yes, honest. Nearly every morning, a bloody great thing would come up and stand up on its back legs and gnaw at something. I used to line the sights up and give them one round of ball. Bang! And blow them to nothing".

Dependent on time of year, either 'stand to' or evening meal occurred first. Evening meal occurred at 6 p.m. and was again hot stew or soup bolstered by the men's emergency tinned rations. Stand-to occurred 30 minutes before sundown and was the same process with all men on the fire step, bayonets fixed ready to defend the line against infantry attack. When full darkness arrived, the men were again 'stood down' and the usual routine of night sentry duty resumed. After their designated spell at the front, another Battalion was guided in to relieve the exiting troops who were then guided out and marched to a rest area.

Life at the rear was not without danger, as camps within artillery range were often targeted and casualties experienced. Hard work in the form of working and carrying parties along with training and compulsory church parades,minimised any leisure time. However, for the men of the British army, this was where they could relax and enjoy life as it was. There were film shows, concert parties touring and Battalions had entertainment groups, who laid on concerts and plays, with the men acting all roles usually to much amusement. Sing songs played an important role in boosting moral and reinforcing camaraderie. Many songs of the day transformed to a bawdy version and became enshrined in British culture. Different versions are today sang around boy scout campfires or in rugby club baths. Men supplemented army rations with food from the locals, who cooked such delights as egg and chips and paid visits to local bars called Estaminets, which were a substitute for a visit to the pub at home. Flemish by origin this was where you could get beer and a good hearty meal, stews of rabbit and chicken, with bread cooked in wood fired ovens or the more popular egg and chips and meet women. These establishments were often run by farmers who had their buildings commandeered for accommodation purposes to make a few Francs in return.

The accommodation was according to rank and the men occupied, barns, halls, schools and anything that was available. Officers were billeted separately and both tented and wooden hut camps were constructed. Occasionally men would find themselves in the luxury of a chateaux,but not very often!

Wherever an army was stationed, the needs of nature are accommodated by women drawn to the oldest profession for various reasons, with money being the common factor. Official brothels were usually kept for the exclusive use of officers an d guarded to prevent entry by other ranks. Whilst the men were accommodated by street girls, resultant disease was a danger for all both men and women. Sexually transmitted disease was a serious problem as it diverted medical resources from where it was most needed. Pleas by army chaplains to abstain on religious grounds was disregarded and substituted with education from medical officers, a free prophylactic kit and encouragement to seek early advice if thought exposed.

I find this poem, written by an unknown Australian soldier and published in a magazine called 'In Billets' in 1918, sums up the mind of a man at the rear;

You say we're mad when we strike the beer!
But if you'd stood in shivering fear
With the boys who bring the wounded back
Cross no-man's land where there ain't no track
You'd read no psalms to the men that fight!
You'd take to drink to forget the sight
Of torn out limbs and sightless eyes
Or the passing of a pal that dies.

About the Author

Author's Picture

Mick is a retired British police officer having served in both Birmingham City and West Midlands forces. He served in both uniform, CID and other specialist units gaining experience and expertise in major investigation. In retirement he has combined two lifelong passions, motorcycling and history, resulting in research trips throughout Western Europe and books about Soldiers of the two World Wars.

A member and supporter of the Royal British Legion profits from this book will donated to that worthy cause.

www.ingramcontent.com/pod-product-compliance
Lightning Source LLC
LaVergne TN
LVHW052344100826
845147LV00012B/746
9781786236593